The Prostitution of Women and Girls

The Prostitution of Women and Girls

by R. Barri Flowers

McFarland & Company, Inc., Publishers
Jefferson, North Carolina, and London

To those long-ago ladies of the evening:
Catherine Eddowes, Elizabeth Stride, Polly Nichols,
Annie Chapman, and Mary Jane Kelly,
whose colorful lives and untimely demise helped inspire this book.

And, as always,
for the exceedingly wondrous "Bell Jar,"
a true queen among princesses.

British Library Cataloguing-in-Publication data are available

Library of Congress Cataloguing-in-Publication Data

Flowers, R. Barri (Ronald Barri)
    The prostitution of women and girls / by R. Barri Flowers.
      p.   cm.
    Includes bibliographical references and index.
    ISBN 0-7864-0490-6 (library binding : 50# alkaline paper) ∞
    1. Prostitution.   2. Prostitutes — Attitudes.   3. Teenage
prostitution.   4. Child prostitution.   5. Sex oriented businesses.
I. Title.
HQ111.F58   1998
306.74 — dc21   98-12338
                                                    CIP

Manufactured in the United States of America

McFarland & Company, Inc., Publishers
  Box 611, Jefferson, North Carolina 28640

Contents

Tables and Figures

Preface

The worldwide sexual exploitation of women and children through sex tourism, sexual slavery, pornography, pedophilia, pederasty, and other means has reached alarming proportions, according to most authorities. The explosion in female prostitution in the sex trade industry is of particular concern. The World Health Organization reports dramatic increases in the prostitution of women and girls in virtually every country.[1] A United Nations report found that violence against women, including forced prostitution, is a growing problem globally.[2]

This rise in the international trafficking of females is largely attributed to a booming sex tourism industry in Asia, Europe, and South America, to Third World poverty, to the economic depression of the former Eastern bloc, and to weak or inconsistent laws that effectively encourage prostitution in many countries by minimizing penalties against pimps, purveyors, panderers, sex tour promoters, brothel owners, customers of prostitutes, and other sexual exploiters of women and girls.

The concurrent growth in the prostituting of children is seen primarily as a response to the AIDS epidemic and the belief that younger and virginal prostitutes are free of infection. In reality, they are the most susceptible to HIV and AIDS exposure, creating a frightening cycle of illicit sex with girls and boys, child sex slaves, drug addicts, sexually transmitted diseases, and HIV infection.

The increasing worldwide attention on the problem of prostitution and sex tourism led Pope John Paul II to warn in 1990, "Women and children must not be used as objects at the expense of their unalienable dignity."[3] A number of antiprostitution efforts have been launched in recent years in an attempt to stem the tide. Some have had an impact. However, most have failed to make a serious dent in the lucrative flesh trade.

With varying results and conclusions, AIDS researchers, criminologists, sociologists, psychologists, anthropologists, and others have examined various aspects of the prostitution subculture and its implications for participants and society. Most prefer to focus their attention on the particular prostitution-related issues relevant to their interests.

The Prostitution of Women and Girls was written as a comprehensive examination of female prostitution in the United States and around the globe. This book seeks to promote a greater understanding of the dynamics of the prostitution of women and girls and the ramifications internationally, including the AIDS virus and the sex-for-sale industry itself, as we approach the twenty-first century.

This book is appropriate as an academic text in undergraduate- and graduate-level studies on prostitution, prostitutes, sexual abuse, and the sex industry. The following fields of college study are recommended for its use: child health and welfare, criminal justice, criminology, human behavior, juvenile delinquency, law, psychiatry, psychology, racial and ethnic studies, sociology, women's studies, and related disciplines. Additionally, it was written for legislators, social scientists, medical practitioners, law enforcement officials, researchers, and laypeople who have an interest in female prostitution and their welfare.

I would be remiss if I did not conclude this preface by offering my sincerest gratitude to my incredibly talented and tirelessly devoted partner in crime-writing and research, the lady with the *long red hair*, whose superb typing skills and ability to turn scribble into professional tables and figures never fail to amaze me. Thank you, my beautiful dear wife, H. Loraine, for your patience, devotion, and loving support.

Introduction

The lines have often been blurred between female criminality and victimization, since they are typically entwined through child abuse, sexual abuse, economic distress, sexism, and differential enforcement of laws. The same is no less true when examining female prostitution, where the perpetrator is at once also a victim. The lines may be even more blurred in the selling of sexual favors, with so many prostitutes facing the serious threat of AIDS infection, drug addiction, pimp domination and violation, and a generally bleak future. These realities are compounded by an increase in the worldwide demand for women and girls in the sex-for-sale industry, as sexual slaves or indentured sex servants; by the widening socioeconomic gap between the haves and the have-nots, putting pressure on females to enter prostitution; and by the seeming indifference of those in positions of compassion or authority.

This book will explore the complex issues surrounding the prostitution of women and girls, both in the United States and abroad. The hope is that it will lead to a greater understanding of the prostitution subculture, the particular nuances and elements of adult and teenage female prostitution, and the global dimensions of female prostitution and encourage future research on the subject matter.

The Prostitution of Women and Girls is divided into five parts and is supplemented with relevant tables, figures, and an index. Part I defines prostitution and examines the extent of female prostitution, types of prostitutes, theories and motivations surrounding prostitution, and the relationship between female prostitution and AIDS.

Part II focuses on women and prostitution, including the scope of prostitution, streetwalkers, call girls, drug use, related crimes, and victimization.

Part III examines the prostitution of girls, including the extent of teenage

1

prostitution, characteristics of girl prostitutes, runaway and throwaway girls, pimps, and the dimensions and dangers of child sexual abuse.

Part IV addresses other dimensions of prostitution and the sex trade industry. These include the relationship between female prostitution and pornography, child pornography, customers of female prostitutes, male prostitution, laws and prostitution, and decriminalization and legalization of prostitution.

Part V explores female prostitution in other countries, including the prostitution of women worldwide, international child prostitution and sexual exploitation, AIDS and the global proliferation of prostitution, and responses to the worldwide tragedy of female prostitution.

As we near the millennium, it is of utmost importance that the world communities work collectively toward dramatically reducing the incidence and exploitation of women and children in the sex trade industry. This book is but one part of that effort.

Part I

Female Prostitution

Chapter 1

Defining Prostitutes
and Prostitution

Prostitution has often been referred to as the "world's oldest profession"; consequently, *prostitutes* may be seen as engaging in the oldest occupation or trade the world has known. The practice of prostitution existed long before the threat of AIDS and meaningful attempts to define, decriminalize, and control prostitution. History is replete with examples of prostitution, which was once closely associated with religious beliefs and customs.[1] In ancient Babylonia, most females were often required to offer themselves sexually to strangers in a worship ceremony.[2] Prostitution among ancient Jews was considered acceptable "without any moral condemnation"[3]; in ancient Cyprus, women became prostitutes as a prerequisite for marriage.[4] In the Orient, prostitution flourished by 300 B.C.,[5] and Greek prostitutes included high-class mistresses and slaves.[6] Even young girls were subjected to forced prostitution in historical times. Indeed, many societies not only considered the practice to be proper but actually "encouraged treating children as marketable commodities and selling them into slavery or prostitution."[7]

The history of prostitution notwithstanding, few today regard this as a legitimate "profession" per se; there are generally no professional skills, study, or training required. Yet prostitution remains a steady, viable occupation for many females today, with no end in sight.

What Is a Prostitute?

When we think of the word *prostitute*, a number of synonyms come to mind, many of them stereotypical and sexist: whore, fallen woman, streetwalker, call girl, white slave, drug addict, runaway, and even victim. What is a prostitute by definition? According to the dictionary, a prostitute is "one hired as a sexual partner"; to prostitute oneself is "to offer oneself to another as a paid sexual partner." Prostitution is thereby the act of sexual relations between a prostitute and a paying customer.

Because today the lines are sometimes blurred between what constitutes prostitution and what does not, it is not always as black and white in real life as the dictionary suggests. For example, not all prostitution involves the direct exchange of money between the participants; nor do all "offers" of prostitution result in actual sexual acts. Hence, some *would-be* prostitutes may not actually be prostitutes in the strictest sense of the definition.

Later we will examine teenage female prostitution and male prostitution. For purposes of this discussion, the emphasis will be on the adult female prostitute, who tends to generate the most attention empirically and by definition. *Women and Criminality* defined the woman prostitute as "any female aged 18 and over who engages in any sexual relations (such as intercourse, fellatio, exhibitionism) primarily for material and/or financial gain, with persons other than their married partners."[8] It should be added that some working prostitutes are known to be married to their pimps. Therefore, if their sexual intimacy is a reflection of "payment" for services of prostitution rendered rather than normal married relations, the definition would include sex acts between married partners.

Defining Prostitution

Prostitution has taken on many definitions as it relates to sex for hire. Some define it explicitly within social or legal terms and parameters; others define prostitution as "at most only a marginal type of vice."[9] Historically, the vast majority of definitions of prostitution have been sex-specific or focused on adult female prostitution. Today these definitions have expanded to include adolescent female prostitution, boy prostitution, adult male prostitution, homosexual prostitution, bisexual prostitution, and even prostitution by phone and on-line services.

Typically, most definitions of female prostitution are divided into two types: social definitions and legal definitions.

SOCIAL DEFINITIONS OF PROSTITUTION

Social definitions of prostitution often regard prostitution as sexual relations that include some form of monetary payment or barter and are characterized by promiscuity and/or emotional apathy. Prostitution was defined by one social scientist as "sexual intercourse on a promiscuous and mercenary basis, with emotional indifference."[10] Edwin Lemert included barter as a variable of the interaction before sexual relations.[11] Charles Winick and Paul Kinsie defined prostitution as the "granting of nonmaterial sexual access, established by mutual agreement of the woman, her client, and/or her employer for remuneration which provides part or all of her livelihood."[12] Paul Goldstein's definition was simply "nonmarital sexual service for material gain."[13] In 1914, Abraham Flexner wrote that prostitution is

> characterized by three elements variously combined: barter, promiscuity and emotional indifference. The barter need not involve the passage of money. ... Nor need promiscuity be utterly choiceless: a woman is not the less a prostitute because she is more or less selective in her associations. Emotional indifference may be fairly inferred from barter and promiscuity. In this sense any person is a prostitute who habitually or intermittently has sexual relations more or less promiscuously for money or other mercenary consideration. Neither notoriety, arrest nor lack of other occupation is an essential criterion.[14]

Flexner postulated that one broad-based definition reflected the harm to society brought on by prostitution. He named four social costs of prostitution in particular: economic waste, spread of sexually transmitted diseases, personal demoralization, and the relationship of prostitution to social disorder and criminality.

Another social definition was advanced by Richard Goodall, who defined prostitution as the selling of sex by a person who "earns a living wholly or in part by the more or less indiscriminate, willing and emotionally indifferent provision of sexual services of any description to another, against payment, usually in advance but not necessarily in cash."[15]

Such socially defined views of prostitution typically influence legally drawn definitions.

LEGAL DEFINITIONS OF PROSTITUTION

Legal definitions of prostitution have traditionally focused largely on female prostitutes and promiscuity and thus could be viewed as biased in their meaning. One researcher notes: "Prostitution is really the only crime in the penal law where two people are doing a thing mutually agreed upon and yet only one, the female partner, is subject to arrest."[16]

This double standard is reflected in early legal perspectives on prostitution. Near the turn of the century, the U.S. Supreme Court defined prostitution as involving "women who for hire or without hire offer their bodies to indiscriminate intercourse with men."[17]

In *Prostitution in the United States*, Howard Woolston posited that before 1918, the only statutory definition of prostitution was Section 2372 of the Indiana Law, which read, "Any female who frequents or lives in a house of ill-fame or associates with women of bad character for chastity, either in public or at a house which men of bad character frequent or visit, or who commits adultery or fornication for hire shall be deemed a prostitute."[18]

A study of court decisions before 1918 indicates the legal dilemma in defining prostitution. "In some cases, the element of gain was considered an essential ingredient of prostitution, and in others it was not the case. Dictionary definitions, whether those of Webster or of the Law Dictionaries, are equally confusing. In Webster the definition varies according to the edition."[19]

As recently as 1968, the Oregon Supreme Court sought to differentiate between the prostitute and the nonprostitute when it ruled: "The feature which distinguishes a prostitute from other women who engage in illicit intercourse is the indiscrimination with which she offers herself to men for hire."[20]

Prostitution is currently illegal in all 50 states. Only in 12 rural counties in Nevada is prostitution legal. Thirty-eight states strictly prohibit payment for sexual relations; solicitation laws exist in 44 states and the District of Columbia; and other states outlaw prostitution through vagrancy and loitering statutes.[21]

Legally, prostitution is a misdemeanor, or an offense that typically results in a fine and/or up to a 30-day jail term. However, other charges related to prostitution can lead to stiffer penalties. These include pandering or pimping and income tax evasion. Recently Heidi Fleiss, dubbed the "Hollywood Madam," was convicted in California of pandering and was sentenced to three years in prison. She was also convicted on federal charges of evading income taxes and laundering call girl profits and was sentenced to 37 months in federal prison.[22]

Many see the Fleiss example as proof of gender-based discrimination in the prostitution laws. The evidence supports this. Females are far more likely to be arrested, prosecuted, and incarcerated for prostitution-related activities than males. In 1995, there were 49,491 females arrested in the United States for prostitution and commercialized vice, compared with 31,573 males.[23] One in 3 women in jails was arrested for prostitution; 7 in 10 women imprisoned for felonies were initially arrested for prostitution.[24]

The disparity in arrests can also be seen apropos of female prostitutes and their male clients. It is estimated that 1 in 5 males solicits prostitution at some point in his life. However, official statistics reveal that only 2 johns are arrested for every 8 prostitutes.[25] A report on female prostitutes in the District of Columbia found that whereas 1,110 women were arrested for prostitution that year, only 4 men were charged with solicitation.[26]

White Slavery

Within the world of prostitution, an even darker phenomenon exists called *white slavery*. The dictionary defines a *white slave* as a woman forced into prostitution — as opposed to those who enter the business voluntarily and are thus free to leave the same way. The term *white slavery* was introduced at the 1902 Paris conference "on traffic in persons and was meant to differentiate the enslavement of white women from the age-old practice of black enslavement."[27] In fact, "white slaves" were not limited to white women but included females and males of all ages, nationalities, and races who "could be tricked, kidnapped, and coerced into prostitution."[28]

The practice of white slave prostitutes has existed for centuries throughout the world. When the British colonized Australia during the 17th and 18th centuries, "shiploads of British women convicted of crimes were sent to the new continent and forced into a life of prostitution."[29]

White slavery remains a serious problem worldwide as millions of females are forced to become prostitutes or indentured sex slaves by pimps, brokers, organized criminals, and even family members. In a 1991 conference of organizations of Southeast Asian women, it was estimated that 30 million women had been sold into sex slavery since the mid–1970s.[30] It is approximated that anywhere from 200,000 to 500,000 women are smuggled from developing countries to the West annually.[31] These women are often lured on false promises of high-paying employment, marriage, and/or a better life, then are forced instead into prostitution.

The problem also exists in the United States and seems to be growing. Asian crime syndicates are believed to be smuggling tens of thousands of females into the United States each year. Once here, the women are often forced into a life of prostitution and sexual slavery behind fronts such as massage parlors and modeling agencies.[32]

Some sex slaves from countries such as Korea are trafficked into the United States legally as brides to American soldiers. These GIs are bribed by Asian flesh traders to marry prostitutes. Typically the soldiers are paid between $5,000 and $10,000 to bring the women here and a similar amount to divorce them.[33] In other instances, GIs may unknowingly marry prostitutes. Either way the women, who usually speak little to no English, are forced into brothels in cities like Detroit and Houston to repay marriage fees and plane fares. Generally, the sums are so high that payment is impossible other than as indentured sex slaves.

The implications of worldwide white slavery and sexual exploitation will be discussed in depth in Part V.

Teenage Prostitution

Of even more concern than adult female prostitution in this country is the prostitution of teenagers. Teen prostitution, also known as child prostitution, is generally defined as the participation, for pay or barter, by minors (usually under the age of 18) in sexual acts with adults or other minors where no force is used. This includes intercourse, oral copulation, and sodomy. What differentiates child prostitution from statutory rape is the exchange of money, drugs, or other goods as payment for services rendered.

It is estimated that there are well over one million teenagers active as prostitutes.[34] Many have been abused and are runaways or throwaways. They often compete with each other and adult prostitutes in selling their bodies and souls. There are at least as many girl prostitutes as boy prostitutes, and likely more. What they share is a life fraught with risks and danger.

Chapter 2

The Magnitude of Female Prostitution

Arriving at the precise number of female prostitutes in the United States would be impossible, given the wide range, and often secrecy, of prostitution operations. These include prostitutes who work the streets, in massage parlors and brothels, as call girls and in escort services, and through other means. There is also the task of attempting to separate adult women from teenage girl prostitutes.

What is known, and generally agreed upon by most authorities and researchers, is that females actively engaged in prostitution number into the millions. The figures may double or triple when we add women who work only part-time or are categorized as mistresses.

The reality is that prostitution is big business and continues to draw countless girls and women, for economic and psychological reasons, because of coercion by pimps and sexual victimization, for sexual needs, desires, or adventure, and because of drug addiction. Hence, we face an epidemic of females selling their bodies, and in spite of the best attempts at curbing or eliminating the problem, there is little indication that prostitution will be disappearing anytime soon.

Arrests of Females for Prostitution

Most experts agree that only a fraction of prostitutes are ever arrested. Nevertheless, official arrest data offers the one steady indicator of the scope of prostitutes' involvement with the legal system, if not their overall numbers. Such figures also allow us some perspective on other prostitution data.

Table 2-1: Female Arrests for Prostitution and Commercialized Vice, by Community Type, 1995

Community Type	Total Number of Arrests	Percent
Cities[a]	47,297	95%
Suburban Areas[b]	4,079	8%
Suburban Counties[c]	2,098	4%
Rural Counties[d]	96	Less than 1%

[a]Arrest totals include those under suburban areas.
[b]Includes cities with under 50,000 inhabitants and unincorporated areas with Metropolitan Statistical Areas (MSAs).
[c]Counties within an MSA, including a central city or urbanized area, of at least 50,000 inhabitants.
[d]Comprised primarily of unincorporated areas with under one percent of total arrests.

Source: Adapted from U.S. Department of Justice, Federal Bureau of Investigation, *Crime in the United States: Uniform Crime Reports 1995* (Washington, D.C.: Government Printing Office, 1996), pp. 234, 243, 252, 261.

Arrest figures for female offenders are compiled by the Federal Bureau of Investigation (FBI) through its annual *Crime in the United States: Uniform Crime Reports (UCR)*. Most arrests for prostitutes are compiled under the *UCR* offense *prostitution and commercialized vice*, defined as "sex offenses of a commercialized nature, such as prostitution, keeping a bawdy house, procuring, or transporting women for immoral purposes. Attempts are included."[1]

According to the most recent *UCR*, 49,491 females were arrested for prostitution and commercialized vice in 1995 (thousands of other female prostitutes are arrested under other offenses, such as runaways).[2]

Arrests by Age

Of the females arrested for prostitution and commercialized vice in 1995, 99 percent were age 18 and over. The vast majority of arrestees fell between the ages of 25 and 34. More than 26 percent were age 30 to 34; 23 percent were age 25 to 29. Women aged 23, 24, and 35 to 39 were slightly more likely to be arrested than those age 19 to 22.

Among females under age 18, arrests peaked at age 17, more than doubling the total for age 16. Arrests declined thereafter the younger the age.[3]

Arrests by Community Size

Most females arrested for prostitution plied their trade in cities. As shown in Table 2-1, 95 percent of the female arrests for prostitution and commercialized vice in 1995 occurred in cities. Eight percent of the arrests took place in suburban areas, while 4 percent were in suburban counties and less than

**Figure 2-1: Total Arrests for Prostitution
and Commercialized Vice, by Sex, 1995**

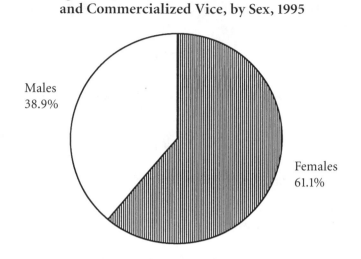

Males
38.9%

Females
61.1%

Source: Adapted from U.S. Department of Justice, Federal Bureau of Investigation, *Crime in the United States: Uniform Crime Reports 1995* (Washington, D.C.: Government Printing Office, 1996), p. 225.

1 percent in rural counties. See the table notes for community size differences and statistical explanations.

ARREST COMPARISONS WITH MALE ARRESTEES

Figure 2-1 compares female and male arrests for prostitution and commercialized vice in 1995. Females accounted for more than 61 percent of all arrests, compared with 38.9 percent for males. Prostitution arrests accounted for about 2 percent of the total female arrests and comprised less than 1 percent of all male arrests.

ARREST TRENDS FOR FEMALE PROSTITUTES

Arrest trends for females arrested for prostitution and commercialized vice can be seen in Table 2-2. From all indications, arrests of females for prostitution have declined in recent years, though the drop was less substantial in short-term figures. Between 1986 and 1995, arrests decreased by nearly 25 percent. Arrest trend from 1991 to 1995 also reveal a drop in arrests for prostitution and commercialized vice, at almost 14 percent. From 1994 to 1995, arrests decreased by just over 2 percent. The last figure reveals that the decline in total arrests for prostitution was considerably less the shorter the trend period.

Table 2-2: Female Arrest Trends for
Prostitution and Commercialized Vice, 1986–1995[a]

1994	1995	Percent Change	1991	1995	Percent Change	1986	1995	Percent Change
50,077	48,896	-2.4%	49,147	42,448	-13.6%	59,805	45,0068	-24.6%

[a]Based on arrest trends data from the three time periods listed, which may differ from arrest
data noted for only 1995.

Source: Adapted from U.S. Department of Justice, Federal Bureau of Investigation,
Crime in the United States: Uniform Crime Reports 1995 (Washington, D.C.: Government Printing Office, 1996), pp. 213, 215, 217.

Shortcomings of Official Data

Though official statistics provide an important measure of female crime
and arrests, the limitations of such data for the study of female prostitution
must be pointed out. For one, arrest data does not reveal the true extent of
female prostitutes, since the majority selling sex are never arrested. A second
shortcoming is that not all people arrested for prostitution are recorded under
the offense of prostitution and commercialized vice. Depending on the jurisdiction, some prostitutes may be arrested and charged with disorderly conduct,
loitering violations, drug abuse violations, or other offenses.

There is also the very real concern that the police may be biased in those
they choose or are able to arrest. For example, a streetwalker is far more likely
to face arrest than a high-class call girl. This may be due to police perception
of different types of prostitutes as much as to accessibility and visibility.

Edwin Sutherland and Donald Cressey have addressed the shortcomings
of official statistics in measuring crime in general: "The statistics about crime
and delinquency are probably the most unreliable and most difficult of all statistics. It is impossible to determine with accuracy the amount of crime in any
given jurisdiction for any particular time."[4] Charles Shireman and Frederic
Reamer noted that the limitations of official statistics include the "unknown
relationship between the number of crimes actually committed, the number
of those reported to the police, and the number of those so reported actually
recorded and reported by the police."[5]

Other drawbacks of *UCR* and police statistics include the following:

• Official data reflects only those offenses that law enforcement agencies are
   aware of.
• The *UCR* statistics vary.
• The arrest statistics include differential enforcement.

• Defining a crime (that is, *arrest, charge, incarceration*) can lead to overlap and sometimes confusion.
• Law enforcement agencies may be politically motivated or otherwise encouraged to inflate arrest figures or underreport crime.

Assessing the Number of Prostitutes in the United States

Aside from official statistics that tell us the number of females arrested for prostitution, few reliable sources assess the actual number of women and girls selling their bodies for purposes of prostitution in America. The best estimates are that at least 2 million females are active as prostitutes, and likely many more. When one considers the means by which prostitution is alive and well in this country (for example, more than 200 known escort services operate in Portland, Oregon), it is anyone's guess just how staggering the problem might be.

It is estimated that there are between 300,000 and 600,000 female prostitutes under the age of 18 in the United States.[6] Some researchers have doubled that number when considering 16- and 17-year-old prostitutes.[7] A recent 50-state survey of teenage prostitution found that it had increased in 37 percent of the "affected" cities.[8]

More than one million girls run away from home annually.[9] As many as 35 percent are believed to be *throwaways*: girls forced out of the home and often unreported as runaways.[10] A majority of these girls end up as teen prostitutes for survival and ultimately swell the number of adult female prostitutes.

Because most prostitutes manage to elude law enforcement and arrest figures, as well as researchers, their true numbers may never be known. What can be ascertained is that in the competitive sex industry, more and more females are being aggressively pursued, often being offered far more than they ever receive. Hence, the number of girls and women entering the profession will likely swell in the coming years as we enter the new century.

Chapter 3

Types of Prostitutes

As we enter the last years of the 1990s, prostitution has found new ways to expand and flourish, making it that much more difficult to contain. Aside from the more traditional streetwalker and call girl, prostitutes can ply their trade under a variety of headings — including student, housewife, and sex slave — and even on the Internet. Prostitutes also vary in terms of psychological and sociological profiles, racial and ethnic attributes, socioeconomic classes, and age. Consequently, there are many *types* of prostitutes making up the world of prostitution.

Prostitute Typologies

Much of the research on types of prostitutes has focused on the motivations for entry into prostitution and on the prostitute's situational and economic circumstances. In *Prostitution and Morality*, Harry Benjamin and R. E. L. Masters divided prostitutes into 2 general types: *voluntary* and *compulsive*. Voluntary prostitutes enter the business rationally and freely. Compulsive prostitutes tend to act under compulsion due to "psychoneurotic" needs or addiction to narcotics. The researchers found that neither type of prostitute was mutually exclusive of the other.[1]

Paul Goldstein described prostitutes in terms of *occupational commitment* and *occupational milieu*. Occupational commitment refers to the frequency of a woman's prostitution and is subdivided into three types:

- *Temporary prostitute*: a discrete act of prostitution, lasting not more than six months in a specific occupational milieu
- *Occasional prostitute*: 2 or more discrete acts of prostitution in a specific

16

occupational milieu, each instance lasting no longer than six months in duration
- *Continual prostitute*: prostitution lasting more than six months in a particular occupational milieu on a regular basis[2]

Occupational milieu relates to the specific types of prostitution in which a female is involved.[3] Goldstein divides these into seven categories:

- *Streetwalker*: a woman who overtly solicits men on the street and offers sexual favors for pay
- *Call girl*: a woman who works in a residence or hotel soliciting clients or who solicits by phone
- *Massage parlor prostitute*: a woman who offers sexual services in a massage parlor, not always limited to massages or fondling
- *House prostitute*: a woman who works in an establishment that is created specifically for prostitution and where male clients are provided sexual favors for payment
- *Madam*: a woman who supplies other prostitutes with male customers for a percentage of the fee
- *Mistress*: a woman who is mainly supported by one man at a time or who sees only one man at a time for paid sexual favors
- *Barterer*: a woman who exchanges sexual relations for professional or other services or for material goods (such as drugs or clothing)

Jennifer James divided prostitutes into two classes: *true prostitutes* and *part-timers*. From these she established roles played by prostitutes. True prostitutes' roles included outlaws, rip-off artists, hypes, old-timers, ladies, and thoroughbreds. Part-timers included prostitutes who had no style and amateurs or "hos."[4] James found that none of the roles were mutually exclusive of one another, since they described different aspects of prostitute behavior rather than complete behavioral sets.

Prostitutes are also categorized by class, money, and the opportunities available to them. Those at the lowest levels of prostitution tend to make the least amount of money and work harder to keep what they make. On the other hand, prostitutes on the high-priced end can make a comfortable, if not financially independent, living while having a lower risk for the dangers often accompanying prostitutes, such as sexual assault and drug addiction.

Types of Prostitutes

Female prostitutes can be grouped into a number of categories — each with distinct qualities, though they can also cross over into one another. These include but are not limited to *streetwalkers, call girls, madams, in-house prostitutes, indentured sex slaves, escort service prostitutes, drug-addicted prostitutes, homeless prostitutes, part-time prostitutes*, and *professional dominatrices.*

STREETWALKERS

Streetwalking prostitutes are perhaps the type we are most familiar with. Hollywood has often portrayed streetwalkers as gum-chewing young women in short skirts, black stockings, and high-heeled shoes. This is considered the lowest form of prostitution. As one researcher noted, streetwalkers "live in a vastly different world" from that of many of their counterpart prostitutes.[5] It is estimated that less than 15 percent of all prostitutes fall into this category.[6]

The majority of teenage prostitutes are streetwalkers. One study estimated that 20 percent of all streetwalking prostitutes are teenagers.[7] Many streetwalkers have pimps, are addicted to drugs, and have little hope for advancing to another level of prostitution.

CALL GIRLS

Call girls are probably depicted just as often in movies as streetwalkers. They represent the elite class of prostitutes, work out of expensive hotels or apartments, and generally have a steady clientele of well-paying customers. Usually in their late teens to mid-twenties, these "high-class" prostitutes "pride themselves on their attractiveness and their ability to look successful."[8] Many call girls boast of their earnings, which are often well above those of many career women in legitimate occupations. Experts estimate that one-quarter of all prostitutes are call girls.[9]

MADAMS

Madams have forever cemented their own place in the public's mind over the years. The madam is defined in the dictionary as "a woman manager of a brothel." Two of the more infamous madams in recent memory are Sydney Barrows, dubbed the "Mayflower Madam," and Heidi Fleiss, known as the "Hollywood Madam." Fleiss, who provided prostitutes to wealthy businessmen sometimes for as much as $10,000, was convicted on state charges of pandering and federal charges of income tax evasion, money laundering, and conspiracy to conceal her crimes.[10]

IN-HOUSE PROSTITUTES

In-house prostitutes usually ply their trade at brothels, massage parlors, modeling agencies, and other establishments fronting for prostitution. Many of the working women and girls are solicited through personal ads, often promising big money and success through legitimate modeling or pornography.

Rarely do they realize the full extent of what they are getting themselves into. A number of these in-house operations are controlled by organized crime and Asian gangs. In Asian communities, thousands of young females are smuggled into this country annually; "gang rapes and narcotics often are used" to force them into prostitution.[11]

INDENTURED SEX SLAVES

Many such girls and women become virtual indentured sex slaves, forced into prostitution to pay off debts to smugglers or simply through fear and intimidation. Although sex slavery and forced prostitution are a far greater problem outside the United States — particularly in Third World countries and eastern Europe — they are of no less concern here as more and more females fall prey to this type of sexual bondage (see also Part V).

ESCORT SERVICE PROSTITUTES

The escort service business is booming in cities across the United States. Most experts agree that the vast majority of these are fronts for prostitution. Escort services dispatch women as "dates" to male customers' homes, hotels, or elsewhere for massages, companionship, and often sexual services. In Portland, Oregon, escorts charge an average of $165 an hour for a date. There are more than 200 such agencies in the city, easily found in Yellow Pages advertisements under such names as "Exotic Entertainment" and "Elegant Babes."

Escort service prostitutes tend to view themselves as superior to their streetwalking counterparts. But they are below upper-class call girls on the prostitution scale in both prestige and income.

DRUG ADDICTED PROSTITUTES

Drug-addicted prostitutes often depend on prostitution to support their habits, using drugs as a secondary practice to prostitution. These females face even greater hazards than non-drug-addicted prostitutes, hazards including drug robberies from other addicts and AIDS from sharing dirty needles. Most drug-addicted prostitutes occupy the lower rung of the prostitution ladder, but prostitutes of all types have problems with drug abuse or addiction. A researcher for the Centers for Disease Control noted the alarming relationship between female crack-cocaine addicts and prostitution: "Women crack addicts are sometimes kept at crack houses and given the drug in exchange for sex with the dealers or clients. The women become virtual slaves to both the drug and the dealers."[12]

It is estimated that as many as 50 percent of all adolescent female prostitutes use drugs regularly.[13] The total is likely even higher for adult female prostitutes, many of whom graduated into prostitution from child prostitution.

Although marijuana is the most commonly used and abused drug by prostitutes, a high percentage use drugs also intravenously or combine various drugs and/or alcohol.[14]

HOMELESS PROSTITUTES

The number of prostitutes who are homeless is on the rise across the country. Described by one writer as "at the bottom of the heap," homeless prostitutes are often runaways, throwaways, and substance abusers.[15] Most must resort to streetwalking to survive. Consequently they face assorted risks including assault, arrest, and exposure to the AIDS virus.[16] It is believed that a high percentage of homeless females ultimately end up as prostitutes.[17]

PART-TIME PROSTITUTES

A growing number of prostitutes can be termed part-timers. This largely hidden class of prostitutes includes housewives, young mothers, college students, women with jobs that provide insufficient income, drug users, and others whose circumstances do not require full-time prostituting. The motivations for being a part-time prostitute include getting easy, sometimes significant, money for tuition, the mortgage, drugs, baby food, and clothes. One article on middle-class prostitution noted, "For women who are short on money and unconventional, hooking has become like waitressing — a means of getting by."[18] Given the relatively low risk of detection, many more females in short-term dire straits may turn to part-time prostitution as a quick fix.

PROFESSIONAL DOMINATRICES

Another kind of prostitute is known as a professional dominatrix. She often uses B&D (bondage and domination) or S&M (sadomasochism), along with other sexual services, to inflict pain and pleasure on her customers. A professional dominatrix can charge $150 or more for a one-hour session. Her clients, often middle- or upper-class men, tend to have a high tolerance for pain and an eagerness to be dominated. One dominatrix spoke about a recent session: "I ordered him to arrive after I had been to my dance class and was nice and sweaty. I had him clean my armpits, my feet, and my inner thighs with his tongue. For further amusement, following my own energy, I worked over his nipples using nipple clamps and weights. The energy between us was roaring. Believe me, this was 'real B&D' for us both."[19]

Race, Ethnicity, and Prostitution

There are no reliable figures on the classification of prostitutes by race and ethnicity. Most studies indicate that the vast majority of females selling sex are white.[20] However, in inner-city red-light districts, the percentage of racial and ethnic minority prostitutes (such as blacks and Hispanics) may increase as much as 50 percent.[21]

Arrest data indicates that poor, black female streetwalkers are most often targeted by police as prostitutes because they are most likely to be "forced onto the streets and into blatant solicitation where the risk of arrest is highest."[22] Black women are seven times more likely to be arrested for prostitution than are prostitutes of other races.[23] Most such arrests occur in the inner cities, where "living standards are low, the level of depression high, and police prejudice endemic."[24]

Studies on streetwalkers show an overrepresentation of black females. After interviewing more than 3,000 New York City streetwalking prostitutes over a three-year period, Joyce Wallace found that half were black, one-fourth Hispanic, and one-fourth white.[25]

White girls are far more likely to engage in prostitution than are girls of other racial or ethnic groups. Studies in Minneapolis[26] and San Francisco[27] found that eight in ten adolescent female prostitutes were white. Black girls have been found to represent anywhere from 10 to 50 percent of the prostitutes sampled in studies.[28] Hispanic, Native American, and Asian girl prostitutes are comparatively rare, with samples ranging from 2 to 11 percent of the girls studied.[29]

Legal Prostitution

Legal prostitution exists in several countries including the Netherlands, Germany, Brazil, England, and Hungary. However, Nevada is the only state in the United States where prostitution is not outlawed. Even then, this legality is only in 12 rural counties in strictly regulated brothels. Female prostitutes working at these brothels are regularly tested for AIDS. Studies have shown the rate of HIV infection to be significantly lower among brothel prostitutes than among streetwalkers. A University of California at Berkeley study of brothel workers and Nevada streetwalkers found that whereas none of the brothel prostitutes were HIV-positive, 6 percent of the streetwalkers were.[30] Studies conducted in Newark, New York City, and Washington, D.C., found that 57 percent, 35 percent, and nearly half the prostitutes, respectively, tested positive for the AIDS virus.[31]

Many have used Nevada brothels as a model example for decriminalization or legalization of prostitution in the entire United States. Such prostitutes' rights organizations as COYOTE (Call Off Your Old Tired Ethics) promote decriminalization, sexual privacy, and the repeal of all laws banning prostitution as well as pimping and pandering laws.[32] Others disagree with any such changes in the status quo. For instance, it is noted that even in Nevada,

prostitutes regularly work illegally in and around casinos and most legal brothels are connected to illegal pimping by "paying a finder's fee to pimps for bringing in new women."[33]

Even in legal brothels, prostitutes complain of less than ideal conditions,
as one brothel worker describes: "We had to live in the house while we were
working, usually for three week stints, and leaving the premises was discour-
aged when it wasn't forbidden. They test the women regularly for sexually
transmitted diseases, but they don't test the clients. The shifts are long — 12 to
14 hours — and the management takes half of the fee, which can be as low as
$40.[34]

Aside from the legal brothels of Nevada, many purveyors of prostitutes
have successfully circumvented laws across the country in the form of escort
services, massage parlors, nightclubs, and other establishments. Even when
police are well aware of the problem, there is often little they can do or seek
to do about it. One writer referred to these services as "disguised prostitution,
at very expensive rates."[35] In other instances, law enforcement doesn't even
attempt to enforce prostitution laws. For example, a mistress to a single male
client rarely, if ever, faces any legal challenges to her prostitution.

Later in the book, the issues of decriminalization and legalization will be
further addressed.

Emerging Types of Prostitution

Aside from the more traditional areas of prostitution, new means of selling sex have emerged in recent years, fueled by demand and largely unregulated territory:

• *Phone sex*: live and taped sex talk by female operators is available 24 hours
  a day, often for anywhere from 99¢ to $3.95 a minute. Services may be
  charged directly to your phone bill or credit card.
• *Lap dancing*: women perform private "lap dances" for male clients at a bar
  or strip club. The dancer's performance usually includes nude or semi-
  nude suggestive body movements, gyrating, fondling, and being fondled
  and caressed by the client. Many men achieve orgasms through this contact. With tips, women can make anywhere from $100 to $250 a night.
• *Cyber sex*: through the Internet and on-line services such as CompuServe and
  America Online, women can have computer sex with men or other women
  in chat rooms or through e-mail. Cyberspace can also be used to adver-
  tise sexual services and sellers of sex through Web pages and message
  boards.

Chapter 4

Theories and Motivations Regarding Female Prostitution

Many social scientists, criminologists, and other researchers have developed theories explaining the existence of female prostitution. Others have focused largely on the motivations for females to become prostitutes as well as stay in the business. In some instances, explanations have been dismissed as sexist or inadequate. Many of the causes of prostitution are gender-neutral, equally attributable to female and male prostitutes alike, given similar circumstances. Virtually all theories and motivational factors can be put into eight categories: (1) *biological*, (2) *psychological*, (3) *sociological*, (4) *economic*, (5) *drug-related*, (6) *physical and sexual abuse*, (7) *sexual adventure* and *promiscuity*, and (8) *mental illness*.

Biological Theories

Italian psychiatrist Cesare Lombroso was among the first to study female criminality scientifically. Believed by some to be the founder of the biological-positivistic school of criminology, Lombroso collaborated with his son-in-law, William Ferrero, to write *The Female Offender* in 1894.[1] Combining quantitative and qualitative data on female criminals, they hypothesized that females, *particularly prostitutes*, were "biologically predisposed" to criminal behavior. Such females were thought to be atavistic, or possessing primitive hereditary characteristics not found in normal women. For example, they believed a prostitute was "likely to have very heavy lower jaws, large nasal spines, simple cranial

23

sutures, deep frontal sinuses, and wormian bones. A 'fallen woman' usually possessed occipital irregularities, a narrow forehead, prominent cheekbones, and a 'virile' type of face."[2]

Lombroso and Ferrero's work has long been rejected, due primarily to the inadequacies of their methodologies, the relatively small sample, and the gender-based atavism theory. More recent biologically based research on female criminal behavior has linked genetic factors to sexual promiscuity in girls, as well as linking menstruation and premenstrual syndrome to female criminality.[3] This research is also generally seen as weak in its methodology and conclusions.

PSYCHOLOGICAL THEORIES

It was the psychoanalytic writings of Sigmund Freud that influenced much of the thinking on female prostitution in the early part of this century. Like Lombroso, Freud regarded prostitutes as biologically deficient and hence unable to resolve the Oedipus conflict. He believed them to be morally inferior and less able to control their impulses than men, implying that an inherent pathology existed in females who prostituted themselves.[4]

Many Freudian disciples came to regard prostitutes as frigid women with "immature psychosexual development and severely deficient object relationships."[5] However, case studies of "sex delinquents and prostitutes failed to indicate any general state of abnormality."[6] Jennifer James's study found that prostitutes experienced a higher rate of orgasm than the general female population, contradicting the notion of frigidity among female prostitutes.[7]

Modern psychiatry and psychology largely rejected Freudian interpretations of prostitution as biased, psychologically weak, and absent of necessary socially and economically recognized variables. Recent studies of prostitutes have found evidence of psychological problems ranging from depression to schizophrenia to suicidal tendencies.[8]

SOCIOLOGICAL THEORIES

Sociologist William Thomas was another significant early contributor to the study of female criminality. He criticized theories of prostitutes' biological inferiority, contending that gender differences in crime were more a reflection of social factors and acquired characteristics. Thomas proposed a dyadic goals-means conflict theory in which he believed every person has four basic desires: the desires for security, recognition, new experience, and response.[9] Criminality was most influenced by desires for new experience and response, the sociologist contended. He attributed female prostitution to the need for excitement and response; for a woman, "prostitution in one form or another was the most likely avenue to satisfy those needs."[10] Contemporary writers have repudiated Thomas's theory as unproven and paternalistic. One critic attacked his work as "sexist in that females were identified as offenders through sexual behavior. The sexual standards of society were rigid, and female deviators were castigated more harshly than male deviators. The significance of this in sociology was that a man's sexual behavior was only one facet of his total character, whereas a woman was actually defined by her sexuality."[11]

Sheldon and Eleanor Glueck studied the backgrounds of 500 Massachusetts female delinquents in the 1930s.[12] Many were prostitutes. The researchers concluded that a high percentage of the females were mentally defective and that their crimes were likely to be intergenerational. Although their research was comprehensive, critics found the findings to be heavily influenced by sexist attitudes and gender biases.

Otto Pollak's *The Criminality of Women*, published in 1950, was considered the definitive work on female crime during the postwar years.[13] Though influenced by Lombroso and Freud, Pollak established new theories on the criminal behavior of females, particularly prostitutes. He argued that women's crimes are primarily sexually motivated, compared with the economic motivation of male offenders. According to Pollak, women's crimes such as prostitution are inadequately reflected in the statistics because of their hidden nature; he theorized that females are addicted to easily concealed crimes and more deceitful than males in this concealment. Pollak's arguments have been rejected by many for their biases and lack of substantiation. In attacking his propositions, one writer argued, "Pollak's theories on causation were heavily influenced by Freudian analysis, [and] therefore are subject to the same criticism."[14]

In *The Lively Commerce*, Charles Winick and Paul Kinsie suggested that the social structure is threatened by prostitution because "people tend to equate sexual activity with stable relationships, typified by the family."[15] Kingsley Davis advanced a functionalist theory of prostitution — that "the function served by prostitution is the protection of the family unit, maintenance of the chastity and purity of the 'respectable' citizenry."[16] Davis theorized that the majority of women do not enter prostitution because "morality is more potent than the financial benefits of prostitution, and that this societal system of morality creates prostitution by defining the sex drive in terms of a meaningful social relationship and denouncing prostitution as a meaningless sexual relationship."[17]

In a social pathology hypothesis, Edwin Lemert described prostitution as a "formal extension of more generalized sexual pathology in our culture, of which sexual promiscuity and thinly disguised commercial exploitation of sex in informal context plays a large and important part."[18] From this perspective, prostitution is seen as situational and the act of prostitution as a reflection of the conflicts and strains inherent in society.

Cultural transmission theories hold that prostitution is the result of a "weakening of family and neighborhood control and the persistence and transmission from person to person of traditional delinquent activities."[19] Although some evidence supports the notion that a prostitute's introduction to prostitution comes from a girlfriend, a relative, or the neighborhood itself,[20] other studies have found that prostitution is not a product of ecological factors but rather is present at all income and occupational levels due to "urban anonymity and the weakening of traditional and moral values."[21]

ECONOMIC THEORIES

Most researchers have found economic influences to be significant in causing females to become prostitutes and to continue in the profession. Winick and Kinsie posited that a person's decision to become a prostitute is based largely on few work opportunities and the recognition of the income potential.[22] According to Lemert, women's inferior power and control over material gains in society make prostitution a viable means to balance this differential in status.[23]

Irrespective of the type of prostitute or prostitution, the primary motive for becoming a prostitute is the money it provides for the female and often others, such as a pimp or boyfriend. The reasons for needing or wanting the money vary from prostitute to prostitute and include supporting a lifestyle, a drug habit, children, or a pimp or merely having the basic necessities of life for a streetwalker or homeless prostitute.

In her comprehensive study of prostitutes, James described five aspects of the social-economic structure that pulls women into prostitution:

• No other occupations available to unskilled or low-skilled women provide an income comparable to that of prostitution.
• Almost no other occupations for unskilled or low-skilled women provide the independent, adventurous lifestyle of prostitution.
• The traditional "woman's role" is virtually synonymous with the culturally defined female sex role, which centers on physical appearance, service, and sexuality.
• The cultural significance of wealth and material items leads some women to desire advantages they are normally not afforded by their socioeconomic position in society.
• The discrepancy between accepted male and female sex roles creates the "Madonna-whore" view of female sexuality, such that women who are sexually active outside the parameters of their normal sex role expectations are labeled as deviants and thereby lose social status.[24]

In her study of teen prostitutes, Joan Johnson wrote: "Money becomes a symbol for love. Just as they could never get enough love as children, prostitutes can never seem to get enough money as teenagers.... This hunger for money helps to explain why some adolescents begin turning tricks while they are still living at home."[25] Because most child prostitutes lack self-esteem, making money "makes them feel good about themselves" as they are astounded that "people will pay for their bodies."[26]

How much money can a prostitute expect to make selling sex? This can vary considerably, according to the type of prostitute and the services offered. A National Task Force on Prostitution put the average "full time gross between $15,000 and $25,000; $200 to $500 weekly for solicitors on the streets; $500 for sauna workers; $300 to $1,200 for brothel hostesses."[27] Call girls make the most money turning tricks, earning anywhere from $1,000 to $2,500 a week at escort services to more than $2,000 a day as an independent operator. Some high-class call girls have been known to gross more than $1 million a year.[28]

DRUG-RELATED THEORIES

There is a strong relationship between substance abuse and prostitution. A number of studies have documented this correlation. One-third of women addicts support their habit by working as prostitutes.[29] A Baltimore study of female street addicts found that 96 percent of the daily users resorted to prostitution and other crime to feed their addiction.[30] Nearly three-quarters of the streetwalkers sampled in a New York study used illegal drugs.[31] Another study found more than 65 percent of the prostitutes were drug addicted.[32]

Teenage prostitution is closely associated with drug and alcohol abuse. Many female runaways were already abusers of drugs and/or alcohol before leaving home. In one study, almost 80 percent of the teen prostitutes surveyed said they were using drugs before becoming prostitutes.[33] Many are then forced into selling their bodies to support drug addiction.[34] Others quickly become addicts or alcoholics after entry into prostitution.[35]

The head of Defense for Children International U.S.A. stated, "The combined impact of the deterioration of the cities and the drug epidemic is driving this phenomenon forward fast."[36] Lower-class teens sell their bodies for drugs, food, shelter, and even status. Once on the streets, where few other alternatives exist for them, even those teenage prostitutes from middle- or upper-class backgrounds become vulnerable to the temptations and addiction of drugs and/or alcohol.

PHYSICAL AND SEXUAL ABUSE THEORIES

The majority of female prostitutes entered the profession as victims of physical or sexual abuse. Studies of runaways reveal that over half were victims of sexual or physical abuse at home, 60 percent had parents who abused alcohol and/or drugs, 25 percent had been raped, and almost all came from dysfunctional families.[37] One study found that 78 percent of the prostitutes sampled were forced to submit to sexual intercourse before age 14, usually with a family member or a close family acquaintance.[38] A Huckleberry House study found that 90 percent of the girl prostitutes had been sexually molested.[39] Maureen Crowley found that two of every three prostitutes in her study had been physically abused at home.[40] Other surveys have produced similar results.[41]

The cause-and-effect relationship between physical and sexual abuse and prostitution cannot be denied. As many such victims leave or are thrown out of abusive homes, they inevitably end up on the streets, in a life of prostitution and drugs. In many instances, the abuse they escaped numbs them to the abuse they face from pimps, customers, drug dealers, addicts, and even police.

SEXUAL ADVENTURE AND PROMISCUITY THEORIES

In spite of the strong negative factors associated with runaway and drug-addicted prostitutes, it would be naive to assume that sex itself or the sex industry is not influential in some females' (and males') decisions and motivations to enter prostitution. For many girls, excitement, adventure, money, and sex are enticements that prove stronger than any risks or any incentives to stay out of the business. In her study of prostitution, Dorothy Bracey found that many girls became prostitutes because of others they knew in the business.[42] A San Francisco social worker who counseled teen prostitutes sadly commented: "Sex is no longer for love and procreation, but solely for enjoyment. But this leads to fleeting sexual contacts which turn out to be meaningless. What gives them meaning is the profit."[43]

Another researcher spoke of the girl prostitute's need for physical affection as well as the camaraderie of other prostitutes — offering a temporary feeling of satisfaction and well-being. "At first, many find their attractiveness to the opposite sex exciting. They like the flattery and the fact that they can gain material wealth for bestowing sexual favors."[44] In James's study, the rise in prostitution among affluent girls is largely attributable to their need for adventure, sexual experimentation, and danger.[45]

The sex industry itself is seen as addictive to many females entering prostitution. The bright neon signs of red-light districts, the fast pace, the action, the drugs, and the lifestyle of the world of prostitution are almost irresistible to some. To others, the addiction to the business and often to drugs makes it nearly impossible to leave — usually until they are forced out by age, AIDS, arrest, incarceration, or death.

MENTAL ILLNESS THEORIES

Only a relatively small percentage of prostitutes are believed to be in the business due to mental illness. Nevertheless, there is strong evidence that many runaways and prostitutes who enter and remain in the business suffer from various mental and emotional disorders including depression, schizophrenia, emotional deprivation, and psychosis.[46] According to research, between 10 and

20 percent of adolescent girl prostitutes have been hospitalized in psychiatric institutions.[47] Half of the prostitutes had been hospitalized on more than one occasion. Studies have shown that as many as 50 percent of all female prostitutes have attempted suicide at least once.[48]

Chapter 5

AIDS and
Female Prostitution

Female prostitutes face their greatest threat not from abusive customers or pimps, substance abuse per se, or the elements that many of them must brave on the streets but instead from the deadly Acquired Immunodeficiency Syndrome, commonly known as AIDS. Just how many prostitutes would test positive for the Human Immunodeficiency Virus (HIV), the precursor to AIDS, is unclear. However, given that the virus is most commonly passed from one person to another through sexual contact or through the sharing of dirty needles between drug users, prostitutes are at particular risk for exposure. Studies have shown a clear link between prostitution, sexually transmitted diseases including AIDS, and intravenous (IV) drug use.[1] There is also evidence that female prostitutes are not in and of themselves spreading AIDS at a greater rate than the general public.[2]

How Is a Prostitute Infected with AIDS?

The majority of female prostitutes become HIV/AIDS infected by having sexual relations with customers (vaginal and anal intercourse and fellatio) and being IV drug users. Prostitutes (and their customers) who use or abuse non-IV drugs such as alcohol and stimulants have been shown to be related to high-risk activity, such as unprotected sex, and AIDS.[3] A study of streetwalking prostitutes and their risk factors for HIV infection noted, "Seventy-five percent of these contacts are limited to fellatio, an activity that clearly puts a woman more at risk than a man: common sense tells us that the AIDS virus gains easy entry through mouth lacerations from crack smoking."[4] For other

30

sexual contact between a prostitute and a male customer and the relationship to AIDS, studies show that the virus is also often passed "through unprotected, vaginal and anal intercourse and through the sharing of 'works' with infected substance abusers."[5] Though the use of condoms lowers the risk for HIV transmission by as much as 99 percent, misuse may lower this percentage considerably.

What happens when a prostitute becomes infected? In *Teen Prostitution*, Joan Johnson provides a frightening account: "The virus multiplies and spreads ... can attach itself to the body's vital T-cells and at the same time evade the body's defensive army of antibodies.... Colds become pneumonia. Tumors grow and multiply. Stomach aches become stomach ulcers. Yeast infections flourish unabated in the mouth or vagina.... Eventually, sick all the time, unable to eat or hold down food, in constant pain, and totally debilitated, the AIDS victim dies.[6] Even more alarming is that many prostitutes (and others) carry the virus for years without being aware of it or its worst symptoms — passing the death sentence on to unsuspecting johns, who then infect their wives and girlfriends and babies.

General Studies on Female Prostitution and AIDS

There is a substantial body of research on the correlation between AIDS/HIV infection and female prostitution. Studies worldwide have revealed cause-and-effect relationships between AIDS and prostitution in a number of areas, including use of alcohol and/or psychoactive drugs,[7] and have revealed variance in the rate and circumstances of infection from one country to another.[8] For example, researchers have found the high rate of AIDS in Africa to be largely a reflection of exposure through sexual activity only; in the United States and Europe, transmission of the AIDS virus is more likely to come from prostitutes or customers who are also IV drug users.[9] (See Part V for more discussion on the AIDS epidemic internationally.)

Here in the United States, AIDS continues to be viewed by many as a gay disease. In fact, the first person diagnosed with HIV infection in this country was a female prostitute.[10] The association between AIDS and prostitutes who are substance abusers is cause for alarm. Estimates of the proportion of female drug-using prostitutes range from 40 to 85 percent, according to Paul Goldstein's research on female prostitutes and drugs.[11] He found that for high-class prostitutes, drug addiction tended to come after entry into prostitution, whereas lower-class prostitutes were more likely to have been addicted before entering prostitution.[12]

D. Kelly Weisberg found drug and alcohol use to be common among teenage prostitutes, with many having experimented with psychedelic drugs and narcotics.[13] Other studies have linked prostitution to the location in which solicitation takes place, such as nightclubs, bars, and hotels.[14] In the book *AIDS, Drugs, and Prostitution*, Martin Plant emphasizes the relationship between prostitution, high-risk behavior, and AIDS: "Available evidence clearly supports the conclusion that alcohol and other drugs are associated with sexual behavior for a host of social and psychological reasons. Further, it is apparent that high-risk sexual activities are frequently associated with heavy alcohol and drug use. The AIDS-related risks of psychoactive drug use are compounded by the fact that high levels of alcohol and some other drugs depress the immune system."[15]

Experts have found that the tripartite relationship between substance abuse, sexual behavior, and AIDS increases the risk to exposure to the virus in two ways. One is that the "relaxing or disinhibiting" effects of alcohol and/or drugs may "increase the prospect of high-risk sexual activity."[16] Second, prostitutes and others who have an inclination to engage in some high-risk actions are also more likely to participate in others as well.[17]

AIDS and the Type of Female Prostitute

The risk of female prostitutes contracting AIDS appears to be closely related to the type of prostitute. Four types of prostitutes generally appear to face the greatest risk of exposure to the AIDS virus: (1) streetwalkers, (2) racial and ethnic minority prostitutes, (3) unregulated prostitutes, and (4) IV-drug-using prostitutes. Studies have found a higher incidence of HIV infection in these classes of prostitutes than in call girls, nonminority prostitutes, regulated (legal) prostitutes, and non-IV-drug-using prostitutes.

STREETWALKERS

Streetwalkers typically have the greatest risk of exposure to AIDS; call girls have the lowest. A University of Miami study of streetwalkers and prostitutes working at an escort service found that of 90 streetwalkers, 41 percent were infected. Comparatively, none of the 25 escort service prostitutes tested HIV-positive.[18] Another study found that 37 percent of the female streetwalking prostitutes who admitted to being IV drug users tested positive for the AIDS virus.[19] In a study of high-class call girl prostitutes, only one woman, who had a history of IV drug use, tested HIV-positive.[20]

RACIAL AND ETHNIC MINORITY PROSTITUTES

Black and Hispanic female prostitutes have been found to have a higher HIV infection rate than white or non–Hispanic prostitutes.[21] The differential is even greater when IV drug use is present. A Baltimore study of prostitutes who were HIV-seropositive with a history of drug abuse found that the rate of HIV infection was highest among blacks in lower-class urban areas.[22] Other studies have found similar results.[23]

UNREGULATED PROSTITUTES

Studies of legal prostitutes indicate that their risk of HIV infection is significantly lower than that of streetwalkers or unregulated prostitutes. In Germany, for example, licensed prostitutes were found to have only a 1 percent rate of HIV infection, compared with a 20 percent infection rate for unlicensed prostitutes.[24] In the United States, female prostitutes can ply their trade legally only in Nevada. A study of Nevada brothel prostitutes and Nevada streetwalkers found that whereas none of the brothel workers tested HIV-positive, 6 percent of the streetwalkers were infected.[25] By comparison, studies of streetwalkers in other cities found even higher rates. In Newark, 57 percent of the streetwalking prostitutes sampled tested positive for HIV; nearly 50 percent in Washington, D.C., and 35 percent in New York City had been exposed to the virus.[26]

The regulations of brothels, which regularly test their prostitutes, are seen as playing an important role in this lower rate of AIDS exposure for brothel workers. However, critics point out that even where there is legal prostitution, "it is matched by a flourishing black market."[27] In Las Vegas, for example, police arrest "between 300 to 400 prostitutes a month."[28]

Although the legalization of prostitution clearly has some serious drawbacks, there is merit in some sort of system in which prostitutes (and their customers) can be regularly tested, as well as supplied condoms to help reduce the risk to exposure and the spreading of the AIDS virus.

IV DRUG USING PROSTITUTES

Among all prostitutes, those who are IV drug users face the greatest risks for developing AIDS. According to a number of studies, the "proportion of IV drug using prostitutes is staggering: 61 percent."[29] A study investigating the rate of HIV infection in former streetwalkers and other women who were IV drug users found that 46 percent tested positive for HIV.[30] The women reported on average a total of 3,062 sex partners over their lifetimes. Those women who tested HIV negative reported having only one-third as many partners. Regarding this alarming finding, one researcher suggested: "Intravenous drug use and promiscuous sex were proving to be a deadly combination."[31]

Other research has also shown the correlation between prostitution, IV drug use, and HIV exposure. In an Amsterdam study, nearly one-third of the sample of IV drug users and drug-abusing prostitutes tested HIV-seropositive.[32] A. Johnson's review of European studies found that female prostitutes' rate of HIV infection was low, except when they were also IV drug users.[33] In their study of prostitutes and AIDS, M. Rosenberg and J. Weiner concluded: "Prostitutes are considered a reservoir for transmission of certain sexually transmitted diseases (STDs).... HIV infection in non drug using prostitutes tends to be low or absent, implying that sexual activity alone does not place them at high risk, while prostitutes who use intravenous drugs are far more likely to be infected with HIV.[34]

Adolescent Female Prostitutes and AIDS

The risks among female prostitutes for contracting AIDS are even greater for teenage prostitutes. "They know they're flirting with disease," noted the writer of an article on teen prostitutes and runaways. "There's an epidemic of old venereal infections, crabs and chlamydia, secondary syphilis and super-gonorrhea, resistant to penicillin."[35]

Now there is AIDS, and the two primary means of infection — unprotected sex and intravenous drug use — are key components in the life of a high percentage of adolescent female prostitutes. One article on young prostitutes notes the gravity of the situation:

> AIDS has a potentially disastrous effect on what is going on in the streets, particularly in the inner cities where sex, drugs and poverty cross paths that often lead out to the suburbs and all across the country. Many of these runaway and homeless adolescents, between 20,000 and 40,000 in New York City, up to 1.2 million nationwide, are caught at the juncture of risks.... Many people believe these adolescents will become part of the third wave of the AIDS epidemic.... The risk related behavior of runaway and homeless adolescents put them directly in the path of the disease.... Not only are these kids at higher risk with every sexual contact ... but they also have higher levels of drug use and sexually transmitted diseases ... [increasing] the risk for developing AIDS.[36]

James Farrow, of the University of Washington's Adolescent Medicine Division, concurred with this assessment. Speaking of teenage prostitutes and AIDS, he called the situation "a time bomb.... Because of their activity, their potential for spreading [AIDS] far and wide is pretty great."[37] The AIDS epidemic of HIV-infected adolescent prostitutes may already have begun. According to an article in the *New England Journal of Medicine*, it can take as long as ten years before the symptoms begin to manifest themselves.[38]

No one knows precisely how many girls selling their bodies have actually been exposed to the AIDS virus. However, some evidence indicates the frightening possibilities. Recently at Covenant House, New York City's largest shelter for runaways, 27 percent of the teens sampled tested positive for HIV.[39] It is estimated that 15 percent of the 11,000 youths that pass through the shelter yearly are HIV-positive.[40] For girls who prostitute themselves nightly, the rate of infection is believed to be more than 50 percent.[41]

Male Customers and AIDS

There is a dearth of research on AIDS and the male customers of female prostitutes. What studies exist suggest that the rate of infection is fairly low and is most prominent among johns who are IV drug users. Joyce Wallace's study of prostitutes' male clients found that of those men who had no other high-risk behavior, less than 1 percent tested positive for HIV.[42] In another study of customers of female prostitutes, approximately 2 percent of the males sampled were HIV-positive. Half the men had additional risk factors, such as being IV drug users or bisexual.[43]

Male Prostitutes and AIDS

Like their female counterparts, male prostitutes also face a high risk for AIDS.[44] In a study of male prostitutes in Denver, of those who tested positive for HIV, most had became infected through IV drug use and homosexual relations with nonclients.[45] Another study found that nearly one in five male prostitutes was HIV-positive.[46] Other research has found an even higher rate of infection among male hustlers who use IV drugs.[47] The impact of AIDS on the male prostitution subculture will be further examined in Chapter 18.

Female Prostitution, AIDS, and Sexism

In spite of the attention given to female prostitutes and to AIDS and its containment, the issue still involves important gender differences. For example, one recent government study found that many "female prostitutes are carrying the AIDS virus," and it warned men to avoid prostitutes.[48] This underscores the sexism that continues to prevail in the fears and misconceptions often associated with the disease.

Women and men differ when it comes to the idea of legalizing prostitution. In a 1991 Gallup Poll on the legalization of prostitution to help reduce the threat of AIDS, six out of ten women were against legalization while almost half the men favored the legalization of prostitution.[49] This suggests that women are at least as concerned with the ramifications of legalized prostitution for women in general as they are with AIDS but that men may be more interested in the possibility that legalization of prostitution could lower the risk of exposure to the AIDS virus.

Reducing the Spread of
AIDS Among Female Prostitutes

Trying to prevent or at least curtail the spread of AIDS between female prostitutes and their johns has proven to be a daunting task. Currently more than two dozen states have laws that require mandatory testing of prostitutes for HIV.[50] In at least 12 states, it is illegal to possess a hypodermic syringe.[51] These legal efforts notwithstanding, the educational approach has been seen as most significant in changing prostitutes' habits regarding the risk of HIV infection and eventually AIDS. Around the country, programs are under way to educate prostitutes, addicts, the homeless, and others who may be at high risk about the dangers of AIDS and about ways to reduce, if not eliminate, the risks of exposure. Literature, seminars, free condoms, disposable needles, toll-free numbers to counselors, and free tests for HIV are being provided to help solve this deadly problem of AIDS.

Studies suggest that this has made a difference among female prostitutes and their attitudes toward high-risk activities. A recent report from the National Research Council concluded that AIDS was not being spread by female prostitutes.[52] However, it is clear that prostitutes are still contracting the disease from johns and IV drug use and are passing it on to others, even if not in massive numbers. What is less certain is how the rate of infection among prostitutes compares with the rate among high-risk women who are not prostitutes. This issue needs to be further addressed in future research in the continuing fight against AIDS.

Part II

Women
and Prostitution

Chapter 6

The Scope of
Women's Prostitution

There are at least one million adult female prostitutes in the United States today. Many experts believe the actual figure could easily be double or triple that number. The number of women selling their bodies to men for cash, drugs, or other payment is unknown due to nonuniform studies, insufficient arrest data, and different standards across the country in defining what constitutes prostitution. The problem is real, it is massive, and the answers used to respond to female prostitution are inadequate.

The Extent of Women's Prostitution Globally

In sizing up the problem of female prostitution on American soil, one must look at the extent of women's prostitution worldwide for perspective and for an awareness of its epidemic nature. Estimates suggest that tens of millions of women around the world are prostitutes at any given time either voluntarily or through forced sexual slavery. According to figures from a 1991 conference of Southeast Asian women's groups, 30 million women had been sold into prostitution since the mid–1970s.[1]

In Japan, 70,000 Thai women work as "virtual indentured sex slaves" in clubs mostly controlled by Japanese organized crime.[2] More than 200,000 Bangladeshi women have been abducted and turned into prostitutes in Pakistan, according to the Human Rights Commission of Pakistan.[3] Ninety percent of the 100,000 female prostitutes in Bombay are believed to be indentured slaves.[4] One writer described this as only "the tip of the iceberg."[5]

Other estimates of women in prostitution internationally are equally alarming. It is estimated that in India alone there are 10 million prostitutes.[6] According to the International Labor Organization, there are 200,000 female prostitutes in Bangkok and 500,000 prostitutes in all of Thailand.[7] The Thai government itself, notorious for its sex tour industry, has been called "the consummate international pimp."[8]

Asia is not the only continent where women's prostitution is flourishing. In Europe and the Americas, the incidence of female prostitution is also high.[9] There are 200,000 female prostitutes in Germany, for example, many of them lured from Latin America and eastern Europe.[10] It is estimated that as many as 500,000 women are smuggled from developing countries annually and forced into prostitution.[11] In assessing the worldwide magnitude of women's prostitution, Wassyla Tamzali of UNESCO, noted bleakly, "The sex industry is a huge market with its own momentum."[12]

The frightening problem will likely get worse before it gets better. See Chapter 21 for further examination into the prostitution of women worldwide and its implications.

The Incidence of Women's Prostitution in the United States

Over one million women are estimated to be selling sex in the United States.[13] Including part-time prostitutes may increase the numbers by three or four times that total.[14] Tens of thousands of other women may be in the profession as well, disguised as mistresses, groupies, dancers, porn stars, students, drug users-abusers or dealers, or in other situations or occupations. Women prostitutes operate on all scales (such as streetwalkers and call girls) and economic levels, come from all walks of life, and are generally not discriminatory in whom they choose to sell their services to so long as the price for such services can be met. Unfortunately, it is the hidden cost — such as AIDS — that in many instances proves to be so high.

Official Data on Women Prostitutes

In spite of the weaknesses of official statistics (see Chapter 1), they offer perhaps the most consistent measurement of female prostitution in terms of arrests, age, gender community, and arrest trends. These breakdowns can give us some context in studying which women are likely to come into contact with the criminal justice system as prostitutes (and perhaps which are not).

According to the *Uniform Crime Reports* (*UCR*), there were 48,987 arrests of females ages 18 and over for prostitution and commercialized vice in the

**Figure 6-1 Female Arrests for Prostitution
and Commercialized Vice, by Age Group, 1995**

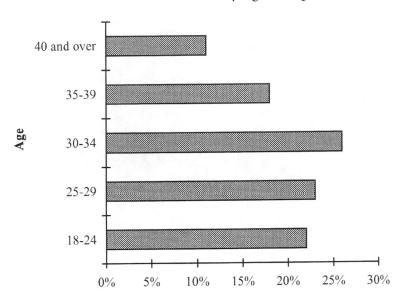

Source: Derived from U.S. Department of Justice, Federal Bureau of Investigation, *Crime in the United States: Uniform Crime Reports 1995* (Washington, D.C.: Government Printing Office, 1996), p. 223.

United States in 1995.[15] Adult females constitute approximately 99 percent of all females arrested for prostitution.

ARRESTS OF WOMEN BY AGE

🌢 Most women arrested for prostitution tend to be in their mid-twenties to mid-thirties. As shown in Figure 6-1, nearly half of all females arrested for prostitution and commercialized vice in 1995 fell between the ages of 25 and 34. Over one-fourth of such arrests were of women ages 30 to 34. The 18-to-24 age group accounted for 22 percent of the women arrested; 18 percent were ages 35 to 39; and only 11 percent of those arrested were age 40 and over. These figures are consistent with the characteristics of prostitutes most likely to face arrest, usually streetwalkers.

ARREST COMPARISONS BY GENDER

Arrest figures indicate that women are significantly more likely to be arrested for prostitution than men (see Figure 6-2). In 1995, women accounted

Figure 6-2   Arrests of Persons 18 and Over for Prostitution and Commercialized Vice, by Gender, 1995

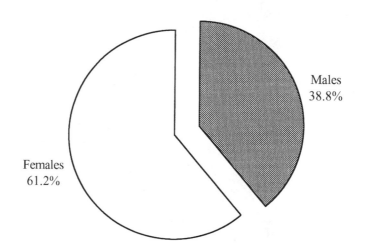

Males
38.8%

Females
61.2%

Source: Adapted from U.S. Department of Justice, Federal Bureau of Investigation, *Crime in the United States: Uniform Crime Reports 1995* (Washington, D.C.: Government Printing Office, 1996), pp. 222, 230.

for 61.2 percent of all arrests of persons age 18 and over for prostitution and commercialized vice, whereas men age 18 and over composed 38.8 percent of the total arrests. The ratio of prostitution arrests relative to gender was 1.6 women for every 1 man. This differential in arrests was not found when considering those under the age of 18. Male juveniles were slightly more likely than female juveniles to be arrested for prostitution and commercialized vice in 1995.[16]

Overall, prostitution-related arrests made up just over 2 percent of the total female arrests in 1995; in comparison, arrests of males for prostitution composed under 1 percent of their overall arrests.[17]

Adult females have a much greater chance to be arrested for prostitution than the men they service or the pimps they work for. In Portland, Oregon, for example, 402 women were arrested for prostitution in 1995, compared with 18 males for pandering and 10 men for soliciting prostitutes.[18] Nationally, statistics show that only 2 male customers of prostitutes are arrested for every 8 arrests of female prostitutes.[19]

Disparities can be found also in incarceration data regarding females jailed for prostitution and males jailed for prostitution, pimping, and/or soliciting prostitutes.[20]

Figure 6-3 Female Arrests for Prostitution
and Commercialized Vice, by Community Size, 1995

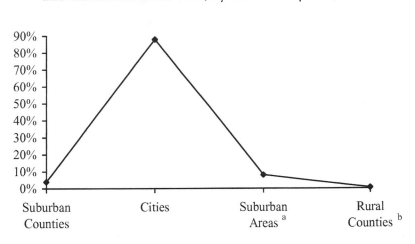

[a]Includes cities with under 50,000 inhabitants and unincorporated areas with Metropolitan
  Statistical Areas (MSAs).
[b]There were 96 female arrests in rural counties for prostitution and commercialized vice in
  1995.

Source: Adapted from U.S. Department of Justice, Federal Bureau of Investigation, *Crime
in the United States: Uniform Crime Reports 1995* (Washington, D.C.: Government Printing Office, 1996), pp. 234, 243, 252, 261.

WOMEN'S ARRESTS BY COMMUNITY TYPE

Women are far more likely to be arrested for solicitation in cities than in
other types of communities. Figure 6-3 distributes adult female arrests for
prostitution and commercialized vice by community type in 1995. Nearly nine
in ten such arrests occurred in cities. Suburban areas accounted for 8 percent
of the arrests and suburban counties 4 percent. Under 1 percent of the arrests
for prostitution and commercialized vice were in rural counties.

At least part of this wide disparity between arrests in cities and those in
smaller communities is a reflection of the fact that there are more prostitutes
to arrest in larger metropolitan areas, as well as more customers and police
stings. On the other hand, fewer police covering a wider area in smaller communities generally means more prostitution can take place, with a lower risk
of detection and arrest.

Many prostitutes are beginning to move out to the suburbs to ply their
trade as city police drive them away from city neighborhoods with tougher
crackdowns on street crime, including prostitution.

Table 6-1 Female Arrests for Crimes
Related to Prostitution, by Offense, 1995

Offense Charges	Number of Arrests
Curfew and loitering law violations	34,011
Vagrancy	3,989
Sex offenses (except forcible rape and prostitution)	5,764
Drug abuse violations	190,729
Liquor laws	82,338
Drunkenness	62,458
Suspicion	1,377
Runaways[a]	108,830

[a]Applicable only to persons under age 18.

Source: U.S. Department of Justice, Federal Bureau of Investigation, *Crime in the United States: Uniform Crime Reports 1995* (Washington, D.C.: Government Printing Office, 1996), p. 225.

OTHER CRIME-RELATED ARRESTS

Many female prostitutes are arrested under statutes other than those for prostitution and commercialized vice. In some cases, there are no specific prostitution laws in effect; in others, the charge is strictly at the discretion of the arresting officer. These include arrests for loitering, vagrancy, runaways, sex offenses (other than forcible rape and prostitution), and suspicion, as well as drug abuse and alcohol-related offenses. Table 6-1 lists such arrests for 1995. Most arrests of adults occurred for drug abuse violations and liquor law offenses.

Although there is no statistical tracking of these crimes in relation to prostitution services, many studies have found that prostitutes commonly abuse alcohol and drugs and that many prostitutes under the age of 18 ran away from home.[21] Conversely, a high percentage of runaways and addicts end up working as prostitutes to survive and to support an addiction.[22]

ARREST TRENDS IN WOMEN'S PROSTITUTION

Arrest trends reveal that fewer women are being arrested for prostitution than in past years. As shown in Figure 6-4, women's arrests for prostitution and commercialized vice declined almost 25 percent between 1986 and 1995. However, the decrease was not as great for the period from 1991 to 1995 and from 1994 to 1995 at 13.6 percent and 2.4 percent, respectively.[23] This slowing rate of decline suggests that female arrests for prostitution may in fact be on the rise again. At this point, it is too early to tell. It may well be that the shorter trends are inconclusive due to inadequate time to allow for true trends to develop.

Figure 6-4 Female Arrest Trends for
Prostitution and Commercialized Vice, 1986–1995

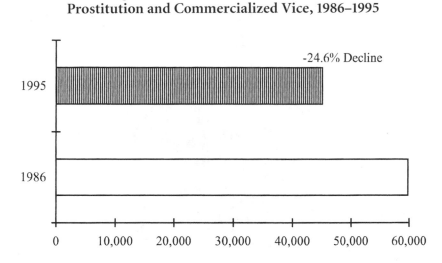

Source: Derived from U.S. Department of Justice, Federal Bureau of Investigation, *Crime in the United States: Uniform Crime Reports 1995* (Washington, D.C.: Government Printing Office, 1996), p. 213.

Women's Prostitution, Race, and Ethnicity

Most women entering prostitution are white. Some studies have found that as many as eight in ten prostitutes are white females.[24] However, among red-light districts in inner cities, the percentage of prostitutes who are minority women increased to as many as 50 percent.[25] Black women seem to be particularly singled out when it comes to arrests. They are seven times as likely to be arrested for prostitution or commercialized vice as women of other races.[26] Most such arrests occur in predominantly poor sections of cities, where streetwalking black prostitutes are most likely to ply their trade and face police prejudice.[27] A recent study of New York City streetwalking revealed that half the prostitutes were black, 25 percent Hispanic, and 25 percent white women.[28]

Arrest data does not reflect arrests for prostitution by race and gender. However, since the majority of adults arrested for prostitution are female, statistics on the race of arrestees can give us a fair indication of the racial distribution of female prostitutes arrested. As shown in Figure 6-5, six out of ten persons arrested for prostitution and commercialized vice in 1995 were white. Nearly 37 percent of the arrestees were black. This figure is disproportionate relative to their population totals. Native Americans and persons of Asian

Figure 6-5 Persons Arrested for Prostitution and Commercialized Vice, by Race, 1995

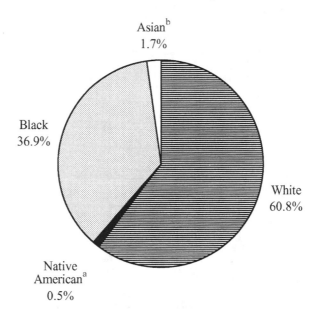

Asian[b]
1.7%

Black
36.9%

White
60.8%

Native
American[a]
0.5%

[a]Includes American Indians and Alaskan Natives
[b]Includes Asians and Pacific Islanders

Source: Adapted from U.S. Department of Justice, Federal Bureau of Investigation, *Crime in the United States: Uniform Crime Reports 1995* (Washington, D.C.: Government Printing Office, 1996), p. 228.

---

descent accounted for just over 2 percent of the arrestees. *UCR* statistics do not measure arrests by ethnicity.

The Prostitution of Women by Class

There are few studies on class differences among female prostitutes. What evidence is available suggests that prostitutes come from all backgrounds and classes.[29] Furthermore, prostitutes ply their trade across the class strata as streetwalkers, call girls, and various levels in between, including prostitution through massage parlors and escort services across the country.

General studies of female criminality have found female offenders to be disproportionately poor and undereducated.[30] A review of 46 studies using arrest data found that lower-class adult women had consistently higher crime rates than did women coming from middle- and upper-class families.[31] However, studies of female prostitutes have shown that a majority actually come from middle- or upper-class backgrounds.[32] In one study, seven out of ten female prostitutes sampled came from families with average or above-average incomes.[33]

Other research has linked the type of prostitute (upper-class or lower-class) with economic necessity, pre– and post–drug use/abuse, and promiscuity.[34]

Chapter 7

Streetwalking Prostitutes

Streetwalkers, often referred to as *hookers*, represent the lowest level of the women's prostitution hierarchy. One social scientist defined the streetwalking prostitute as "a woman who overtly solicits men on the street and offers sexual favors for payment."[1] Streetwalkers typically can be found on busy inner-city street corners wearing "ankle-length coyote and raccoon coats over Victoria's Secret–type chemises of shimmering satin, black stockings, and five-inch red heels or boots" or "G-strings with sparkling pasties on their nipples, or in lace panties and bras."[2] Recently one Hollywood streetwalker, "Divine Brown," made headlines when the 24-year-old black mother of three and actor Hugh Grant were taken into custody after police caught them in a sexual act in Grant's car.

Unlike high-class call girls, who operate on the upper end of the world of prostitution amid expensive hotels and clients, streetwalkers enjoy few advantages in plying their trade. They are often young women or adolescent girls, have pimps, abuse alcohol and/or drugs, and "negotiate" with "dates" for services ranging from fellatio to masturbating to intercourse.

In an article about one drug-addicted streetwalker, Adrian LeBlanc summed up the reality of working the streets: "The Cinderella experience of Julia Roberts' character in the movie *Pretty Woman* is a fantasy far away from any real world. No one is coming to rescue Trina, and though she's tried to escape the street and quit the drugs, she, like most of the girls who inhabit this dark world, has been unable to break the cycle herself.... Many young streetwalkers are born and raised in an environment of poverty, drugs, and violent crimes."[3]

It is unknown just how many women sell sex on the streets in the United States. Estimates of streetwalkers range from 10 to 15 percent of all prostitutes[4] to as many as three-quarters of the "working women."[5] In New York City alone, there are an estimated 5,000 to 8,000 streetwalkers.[6] In all, hundreds of thousands of women across the country are estimated to be making a life (and sometimes a living) as streetwalking prostitutes. Many others may turn tricks part-time as streetwalkers. All such women often face a life of drugs, despair, and danger.

The Dynamics of Streetwalkers

In spite of some notions to the contrary, streetwalking prostitutes are heterogeneous in their races, ethnicities, ages, backgrounds, motivations, and inspirations. One writer found that they "come from a range of backgrounds: rich or poor; well-educated or illiterate; urban, suburban, or rural."[7] According to a sociologist for the Centers for Disease Control and Prevention, many streetwalkers "have lived the typical all–American family life. They grew up in the suburbs, went to ballet school — the whole thing."[8]

Most streetwalkers are in their mid-to-late twenties. It is estimated that 20 percent are teenagers.[9] Many have moved into prostitution as runaways, throwaways, or drug addicts.[10] Others have rebelled against authority or the constraints of family life by choosing the perceived independence of life on the streets.[11]

What virtually all streetwalkers have in common is that they were victims of physical and/or sexual abuse before and after their entry into prostitution; they all also have low self-esteem and find themselves more or less forced to walk a thin line between prostitution, substance abuse, arrest, and violence at the hands of customers and pimps. A study of female prostitutes concluded that 70 percent are raped repeatedly by johns — an average of 31 assaults a year. Sixty-five percent are physically abused by johns, with an even higher percentage commonly assaulted by pimps.[12] According to the Justice Department, the rate of mortality for prostitutes is 40 times the national average.[13]

As the executive director of the Foundation for Research on Sexually Transmitted Diseases, Inc., Joyce Wallace has worked extensively with New York City streetwalkers. In interviewing and HIV testing more than 3,000 streetwalkers, she found the following:

- The average age of the streetwalker was 29.
- Half were black.
- Twenty-five percent were Hispanic.
- Twenty-five percent were white.
- Three out of four used illegal drugs.
- Thirty-five percent were HIV-positive.
- The majority had been physically or sexually abused.[14]

Additionally, studies have found that nearly eight out of ten female prostitutes were sexually assaulted before the age of 14, usually by a relative or close friend of the family.[15] Many are mothers through molestation, rape, or sex with pimps. In New York, 70 percent of the streetwalkers are mothers, giving birth to two children on average.[16] A high percentage of these prostitute mothers end up sterile due to infections caused by sexually transmitted diseases such as syphilis and gonorrhea.[17]

Types of Streetwalkers

Researchers have established various types or classes of streetwalking prostitutes. One article noted streetwalkers' "strolls" or "tracks" in relation to their movement on the streets in attempts to attract and secure johns.[18] Anthropologist Jennifer James, who has studied streetwalkers comprehensively, divided them into two classes: (1) true prostitutes and (2) part-timers. She subdivided streetwalkers into 13 roles. True prostitutes included: outlaws, rip-off artists, hypes, ladies, old-timers, and thoroughbreds:

- *Outlaws*: prostitutes who are independent of pimps
- *Rip-off artists*: thieves disguised as prostitutes; prostitution is not their main source of income
- *Hypes*: prostitutes who work to support drug addictions
- *Ladies*: prostitutes identified by their class, carriage, finesse and professionalism
- *Old-timers*: seasoned prostitutes who lack the class of ladies
- *Thoroughbreds*: young, professional prostitutes.

Part-timers included women who had no style and amateurs, or "hos."[19] None of the roles are mutually exclusive of one another. They refer to different behavioral dimensions of streetwalkers, as opposed to complete behavioral types, each having elements from all streetwalker modes of behavior.

Streetwalkers and Pimps

Pimps are not key players in many adult female prostitutes' lives. In some instances, the prostitute has managed to maintain independence from the myriad of local pimps competing for her services. In most cases, the woman prostitute is between pimps, is estranged from a pimp-lover, or has become shrewd enough to be able to ply her trade without the mental and physical impediments that often accompany younger prostitutes. Studies show that when it comes to teenage prostitution, as many as nine out of ten girls enter or remain in the business through the coercion and/or charms of a pimp.[20] Virtually all streetwalkers, independent or not, have contact with pimps or panderers over the course of their prostitution.[21]

For adult female streetwalkers who have pimps, the dynamics are the same as for adolescent streetwalkers. Often as teenagers, they are wooed, cajoled, and intimidated into prostitution. Once in the pimp's stable, they are kept there by love, drug dependency, pregnancy, fear, degradation, and anything else the pimp can use to hold on to his "property." Often it is the shame of being a prostitute that makes it difficult for many women to leave the business. "They don't feel good enough to go back to school, their family, or fit into society," says a detective who tries to help prostitutes. "A lot of them don't know what a family is. The only place they feel they fit in is on the streets with other prostitutes and pimps."[22]

Studies indicate that the vast majority of streetwalking prostitutes are physically abused by their pimps on a regular basis, from beatings with "coat hangers to lashings with a six-foot bullwhip."[23] The pimp's violent actions are often unpredictable and can result from a prostitute's perceived lack of respect, from her insufficient earnings, or even from the pimp's being under the influence of alcohol and/or drugs. Sometimes the prostitute's abuse can result in death.

Threatening or attempting to leave a pimp generally puts the streetwalking prostitute at her greatest risk of bodily harm. In one example of a streetwalker in her early twenties who tried to escape her pimp, the results were terrifying. She painfully recounted: "He told me to take my clothes off. I wouldn't, so he punched me so hard he lifted me off the ground.... My skin split. Blood was spraying and it was like a horror movie."[24]

Some studies have contradicted the notion of a violence-coercive pimp-prostitute relationship. Based on her research, James concluded, "It is not true that pimps force women to work against their will, seduce young girls, turn women into drug addicts for the purpose of control, give no sexual satisfaction to their women, keep them from ever leaving their stable, and are never married to prostitutes who work for them."[25] Many prostitutes are seen as entering and remaining in the pimp's world not because of intimidation, addiction (to drugs or the pimp), or even economic survival but rather because of the "severe isolation that pre-prostitutes feel [that] predisposes them to join up with someone who 'plugs' them into the world, gives them a set of social relations, a place to call their own, and an ideology to make the world intelligible."[26] According to James, the structure of the prostitute's social environment is a greater determinant in her prostitution than the pimp's actions.

Though James's work has made a significant contribution to understanding the dynamics of streetwalkers, few can realistically dismiss altogether the important role that the pimp's persuasive and manipulative powers play in controlling his prostitutes. This often extends over and above the lack of social ties or other factors that may contribute to her entry into prostitution. An example of the pimp's psychological hold on a prostitute can be seen in this ex-streetwalker's reflections: "My pimp took all my money. If I needed a coat or pantyhose, I had to ask him. The illusion was that he was taking care of me. I thought this arrangement was okay till I got arrested and sent to a treatment center for alcoholics. That stopped me long enough to get a look at what was really happening."[27] The relationship between prostitutes and pimps will be examined more closely in Chapter 13.

Streetwalkers' Motivations for Becoming Prostitutes

Women are motivated to sell their bodies on the streets for a variety of reasons including financial needs — food, shelter, clothing — drugs, alcohol, sex, adventure, freedom, rebellion, and abusive homes. James divided streetwalkers' motivations into three groups: (1) conscious, (2) situational, and (3) psychoanalytic:

- *Conscious*: economics, working conditions, adventure, and a persuasive pimp
- *Situational*: early experiences in life, child abuse and/or neglect, occupation
- *Psychoanalytic*: general factors, oedipal fixation, latent homosexuality, and retardation[28]

According to Claire Elifson, a researcher on the association between prostitution, drugs, and AIDS, the "driving force" behind most streetwalkers' prostitution is drug use, abuse, and addiction.[29] Most studies seem to bear this out. The relationship between streetwalking and drugs has been well documented.[30] In LeBlanc's profile of a 19-year-old streetwalker, she wrote: "Trina's childhood was tumultuous. By nine, she started to use drugs, mostly pills. When she was eleven, she once had to be hospitalized after drinking until she passed out.... Whether the drug use led to prostituting or the prostituting inspired more frequent use of the drugs isn't wholly clear. Whatever the case, drugs — and the mission to do what she needed to get them — became routine.[31]

It is estimated that 5 percent of all prostitutes die every year.[32] Most of these deaths are the result of drug overdoses or homicide related to drug deals gone sour.[33]

Streetwalking Prostitutes and HIV Infection

Streetwalkers have the highest rate of HIV infection among prostitutes.[34] This is closely related to higher rates of IV drug use among streetwalkers than among other classes of female prostitutes.[35] In a study of 110 ex-IV-drug-using streetwalkers, 46 percent tested positive to the precursor to AIDS.[36] Another study reported that 37 percent of the streetwalkers who were IV drug users were infected with HIV.[37] Other findings reveal that 61 percent of the streetwalking prostitutes sampled were HIV-positive.[38]

Racial minority streetwalkers who are IV drug users have been shown to have an even higher rate of HIV infection. In a sample of Baltimore street-walkers with HIV, the rate of exposure was highest among black prostitutes.[39] Other studies have found similar results.[40]

Chapter 8

Call Girl Prostitutes

Call girl prostitutes are considered the cream of the prostitution crop and the least visible. Unlike streetwalkers — who usually conjure up images of overly made-up, underdressed, high-heeled, black or Hispanic women or white teenage girls, often high on drugs as they stroll the boulevards in big cities like Los Angeles or New York in search of johns cruising the streets — call girls offer us a much more glamorous image. Linda Lee notes: "What distinguishes call girls from streetwalkers is appearance, money and class (and the possession of a telephone). An appropriately dressed call girl can walk into a good hotel or drive into a residential neighborhood without attracting police attention. The gear of street prostitution — revealing clothes, excessive makeup, a garish hairstyle — is not for her."[1] Emphasizing the importance of clothing, one call girl declared simply: "The better you dress, the more money you make.... When you dress well, 'Two hundred dollars? No problem.'"[2]

Call girl prostitution has received a boost in attention, and some would say prestige, in recent years thanks to a few well-publicized cases of call girl operations busted by the police. Ex-madams Heidi Fleiss and Sydney Barrows, cop-turned-call-girl Norma Almodovar, and Sherry Rowlands, call girl to an ex–presidential advisor, among others, have become household names. Hollywood has been quick to add to the fanciful allure of the call girl — creating such memorable high class prostitutes as Julia Roberts in *Pretty Woman* and Tina Louise as J. R. Ewing's mistress call girl in *Dallas*.

Most call girls tend to be in their late teens to mid-twenties. Whereas the racial and ethnic makeup of streetwalking prostitutes can be evenly divided between white, black, and Hispanic women particularly in cities, call girls are by and large white women. They are also more likely to be college-educated than their streetwalking counterparts. Barrows boasted of her one-time employees, "Most of my girls were college grads ... good, nice people with serious goals

54

in life — the kind mothers would be proud to have as daughters."[3] Others work the business secretly as married and/or otherwise successful women, as attested to by the operator of a New York escort service: "Some of our escorts are married women. Their husbands think they're working as hostesses. One of our girls is the daughter of a diplomat. She has two art galleries, but she's bored with her life, and she wants to meet executives."[4]

How Many Call Girls Are There?

Because call girl prostitutes can often afford to ply their trade in four-star hotels and luxury apartments where detection, arrest, and estimates are hard, if not impossible, to come by, it is difficult to know how many women are selling high-class sex in the United States. Some estimates put the total at 20 to 25 percent of all prostitutes.[5] Others suggest that there are at least as many call girls in the prostitution business as streetwalkers, if not more.[6] This is probably more accurate when one considers the array of women who, unlike streetwalkers, can easily go into the call girl business while maintaining a low profile: college students, married women, part-time call girls, and those operating inconspicuously behind escort services, brothels, clubs, and massage parlors.

The image of the call girl as a beautiful, smart, articulate, marriage material a "psychotherapist" or "social worker" who also happens to be financially secure, with very flexible hours to see her johns, is no doubt enticing to many women, if only in theory. Just how many turn theory into practice, prostitution, and profit may never be known.

The Dynamics of the World of Call Girls

Call girl prostitutes often enter the business for profit, pleasure, fun, travel, and to escape from boredom. They are usually able to minimize the downside, such as labeling, discovery, arrest, and victimization, commonly experienced by streetwalkers. Nevertheless, call girls do face risks to their health and well-being, including sexual assaults, crime, public exposure, and AIDS.

Even arrest and incarceration are possible, as evidenced by the example of Heidi Fleiss, who was sentenced to several years behind bars for charges ranging from pimping to income tax evasion.[7] In another case, a San Francisco ring of 150 call girls, consisting of housewives, nurses, secretaries, and other women, was broken up by police.[8] However, these cases are more often the exception than the rule.

In some instances, call girls are former streetwalkers who got wise and found that prostitution could be much more profitable and safe away from pimps and the streets. By and large, however, there is little moving back and forth between types of prostitution.

Drugs play a large part in the lives of many call girls, similar to street-walkers. This is underlined by one high-class call girl who admitted: "Cocaine was a big part of the scene. Most of the johns had it, and all the girls wanted it. If you did too much, though, you'd have to come down with booze or pills. No saint, I was still considered pretty clean and managed to stay off the roller coaster by never doing more than a couple of lines a night."[9] In some cases, the primary motivation to become or remain a call girl was to support an existing or developed drug habit. A study of 60 prostitute drug users concluded that the high-class prostitutes were most often addicted to stimulants.[10]

The Financial Lure of Call Girl Prostitution

The money (real or perceived) derived from upper-class prostitution is seen as the primary motivation for women entering the profession and continuing to service well-paying clients. In a study of high-class prostitutes, money (or something else of value such as luxury items or rent payment) was reported to be the most important factor in the prostitution.[11] One high-class call girl described money as "a powerful aphrodisiac."[12]

How much money can a woman make as a call girl? Many can earn six or seven figure incomes. An upper class prostitute who reportedly made $2,000 an hour and up boasted that she "loved all her clients, and was proud of being told she had magic fingers."[13] Madams can make even more. Barrows and Fleiss reportedly raked in millions renting out high-priced call girls to wealthy businessmen before their operations were shut down.

In a *Cosmopolitan* article, a call girl claiming to have worked for Heidi Fleiss recounted her entry into Heidi's stable of money, sex, johns, and drugs:

> When I first moved to L.A., I was one of a million MAWs — model-actress-waitress.... I wanted to be a star.... After I'd been waitressing a couple of months, I went to a Sunset Strip club.... Who should walk in but Heidi Fleiss ... the most dynamic person in the room: cocaine-thin, suntanned, dressed in black.
>
> Heidi looked me over the way a man would.... After a moment, she nodded in vague approval, scribbled her address on a napkin, and invited me to come over the next day.... Heidi's house turned out to be an incredibly cool spread in Benedict Canyon. [She] introduced me around, then quickly got down to business. She charged a minimum of fifteen hundred dollars a night, which meant *all* night. If the men were in the mood — or a little high — they'd often shell out more than they bargained for. Regardless, my take was 60 percent.[14]

During Fleiss's trial, some call girls testified to making as much as $10,000 for a single "date." Clients also testified, including actor Charlie Sheen, who claimed to have spent at least $53,000 for sexual services with Fleiss's prostitutes one year. With Fleiss's made-to-order call girls, there was always a money-back guarantee.[15]

Middle-Class Call Girls

Aside from the upper-class call girls of madams such as Heidi Fleiss and others who operate independently as the elite of the profession, a more middle-class group of prostitutes has emerged in recent years. They are considered above the streetwalker and below the best-paid high-class prostitutes. Many middle-class call girls turn to prostitution to pay for college tuition, the mortgage, or diapers and/or to supplement income from a legitimate job. Some prostitute themselves to support drug habits (or their spouse's addiction). Though there are no reliable figures on the number of middle-class women turning tricks in this country, some believe they may represent the largest group of prostitutes.

Middle-class prostitutes work for pimps, madams, escort services, brothels, massage parlors, and/or on their own. They include women from all socioeconomic backgrounds and circumstances, including "nursing students, housewives in the process of getting a divorce, a teacher with a sick husband who is trying to raise money to bring a relative to the United States."[16] Many college students, college graduates, struggling actresses, aspiring writers and artists, single mothers, and unemployed, underemployed, or part-time employed middle-class women have found themselves resorting to prostitution. In one article on middle-class prostitution, the author wrote, "For women who are short on money and unconventional, hooking has become like waitressing — a means of getting by."[17]

Contrary to most streetwalkers, middle-class prostitutes tend to be more educated, sophisticated, self-respecting, and discriminating in who they sell sexual favors to and where they perform these favors. Many cater to the convention center and high-priced hotel crowds, charging their male clients anywhere from $50 to $250 an hour. Others ply their trade through escort services. These are largely fronts for prostitution, often advertising — in phone books and newspapers — their escorts or dates as "gorgeous" or as "models" selected for their "beauty, personality, and charm."

One escort service call girl recently described her life of leisure and luxury, supported by a $250-an-hour fee for her services:

> I live a pampered kind of life: get up around noon, work out for a couple of hours with my personal trainer, spend the rest of the day shopping

or having a manicure, pedicure, and facial. Around five in the afternoon, I go for a three-mile jog, then return to my sumptuously furnished apartment that's been meticulously cleaned by my housekeeper. I hop in the tub for a refreshing bubble bath, dress in one of my designer suits, apply makeup, and style my hair.

Then I call the escort service. "This is Olivia," I tell my supervisor. "I'm ready for work."[18]

There are tens of thousands of escort services operating brazenly across the country. According to a New York Police Department official, several hundred escort services in New York City alone can each call on anywhere from 50 to 150 female prostitutes "from as far away as Rhode Island."[19]

A typical example of a middle-class woman turned middle-class call girl can be seen in the following account of a young woman who started working for a massage parlor after months of struggling to become a singer: "It was so simple, so natural, I got right into it.... I'd always been promiscuous, ever since I first got started sexually as a teenager. I had a need for security—you know, problems with self-hatred, lack of confidence, and all that stuff—and sex made me feel worthwhile.... I decided, if I'm going to be obsessive about sex, I might as well get paid for it. You know, why give it away?"[20] Another part-time call girl working for an escort service found prostitution to be beneficial for a low self-esteem: "In a way, it was good for my ego. These men were telling me that my presence was worth money, that I was a desirable person to be with."[21]

Though middle-class prostitutes have a lower risk of encountering many of the dangers often associated with streetwalking prostitution, they do not have a lifestyle without peril. Substance abuse and addiction, rape, and sexually transmitted diseases are common in the business at all levels. Emotional stress has also been found to be high among prostitutes, whether high-class, low-class, or middle-class hookers. In describing how she dealt with the stress of turning tricks, one ex-middle-class prostitute explained: "You have to do something to deal with it. I did a lot of drugs, mostly cocaine, during the period I was working. And I drank a lot too."[22]

Pathologies and the Call Girl Prostitute

Researchers have found that call girl prostitutes appear to have few, if any, pathologies in relation to their profession, whereas streetwalkers have been shown to possess any number of pathologies: "At the upper level, among the full time call girls and part-time housewives who appear to lead economically secure, stable, arrest-free lives, there is no evidence of special pathology. At the lower levels, inhabited by streetwalkers, drug addicts, juvenile runaways, and deviants of many different stripes, the population is so prone to psychological pathology that it is difficult to know what part, if any, prostitution contributes to their many difficulties."[23] Coramae Mann, in her study of white-collar prostitutes, found no evidence of pathology among the women or hostility toward males.[24] Another study that examined the psychological characteristics of prostitutes found that full-time call girls were "probably as mature and well adjusted as demographically similar females engaging in other occupations. In fact, if financial success is added to any criteria of successful adjustment, these kinds of prostitutes have a clear edge."[25]

Evidence does exist, however, of pathologies among call girl prostitutes. For example, in her study of call girls and streetwalkers, Jennifer James found that 42 percent of the prostitutes had been victims of sexual abuse and a high percentage were from broken homes.[26]

Other studies have shown a correlation between call girl prostitution and psychological and sociological determinants. In his book *The Elegant Prostitute: A Social and Psychoanalytic Study*, Harold Greenwald found severe personality disorders in his call girl patients but was unclear if these disorders had developed before or after entry into prostitution.[27] He proposed that upper-class prostitution "was not necessarily more degrading than working at a job one hated or being married to a man one found physically repulsive."[28] In spite of the complex etiology, Greenwald believed that there was a relatively easy means to prevent women from becoming high-class prostitutes, for he had "never known a call girl who had strong bonds of love and affection with her family."[29]

James Bryan studied call girls in terms of apprenticeship and individual attitudes.[30] He found that call girl prostitutes generally learned their trade by serving as an apprentice to an established call girl. This apprenticeship usually ended once the apprentice had developed her own "book" of clients or ran into friction with her trainer call girl. The training focused on two areas: *verbal behavior* and *attitude*. "The verbal behavior was difficult for many apprentices to master because it was more contrary to traditional sex roles than the overt sexual activity that was sold. Call girls had to learn to be verbally aggressive on the phone and to ask directly for dates."[31]

Bryan found that with respect to attitude, call girls often saw themselves as social workers, counselors, and sex therapists whose services were sorely needed.[32] Delores French, a call girl prostitute, concurs, dismissing any notion of victimization as a motivational factor of her chosen occupation: "I'm from a very middle class background. I wasn't raped, I'm not a victim of incest. I do this because I choose to do it, and I plan to do it for the rest of my life. I love it. There aren't many careers where your job is to renew people's self-esteem. That's really what this job is all about — renewing people's self-esteem."[33]

The view of the call girl as a sort of counselor, social worker, and/or sex therapist appears to have some merit. Following a four-year study of call girls and their clients, a real social worker concluded that high-class prostitutes served as "paraprofessional therapists" or as an "underground sexual health service" and should actually be trained in "mental health principles."[34] She posited that the women met their clients' needs for crisis intervention, venting of problems, and sexual counseling, as well as raised self-esteem and restored confidence "in their own sexuality."[35]

In a study of call girls, Karen Rosenblum found that the cause of their prostitution included a strong need to be independent of men and to make as much money as possible.[36] Another study of call girl prostitutes concluded that they were neither exploited nor "self-destructive, frigid, nymphomaniacal, or desperate."[37] Regarding exploitation, the author commented flatly: "Someone who makes $50,000 to $100,000 a year, lives in luxury, and has a work life considerably more interesting than that of a secretary or even many executives, can hardly be called 'exploited.'"[38]

Call Girls and HIV Infection

Most studies of prostitutes and HIV/AIDS have shown that call girls face the lowest risk among prostitutes of exposure to the AIDS virus. One study of escort service call girls and streetwalkers found that none of the call girls tested positive for HIV, compared with 41 percent of the streetwalkers.[39] Another study of high-class call girls found that only one woman — an IV drug user — was HIV infected.[40]

This evidence notwithstanding, call girls do risk exposure to the AIDS virus every time they have unprotected sex with johns (including fellatio and anal sex). The risky business of multiple sex partners for pay and substance abuse has also exposed call girl prostitutes, like streetwalkers, to sexually transmitted diseases, HIV infection, AIDS, and short lives.

Chapter 9

Drugs, Crime, and Victimization

Female prostitution carries with it not only the stigma of selling sex and the risk for contracting HIV and eventually AIDS but also other negative and dangerous elements. Few prostitutes, particularly streetwalkers, can ply their trade without involvement with some form of drugs, other criminal activities, or victimization. For most, these risks simply come with the territory. Others enter the business unprepared and often leave it when the damage is irreparable.

Drugs and Women's Prostitution

Drugs play a major role in the prostitution of women, regardless of the type of prostitution. Studies show that most prostitutes use and/or abuse drugs.[1] Many are addicted to drugs such as crack and heroin;[2] others are alcohol abusers.[3] Drug addiction draws many women into prostitution,[4] whereas other women become drug abusers after entry into the sex-for-sale profession.[5] Many female prostitutes must resort to other crimes to support drug habits.[6] In other instances, women who are smuggled into this country and turned into sexual slave prostitutes are often forced into narcotics addiction as a form of control.[7]

One study estimated that nearly seven in ten prostitutes were drug addicts.[8] Another study reported that almost 80 percent of the prostitutes sampled used drugs before becoming prostitutes.[9] Nearly 75 percent of the streetwalkers Joyce Wallace interviewed admitted to using illicit drugs.[10] Anywhere from one-fifth to one-half of all female prostitutes are believed to use drugs regularly.[11]

In Paul Goldstein's study of drugs and prostitution, he found that drug addiction usually came before prostitution among streetwalkers, whereas call girls tended to be in the business before becoming addicts.[12] The major forms of addiction for streetwalkers and call girls were heroin and stimulants, respectively.[13]

Prostitutes use virtually every type of drug — with marijuana being the most popular — including mind-altering drugs such as alcohol, PCP, and LSD and psychotropic drugs such as Valium and Demerol.[14] The result often becomes drug dependency and prostitution to pay for the habit.

A review of literature on the relationship between female prostitutes and drug users found that estimates of female drug users who were also prostitutes ranged from 30 percent to 70 percent.[15] Among female prostitutes who were also drug users, the estimates varied from 40 to 85 percent.[16] Researchers have found the choice of drug to be important to the prostitute in serving real or perceived functions, as noted below:

> Heroin use may help a prostitute adjust to a life she resents; increase her ability to withstand emotional and physical stress; help her relax.... Heroin seems to relax the anal sphincter muscles. Prostitutes who are heroin addicts are likely to have minimal problems in engaging in anal intercourse.... Cocaine and other stimulants have been reported to increase the confidence of streetwalkers to solicit strangers on the street and ... enable massage parlor prostitutes to maintain their "energy level." ... Valium aided some call girls in "getting through the day." ... New York call girls got "protection from insults to their bodies and minds" by drinking steadily.[17]

D. Kelly Weisberg further reported that female prostitutes used drugs to help them to relax and/or to help make selling their bodies more bearable.[18] Goldstein postulated that female prostitutes' use of alcohol was primarily to "enhance sociability" with customers.[19]

Drugs, HIV Infection, and Women's Prostitution

The link between drugs and HIV infection among prostitutes is strong. IV drug use puts women prostitutes at particular risk for exposure to the AIDS virus. Studies have found that the proportion of HIV-infected women prostitutes who are IV drug users is a frightening 61 percent.[20] Wallace's study of the rate of HIV infection among New York IV-drug-using streetwalkers was 46 percent.[21] Another study found that an increasing number of drug-abusing prostitutes were testing positive for HIV.[22]

Some researchers have found that minority female prostitute IV drug users have an even higher rate of HIV infection.[23] A study of Baltimore IV-drug-addicted prostitutes found the percentage of HIV-seropositive prostitutes to be highest among black women.[24]

International studies have further supported the association between drugs, female prostitution, and HIV infection. Studies of women prostitutes in Germany and Pordenone, near Venice, found that half the HIV-infected prostitutes were IV drug users.[25] Another study of Amsterdam IV-drug-using prostitutes found that 28 percent were HIV-seropositive.[26]

Women's Prostitution and Other Crimes

Aside from the criminal act of prostitution itself, women in the profession frequently commit other criminal offenses. These include using and dealing illegal drugs, loitering, vagrancy, running away from home (minors), shoplifting, robbery, assault, and occasionally murder.[27] Many prostitutes were already perpetrating other crimes before entering the profession. Others turned to additional crimes after they became prostitutes, in order to support drug habits, please pimps, or make more money. In the recent case, the "Hollywood Madam," prostitute Heidi Fleiss, was convicted not only of pandering, but also of evading income taxes and laundering profits from her call girl operation.

Most female prostitutes think lowly of the men they service and, thus, will use every opportunity to leave them with more to remember than the sex act. Robberies, thefts, and blackmail are common offenses of prostitutes against their johns.[28] Some customers face "knife-wielding" women prostitutes in search of drugs, more money, or even their lives, often to support drug addictions or on orders from pimps.[29] Some HIV-infected prostitutes have been known to have unprotected sex with male customers in the hope of passing on the disease and punishing both themselves and the johns for their illicit sex acts.

Few women who sell sex are able to remain in the profession without committing other crimes as part of the world of prostitution and the sex trade.

The Victimization of Women Prostitutes

Many prefer to view prostitution as a "victimless" crime. In fact, female prostitutes are victimized in a variety of ways — before and after they enter prostitution. One study reported that 90 percent of the female prostitutes had been sexually molested at some point in their lives.[30] Another study found that nine out of every ten female prostitutes were victims of childhood sexual assaults.[31] A number of studies have revealed that over three-quarters of prostitutes were sexually abused or raped before the age of 14 — often by a family member or someone near to the family.[32]

The majority of women prostitutes have been physically abused by parents, relatives, lovers, customers, and pimps.[33] According to statistics, approximately 70 percent of all female prostitutes are victims of repeated rape by their male customers, on average 31 times a year.[34] A law journal reported that 65 percent of women prostitutes are subjected to frequent beatings by customers and pimps.[35] Prostitutes being gang-raped has also been reported.[36]

Recently an article about female streetwalkers stated, "Violence is a part of the routine — slapping, beating, tugging, scratching, twisting, forcing, kicking."[37] In referring to one streetwalker's ordeal, the author wrote: "Trina has yellowed black-and-blue marks as well as fresh purple bruises from recent beatings. More than once she has been cut — on the face, the hands — with pocket knives."[38]

Death is also a distinct possibility for female prostitutes worldwide. In Michigan recently, the strangulation death of a call girl by one of her male customers made headlines.[39] An Oregon newspaper article warned prostitutes about the deadly danger they face almost daily and reported, "A body found on Mount Spokane was the fourth unsolved killing of a prostitute in the past six years."[40] In Victorian England, five streetwalking prostitutes met violent deaths at the hands of a serial killer who became known as "Jack the Ripper."

It is unknown how many prostitutes are killed in relation to the sex-for-sale business each year in this country. One estimate placed the number that die annually at 5 percent of all prostitutes.[41] The Justice Department reported that the rate of mortality for female prostitutes is 40 times the national average.[42]

Women prostitutes also face other perils to their health and well-being. Besides AIDS, prostitutes are frequently exposed to sexually transmitted diseases such as syphilis, herpes, and chlamydia.[43] They are also often sick from such illnesses as pneumonia and hepatitis.[44] Studies have found a relationship between prostitution and certain types of cancer, such as cervical cancer.[45]

Many female prostitutes become mothers during the course of their prostitution. Frequently their babies are born drug-addicted, with AIDS, or with other physical or mental impairments resulting from the mother's condition at the time of birth.[46] Other women prostitutes entered the profession with children or added to an existing family. Often the mother and child are impoverished. In New York, 70 percent of prostitutes are mothers.[47] Only 10 percent of these children actually live with their prostitute mothers.

Female prostitutes also tend to be victimized by differential enforcement of the law. Studies indicate that they are more likely to be arrested and to face jail time than are their male counterparts, customers, and pimps.[48]

Finally, women prostitutes suffer victimization through economic discrimination. Many believe that the gender-based inequality of our economic structure forces women into prostitution and pornography. The financial rewards afforded by prostitution — especially for unskilled, low-skilled, uneducated, and poor women but other women as well — make it a tempting alternative to traditionally low-paying, typically women's occupations.[49] Discrimination in the workplace, coupled with increasing demands for economic survival, material items, and support for addiction, will continue to compel some females into a life of prostitution.[50]

According to many studies, much of the victimization that women prostitutes face in the United States is a microcosm of what female prostitutes are facing worldwide.[51]

Part III

Girls and Prostitution

Chapter 10

The Extent of Teenage Prostitution

If prostitution is the world's oldest profession, then child prostitution is the world's greatest tragedy. History has shown the sexual exploitation of children to be one of our most enduring shameful phenomenons. Many societies have condoned and actively encouraged the use of minors for sexual purposes.[1] In ancient Egypt, the "most beautiful and highest born maidens were forced into prostitution as a religious practice, and they continued as prostitutes until their first menstruation."[2] In China and India, children were routinely sold into prostitution by their parents,[3] and for centuries Persia was renowned for its boy brothels.[4] Child brothels and freelance teen prostitution flourished in Europe during the nineteenth century.[5]

The prostitution of children in the United States did not become widespread until the early nineteenth century, when men "demanded more esoteric forms of sexual titillation."[6] Today, teenage prostitution is a staple of American society as millions of runaways, homeless children, drug-addicted teens, and perverse male customers converge, even with the threat of AIDS, to keep the child sex industry alive and well.

Defining Teen Prostitution

Teenage prostitution is commonly called child prostitution, though the vast majority of minors involved in prostitution are in their teens. For the purposes of this chapter, teen prostitution will be defined as the use of or participation of persons under the age of 18 in "sexual acts with adults or other minors where no force is present, including intercourse, oral sex, anal sex, and sadomasochistic activities where payment is involved."[7] Contrary to other types of child sexual exploitation, such as statutory rape and incest, teen prostitution involves the selling of sexual favors, which makes the sexual acts prostitution. Payment generally comes in the form of cash (or credit) but also may include drugs, shelter, clothing, jewelry, or other items.

In some instances, teenagers have been turned into prostitutes by their own parents or other family members.[8] In other cases, they have literally been sold into sexual slavery prostitution after being abducted.[9] Only a minority of juvenile female prostitutes are in business for themselves (as opposed to the majority of male prostitutes who generally are independent operators). The vast majority of female teen prostitutes have pimps, pimp boyfriends, or someone else in a position of authority and control.[10]

Girl prostitutes ply their trade in big cities, small towns, and rural areas. They come in all shapes, sizes, races, and ethnicities and from all socioeconomic backgrounds. They are streetwalkers, call girls, dancers, students, and young mothers. Many can be identified simply by their "working the streets" outfits and makeup, including "thickly painted red lips and extravagant wigs"; "they wear brocaded jackets and fish-net stockings, and totter on the inevitable five-inch heels."[11] However, others may be far less conspicuous, plying their trade in dingy motels or first-rate hotels, massage parlors or alleyways, car seats and elsewhere.

The Incidence of
Teen Prostitution Worldwide

The problem of children (mostly female) being forced or sold into prostitution is of global magnitude. One need only look at the statistics to understand the dimension of the sex-for-sale industry. It is estimated that there are at least 800,000 juvenile prostitutes in Thailand, 400,000 in India (some as young as nine years old), and 80,000 in the Philippines.[12] In Brazil, there are an estimated 250,000 to 500,000 underage prostitutes;[13] the number of juvenile prostitutes in Canada is placed at approximately 200,000.[14] In Tokyo, Japan, 8 percent of the schoolgirls are estimated to be prostitutes.[15]

Many believe the numbers greatly underestimate the extent of teenage prostitution in these countries. Experts fear that the booming international child sex trade industry may soon spiral out of control as sex tourism and white slavery continues to spread like the plague in new locations such as China and the Dominican Republic.[16]

"Having sex with children provides a greater sexual thrill to many men," observed the secretary general of the Indian Health Organization. "They find it more titillating, and it gives them an added sense of power."[17] This power, in numbers and money, has led to the continued growth of the child sex-for-sale business and to the spread of AIDS around the world. The international sexploitation and prostitution of children will be examined more closely in Chapter 22.

The Scope of Teen Prostitutes in the United States

The sexual misuse and exploitation of children has become a multimillion-dollar industry in America, with prostitution accounting for much of the revenue. Just how many teen prostitutes are selling sex in the United States varies according to the source. The Department of Health and Human Services estimates that there are 300,000 prostitutes under the age of 18.[18] Police figures have placed the number at between 100,000 and 300,000 juvenile prostitutes.[19] Other, nonofficial but likely more accurate, sources estimate that as many as half a million children under 16 are involved in prostitution, with that number doubling or tripling when including 16- and 17-year-old prostitutes.[20]

A recent survey of child prostitution in all 50 states concluded that it had increased in 37 percent of the cities.[21] This growth was attributed to greater numbers of teenagers running away from troubled, dysfunctional homes. The survey found that most child prostitutes were

- runaways with alcohol and/or drug problems;
- ages 13 to 17, though many were found to be much younger; and
- selling sex primarily in central business districts, arcade game rooms, and bus and train stations.

Stiffer teenage curfew and loitering laws, more runaway shelters, and tougher penalties for pimps and juvenile prostitutes' customers were recommended.

Experts generally agree that the majority of teen prostitutes are female. Some estimate that females account for as many as two-thirds of the juvenile prostitutes in this country.[22] And there is a strong relationship between runaways and prostitution.[23] More than one million girls run away from home each year — often coming from midwestern cities and rural communities — due to sexual, physical, and/or mental abuse, neglect, rebellion, loneliness, lack of communication, or a need for adventure and independence. Some are throwaways — forced out of the home by parents, guardians, or other family members.

Within weeks (sometimes days or hours), many of these runaway girls have become prostitutes — selling their bodies for money, food, drugs, shelter, companionship, or false promises. In the process, some will turn to petty (or serious) crimes, substance abuse, and selling drugs. The less fortunate will end up in juvenile detention or jail, victims of customer or pimp rape and beatings — or worse, will become HIV infected through sex or shared dirty needles.

**Figure 10-1 Arrests of Persons Under 18
for Prostitution, by Gender, 1995**

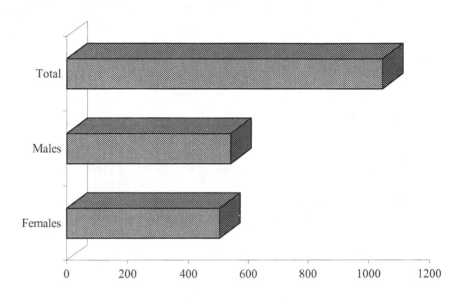

Source: Derived from U.S. Department of Justice, Federal Bureau of Investigation, *Crime in the United States: Uniform Crime Reports 1995* (Washington, D.C.: Government Printing Office, 1996), pp. 218, 220, 222.

Official Statistics on Teen Prostitutes

Police arrest statistics compiled by the FBI's *Uniform Crime Reports* (*UCR*) offer us only a fraction of the true incidence of teenage prostitution. However, they generally can provide a more accurate composite of teenage prostitutes than of adult prostitutes, since most teen prostitution occurs at the street level, where arrests are most likely.

In 1995, there were 1,044 arrests of persons under the age of 18 for prostitution and commercialized vice, according to the *UCR*.[24] This represented a sharp decline since 1986.[25] Comparatively, 189,696 persons under the age of 18 were arrested as runaways in 1995, rising by more than 50 percent since 1986.[26] The increase in the number of runaways is particularly alarming, since we know that a high percentage of these runaways will turn to prostitution at some stage of their street life. Arrest data on juvenile prostitutes suggests that many prostitute runaways are managing to evade the arm of the law, even as they actively sell their bodies.

Figure 10-2 Arrests of Runaways, by Gender, 1995

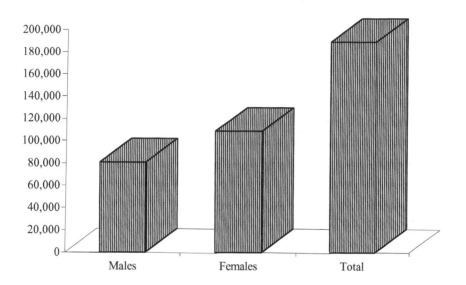

Source: Derived from U.S. Department of Justice, Federal Bureau of Investigation, *Crime in the United States: Uniform Crime Reports 1995* (Washington, D.C.: Government Printing Office, 1996), pp. 218, 220, 222.

ARRESTS BY GENDER

As shown in Figure 10-1, arrests for prostitution and commercialized vice of persons under the age of 18 were roughly divided between female and male juveniles in 1995. There were 540 male arrests, compared with 504 female arrests. These totals reflect an overall decline in juvenile arrests for prostitution since 1986. They also indicate somewhat of a shift in arrest of juveniles by gender for prostitution and commercialized vice.[27] Long-term arrest trends have typically shown more young females arrested for prostitution than young males.[28] At least part of this change may have been due to differential arrest patterns for teenage girl prostitutes compared with arrest patterns for teenage boy prostitutes.[29]

Arrest statistics for runaways reveal that far more girls are being arrested than boys, as seen in Figure 10-2. In 1995, nearly 28,000 more female juveniles than male juveniles ran away from home. This differential has remained relatively consistent over the years.[30]

Many believe that girls tend to run away more often than boys and turn to prostitution because of a greater incidence of sexual or physical abuse at home. Others see this gap in running away due more to girls' rebellion and need for adventure. The truth probably falls somewhere between the extremes.

Table 10-1 Juvenile Arrests for Prostitution
and Commercialized Vice, by Age and Gender, 1995

	Arrests	Ages under 15	Ages under 18	under 10	10–12	Age 13–14	15	16	17
Female	49,491	78	504	16	6	56	74	114	238
Male	31,573	103	540	15	19	69	78	133	226
Total	81,064	181	1,044	31	25	125	152	247	464

Source: Compiled from U.S. Department of Justice, Federal Bureau of Investigation, *Crime in the United States: Uniform Crime Reports 1995* (Washington, D.C.: Government Printing Office, 1996), pp. 218, 220, 222.

Also, girl runaways may be more often reported as missing than boy runaways — many of whom may really be throwaways.

Arrests by Age and Gender

Table 10-1 distributes juvenile arrests for prostitution and commercialized vice in 1995 by age and gender. Arrests of persons under the age of 18 peaked at age 17. This peak at age 17 was true for both genders. Slightly more females than males were arrested at age 17. Most prostitution and commercialized vice arrests of persons under the age of 18 occurred in the 16-to-17 age range. More than two-thirds of all juveniles arrested were between the ages of 16 and 17. Studies support this arrest trend. Jennifer James found the mean age for female prostitutes to be 16.9.[31]

Over 80 percent of the total arrests of persons under age 18, female and male, were of juveniles ages 15 to 17. In spite of this, there were still 31 children younger than 10 arrested as prostitutes in 1995. This underscores the prevalence of the problem of child prostitution, as many more young and older children in the prostitution business fail to show up in the statistics.

Arrests by Race

White teenagers compose the majority of juveniles arrested for prostitution, as reflected in Figure 10-3. More than 63 percent of the persons under the age of 18 arrested for prostitution and commercialized vice in 1995 were white. One-third of the youths arrested were black. This figure is disproportionate to their numbers in the general population. Asian and Native American juveniles accounted for less than 3 percent of the arrests.

UCR data does not provide race breakdowns by gender in arrest statistics. However, other studies indicate that white girls account for anywhere from 60 to 80 percent of female teenage prostitutes.[32] Black and Hispanic girl prostitutes tend to be overrepresented in many large cities. Among streetwalkers in

Figure 10-3 Juvenile Arrests for Prostitution and Commercialized Vice, by Race, 1995

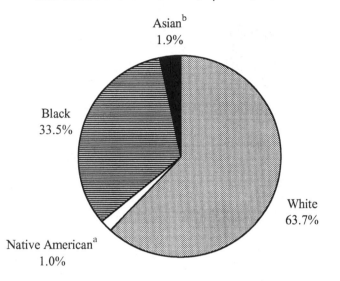

Asian[b]
1.9%

Black
33.5%

White
63.7%

Native American[a]
1.0%

Source: Adapted from U.S. Department of Justice, Federal Bureau of Investigation, *Crime in the United States: Uniform Crime Reports 1995* (Washington, D.C.: Government Printing Office, 1996), pp. 227.

some red-light districts, racial and ethnic minority prostitutes may account for as many as half the teenagers selling sex.[33]

ARRESTS BY COMMUNITY TYPE

Most juvenile prostitution occurs in cities. This is supported by arrest data (see Figure 10-4). In 1995, over 81 percent of the juvenile arrests for prostitution and commercialized vice occurred in cities. Nearly 12 percent of the arrests were in suburban areas. Suburban counties accounted for just over 5 percent of the arrests for prostitution (see notes in Table 2-1 for an explanation of the difference between suburban counties and areas). Less than 2 percent of the arrests of persons under age 18 occurred in rural areas.

In spite of the heavy representation of cities in juvenile arrests for prostitution and commercialized vice, there is some evidence that teen prostitution is growing in the suburbs and rural communities.[34]

RELATED-CRIME ARRESTS OF JUVENILES

In addition to arrests of runaways and juveniles for prostitution, many young prostitutes are arrested and charged with other offenses, such as curfew

Figure 10-4 Juvenile Arrests for Prostitution
and Commercialized Vice, by Community Size, 1995

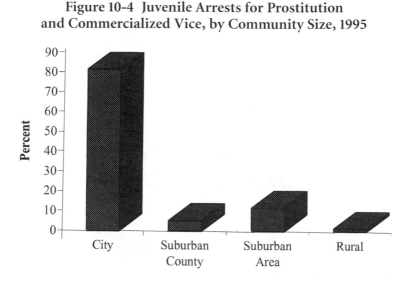

Source: Adapted from U.S. Department of Justice, Federal Bureau of Investigation, *Crime in the United States: Uniform Crime Reports 1995* (Washington, D.C.: Government Printing Office, 1996), pp. 233, 242, 251, 260.

---

and loitering law violations, vagrancy, suspicion, and drug- and alcohol-related crimes. Table 10-2 provides arrest figures for persons under the age of 18 accused of these crimes. Considerably more juveniles were arrested in 1995 for loitering, vagrancy, and suspicion than for prostitution and commercialized vice. The numbers are even higher for substance-abuse violations; with the exception of runaways, drug offenses represent more arrests than any other offense. Some juveniles may be charged with sex offenses other than prostitution or rape, though the crime may have involved an act of prostitution.

In every offense category other than runaways and prostitution, arrests of male juveniles far surpassed that of female juveniles. This could help account for the gender differences in runaway and prostitution figures.

Overall, these offenses illustrate the nonuniformity from jurisdiction to jurisdiction in arresting and charging juvenile offenders. Most experts believe that a high percentage of adolescent prostitutes are represented and hidden in many of these collateral offenses to prostitution.

Arrest Trends in Adolescent Prostitution

An important way to track juvenile prostitution arrests is through arrest trends. The most recent trends for arrests of persons under the age of 18 for prostitution and commercialized vice can be seen in Table 10-3. Between 1986

Table 10-2 Juvenile Arrests for Selected Crimes Associated with Prostitution, by Offense and Gender, 1995

	Total	Female	Male
Curfew and loitering law violations	114,946	34,011	80,935
Vagrancy	2,776	313	2,463
Suspicion	1,527	322	1,205
Sex offenses (except rape and prostitution)	12,307	894	11,413
Drug abuse violations	147,107	18,614	128,493
Drunkenness	15,337	2,430	12,907
Liquor laws	87,843	25,448	62,395
Prostitution and commercialized vice	1,044	504	540
Runaways	189,696	108,830	80,866

Source: Developed from U.S. Department of Justice, Federal Bureau of Investigation, *Crime in the United States: Uniform Crime Reports 1995* (Washington, D.C.: Government Printing Office, 1996), pp. 218, 220, 222.

and 1995, arrests of juveniles decreased by nearly 50 percent. For females, the decline was more than 62 percent, compared with just over 28 percent for males.

These figures, impressive as they are, contradict runaway arrest trends for the same period of time. As shown in Figure 10-5, from 1986 to 1995, total juvenile runaway arrests rose more than 53 percent. Both female and male arrests increased by over 50 percent. This suggests that the ten-year arrest trends for prostitution may be misleading, since a rise in runaways generally means more youths will be forced to sell their bodies for food, shelter, and drugs. It is entirely possible that the conflicting arrest trends may both be accurate, with runaway teens becoming more savvy in avoiding arrest for solicitation and with shrinking police budgets meaning fewer officers on the streets to arrest

Table 10-3 Juvenile Arrest Trends for Prostitution and Commercialized Vice, by Gender, 1986–1995[a]

	1994	1995	Percent Change	1991	1995	Percent Change	1986	1995	Percent Change
Total	932	1,033	+10.8	920	867	-5.8	1,945	976	-49.8
Female	445	501	+12.6	471	434	-7.9	1,231	466	-62.1
Male	487	532	+9.2	449	433	-3.6	714	510	-28.6

[a]Includes data from the three time spans identified. Based on arrest trends which may differ from data noted for only 1995.

Source: Adapted from U.S. Department of Justice, Federal Bureau of Investigation, *Crime in the United States: Uniform Crime Reports 1995* (Washington, D.C.: Government Printing Office, 1996), pp. 212–17.

Figure 10-5   Arrest Trends for Runaways, by Gender, 1986–1995

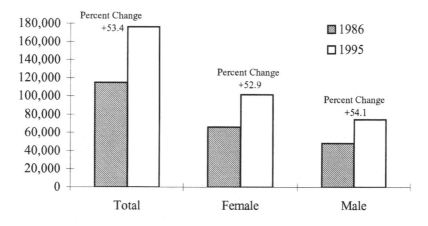

Source: Derived from U.S. Department of Justice, Federal Bureau of Investigation, *Crime in the United States: Uniform Crime Reports 1995* (Washington, D.C.: Government Printing Office, 1996), pp. 212–13.

prostitutes. Refer to Chapter 1 for additional shortcomings of official statistics.

Ironically, the five-year arrest trends for juvenile prostitutes show a much lesser decrease. For the one-year trend from 1994 to 1995, there is actually an increase in juvenile arrests for prostitution and commercialized vice. Arrests rose nearly 11 percent for all persons under the age of 18 and over 12 percent for girl prostitutes.

The latter figures indicate either that juvenile arrests are once again on the rise or that the one-year trend is inadequate for reliability. What is clear by most accounts is that many more girls and boys are in the sex-for-sale business than the statistics would have us believe.

Chapter 11

The Characteristics of Girl Prostitutes

Over one million teenage girls are estimated to be turning tricks in the United States at any given time. Because these girls come in all shapes, sizes, and colors and are from every conceivable background, they cannot be singularly categorized. Girl prostitutes represent every corner of this country. They are inevitably united as one in their common selling, as minors, of sexual favors — whether they are runaways, throwaways, or simply bored and looking for excitement on the streets in neon-lit big cities. Female juvenile prostitutes also share the dangers of HIV and AIDS, shattered lives, and men who hurt children by the very nature of the sexual contract between them. For many, tomorrow will bring only more misery. For others, there will be no tomorrow. Yet others will somehow escape and reestablish a life outside prostitution, even as the scars remain.

Typology of Girl Prostitutes and Prostitution

The vast majority of female prostitutes under the age of 18 are streetwalkers.[1] At least one-fifth of all streetwalkers are believed to be teenage girls. Adolescent female prostitutes can also be found working as call girls through escort services or brothels and plying their trade in massage parlors, saunas, nightclubs, hotels, and just about anywhere else where sex is bought and sold.

They offer a range of sexual services, including sexual intercourse, "oral sex, anal sex, homosexual activities, multiple partner sex, sadomasochistic activities, urination or defecation, and obscenity related sexual performances."[2] One study estimated that 75 percent of streetwalkers' sexual contacts are fellatio only.[3] According to an article on adolescent prostitution, the girl prostitute's primary service is oral sex because "it is what her customers want and the most practical for working in cars. It's also quick, which is a concern, because street prostitution is illegal, and when the cops show up, it's sometimes necessary to run."[4]

Most teenage prostitutes enter the business as part-time prostitutes, usually hoping to earn a few quick bucks for food, cigarettes, drugs, shelter, or pocket money. For many, this part-time work quickly becomes a full-time profession. Studies indicate that the typical female teen prostitute will be turning tricks on a full-time basis within eight months to a year after her initial prostitution experience.[5]

In a study of teenage prostitution, Joan Johnson described the conditions in which a girl becomes a full time prostitute.[6] Girl prostitutes undergo a change in self-image, she noted. Adapting to the reality of being prostitutes, along with the negative self-image this brings, adolescent females become, in effect, what they are labeled by society: sluts, whores, or hookers. The more they become a part of the prostitution subculture — including pimps and customers — the more they come to regard themselves as prostitutes and the more committed they become to working the streets, selling their bodies full-time.

Although a small percentage of female teenage prostitutes operate independently of a pimp or other controlling figure, most girl prostitutes have been turned out by pimps or others. It is believed that as many as 90 percent of female teen prostitutes entered the business through the coercion and charms of a pimp or eventually established a relationship with a pimp.[7] One study reported that nearly every girl prostitute respondent had some association with a pimp, either directly or indirectly.[8]

Pimps (or the stereotypical image of them) are not the only ones to draw girls into prostitution. In some instances, a relative or family acquaintance is responsible for turning a girl out. In 4 of every 100 cases of girls entering prostitution, the "pimp" or influencing person was a relative.[9] The relative may include a mother, a sister, or an in-law who is a prostitute. Ten percent of teenage prostitutes are believed to have started selling sexual favors by being propositioned by a john.[10] Another 20 percent of runaway girls become prostitutes through their acquaintance with other female adolescent streetwalking prostitutes.[11] These girls may be working as recruits for a pimp, or they may honestly be trying to help a runaway girl — who is often homeless, hungry, lonely, and desperate — find a way to survive the mean streets, just as they themselves were once initiated into the business. Given the alternative of perhaps starving to death, many fresh-faced, naive girls turn to prostitution as an easy way out.

Of course, they soon learn there is nothing easy about the life of a prostitute — which may be doubly or triply hard for a juvenile prostitute.

Figure 11-1 Arrests of Girl Prostitutes, by Age, 1995

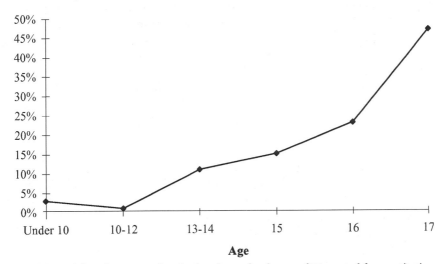

Note: Figure is based on arrest data for females under the age of 17 arrested for prostitution and commercialized vice.

Source: Derived from U.S. Department of Justice, Federal Bureau of Investigation, *Crime in the United States: Uniform Crime Reports 1995* (Washington, D.C.: Government Printing Office, 1996), p. 222.

Girl Prostitutes by Age

Some girl prostitutes are as young as 5 or 6. However, the vast majority of female teens selling sex fall between the ages of 15 and 17. In 1995, over 80 percent of the girls arrested for prostitution and commercialized vice in the United States were ages 15 to 17 (see Figure 11-1). Over two-thirds were 16 and 17, with the number of 17-year-olds arrested more than doubling the number of arrests of 16-year-old prostitutes.

In the book *Entrance into Juvenile Prostitution*, Jennifer James found the median age of girl prostitutes to be 16.9 years.[12] However, most girl prostitutes entered the business before age 16. In a study for the Delancey Foundation in San Francisco, Mimi Silbert and Ayala Pines found that the average age of a girl's first experience as a prostitute was 14.[13] Other researchers have supported this finding.[14]

Girl Prostitutes by Race and Ethnicity

Girls who sell their bodies in this country include every racial and ethnic persuasion — white, black, Hispanic, and interracial or interethnic. They come from as far away as Europe, Asia, and South America. Most are homegrown girls who often leap into both prostitution and womanhood in a single bound.

Studies reveal that, by and large, most adolescent female prostitutes are white. Studies in San Francisco[15] and Minneapolis[16] found that 80 percent of the prostitutes sampled were white girls; James reported that 62 percent of the girl prostitutes in her study were white.[17]

Black teenage girls make up the second-largest group of adolescent female prostitutes, with estimates ranging from 10 percent to 50 percent of those sampled.[18] The larger the sample, the lower is the percentage of black girl prostitutes.

Teen prostitutes of other racial and ethnic groups tend to be relatively low by comparison. Various studies have found Hispanic and Native American girls to constitute between 2 and 11 percent of the adolescent female prostitute population.[19]

Asian girl prostitutes are generally considered to be the smallest minority, by race, of teen prostitutes in this country (as opposed to elsewhere in the world, where Asian teen prostitution is flourishing). However, the prostitution of Asian girls has been on the upsurge in recent years as Asian gangs (sometimes with the deliberate or unwitting help of American soldiers) have smuggled girls from Vietnam, the Philippines, and elsewhere into the United States to work as sex slaves and indentured-servant prostitutes.[20]

Girl Prostitutes by Social Class

It is commonly assumed that most girl prostitutes are products of the lower classes. In reality, all classes of society are represented in the adolescent prostitution subculture. Although a number of studies featuring small samples have reported a higher incidence of girl prostitutes from working- and lower-class backgrounds,[21] research involving larger sample groups has found that the majority of female teen prostitutes emerge from the middle and upper-middle classes. In a study of girl prostitutes in Minnesota, nearly one in four had parents with some college education. Many had fathers who were in professional or skilled occupations.[22] Silbert found that 70 percent of her sample of girl prostitutes came from families with average or above-average incomes.[23] James reached a similar conclusion, noting a "phenomenal" increase in the number of "affluent and overindulged" girl prostitutes.[24]

Family Dynamics of Girl Prostitutes

Studies reveal that the majority of teen prostitutes come from broken and/or dysfunctional homes. In Maura Crowley's study, 85 percent of the girl prostitutes reported the absence of at least one parent during their upbringing.[25] The Huckleberry House Project found that 70 percent of the respondents indicated coming from homes with one or both parents missing,[26] as did also James's research.[27]

Other studies have shown a correlation between teen prostitution and a parental relationship characterized by stress and conflict. The Huckleberry House researchers found that few girl prostitutes had positive, caring relationships with their parents.[28] In Diana Gray's study of teenage prostitutes, she found that 75 percent of the girls described the relationship with their parents as "poor" or "very bad."[29] Crowley's study revealed that mothers were almost twice as likely as fathers to be the source of the child-parent dysfunction, with 42 percent of the mothers, compared with 25 percent of the fathers, reported as being responsible for the girl prostitute's poor relationship with her parents.[30]

Prostitution and/or promiscuity of the mother has also been linked to female teen prostitution, as has also family stresses.[31]

Child Sexual and Physical Abuse and Victimization

Nearly all girl prostitutes have been sexually molested, assaulted, or physically abused before entering the profession.[32] The literature is replete with findings that associate adolescent prostitution with intrafamilial and non-familial sexual and physical mistreatment, including incest, rape, sexual exploitation, and child abuse.[33] The Huckleberry House study found that 90 percent of the girl prostitutes had been sexually molested.[34] Two-thirds of Silbert's sample were victims of incest and child abuse.[35] Other research has found a high percentage of teen prostitutes to be victims of rape, child pornography, and other forms of sexploitation.[36]

A strong relationship between girl prostitution, child battering, and domestic violence has also been well established.[37] In both the Crowley study[38] and the Huckleberry House Project,[39] two out of every three female teens reported being physically abused at home.

Running Away and Girl Prostitution

There is a clear relationship between female runaways and girl prostitutes. Most studies show that the majority of adolescent female prostitutes are runaways — having often fled from home to escape abusive situations.[40] One study found that two-thirds of the teen prostitutes were runaways.[41] Other research suggests the percentage of girl runaway prostitutes is even higher.[42]

Arrest statistics routinely show far more female runaways than male.[43] Many of these runaways show up in prostitution, loitering, vagrancy, and drug- and alcohol-related arrest data.[44]

Anastasia Volkonsky, a director of an organization fighting sexual exploitation, gave a grim view of the typical runaway girl turned prostitute: "Most have experienced a major trauma: incest, domestic violence, rape, or parental abandonment. At an age widely considered too young to handle activities such as voting, drinking alcohol, driving, or holding down a job, these children survive by selling their bodies to strangers. These formative years will leave them with deep scars — should they survive to adulthood."[45]

Another researcher writing about street life for girl prostitutes spoke of one runaway's path to a dead-end life in the sex-for-sale industry: "At 9, Diane ran away from home.... By age 12, she was smoking pot.... By 16, she was a hooker and a junkie, sleeping under benches on the streets.... Everything had become incidental to the drugs — sex, friendships, plans, promises, security.... The first thing on her mind when she woke up was how long she would have to work for her first fix. On cocaine, she could turn tricks for 12- or 14-hour days, the most intense part of the high lasting 15 or 20 seconds."[46]

Further examination of the runaway as part of the female teenage prostitution subculture can be seen in Chapter 12.

Substance Abuse and Girl Prostitution

Drug and alcohol use and abuse are common features of the girl prostitute's life. In many instances, the teen was already using or abusing drugs before becoming a prostitute to support a habit. One study found that almost eight in ten juvenile prostitutes were using drugs before entering the prostitution business.[47] Forty percent of the youths reporting drinking alcohol as well, with 40 percent admitting to taking amphetamines or "uppers" or "speed."

Virtually all teenage prostitutes have tried at least one illicit drug (many have also abused legal drugs). Estimates are that between one-fifth and one-half of all underage prostitutes use drugs regularly;[48] at least 70 percent of girl prostitutes consume some form of alcohol.[49] Marijuana is the drug of choice for most young prostitutes, along with alcohol.[50] However, many teenage prostitutes abuse other mood-altering drugs such as narcotics, heroin, and cocaine.[51]

Girl prostitutes are often introduced to drugs (or new, more powerful drugs) through pimps or other prostitutes. This can often lead to addiction, the sharing of dirty needles and HIV-tainted blood, and continued prostitution and other crimes, in what can be a vicious cycle.

Researchers have studied the reasons so many teenage prostitutes use drugs.[52] These reasons include the following:

- To help relax
- To enhance sexual performance
- To make the selling of sex more bearable
- To help overcome fears of johns or pimps
- To do as other prostitutes and homeless do
- To follow in the footsteps of family members or friends
- To maintain an addiction
- To feel good

In addition, alcohol and drugs are easily obtained, and many girl prostitutes want to become part of the drug and alcohol world glamorized in music and Hollywood. Additionally, some girl prostitutes have reported abusing alcohol or drugs before and after becoming prostitutes in order to "deaden memories" associated with sexual or physical abuse they experienced.[53] Others have turned to drugs to "desensitize present experiences" in the often dehumanizing world of teen prostitution.[54]

A recent article in *Time* magazine illustrated the descent into prostitution for one female teenage addict:

> "Eva" is a 16-year old patient at New York City's Phoenix House drug rehabilitation center who got hooked on crack two years ago. The product of a troubled middle class family, she was already a heavy drinker and pot smoker when she was introduced to coke by her older brother, a young dope pusher. "When you take the first toke on a crack pipe, you get on top of the world," she says.
>
> She started stealing from family and friends to support her habit. She soon turned to prostitution and went through two abortions before she was 16. "I just didn't give a damn about protecting myself," she said. "I just wanted to get high. Fear of pregnancy didn't even cross my mind when I hit the sack with someone for drugs."[55]

Girl Prostitution and Other Crimes

Aside from the illegal acts of selling sexual favors, girl prostitutes often find themselves involved in a variety of other criminal and delinquent activity. Some crimes are a natural progression as they become more deeply ensconced in the dark world of prostitution, drugs, and street crime. Others are the result of supporting drug habits or surviving on the streets. Yet other criminality or delinquency comes as directives from pimps, who often use young prostitutes for stealing drugs or money in addition to turning tricks.

Typical crimes for many girl prostitutes include theft, robbery, drug dealing, assault, and of course, using illegal drugs.[56] Some carry knives or guns to use as in self-defense from violent johns or pimps or during the course of a robbery. One study found that half the teenage female prostitutes admitted to robbing customers regularly.[57]

Many girl prostitutes are hidden in arrest statistics, having been charged with curfew and loitering law violations, vagrancy, suspicion, and often drug- and alcohol-related charges.[58]

Girl Prostitutes, Promiscuity, and Sexual Adventure

In spite of the horror stories often associated with young girls being turned out by violent johns after running away from dysfunctional homes where they were sexually abused, the reality is that not all girl prostitutes entered the profession under such adversity and negative circumstances. One study found that only 5 percent of the girls turning tricks were forced into prostitution by a pimp's threats, intimidation, or physical coercion.[59] In James's study of the relationship between prostitutes and pimps, she found that most pimps do not force or reduce girls into becoming prostitutes or prevent them from ever leaving the stable.[60] This contention was further supported by Dorothy Bracey, who noted the pimp's charm, flattery, and emotional exploitation in enticing a girl into prostitution but concluded, "Although we have heard stories of kidnapping and of totally innocent girls being raped and then 'turned out,' none of the girls interviewed claimed to know anyone who had started in prostitution in these ways."[61]

There is also evidence that a growing number of girls are becoming prostitutes not because of past sexual and/or physical abuses, broken homes, or poverty but for the money, fun, adventure, excitement, and sexual opportunities that present themselves in the adult world of the sex industry. Bracey found that many girls entered the profession because they knew other girls who were prostitutes.[62] One article noted, "A lot of kids take to prostitution as an 'on and off job'—when you need a few bucks."[63]

For many adolescent females, the relative ease with which one can enter prostitution, combined with the money that can be made (often more than the typically low-paying jobs for young people) and the joy derived from sexual coming of age and sexual experimentation, makes the sex-for-sale industry a tempting choice. This is made all too clear in the following commentary by an authority on teen prostitution: "There are more younger hookers, thirteen and fourteen-year-olds. They just don't care. It's a way they can have all the clothes they want, all the blue jeans and shoes they want.... Girls sell their bodies to get money. If it was legal and had a tax on it, they would find something else."[64]

The rise in prostitution among affluent girls is seen as a type of sexual adventure and promiscuity, as opposed to the motivations typically associated with lower-class prostitutes. According to James, for upper-class girls, "it is basically entertaining to dress up with your friends and go down on the street and con, cajole, and be the aggressor. The extravagant sensations from the illegality, projected immorality, and danger of prostitution [are] a relief from the neutrality of suburbia."[65]

Addiction to sex and the sex industry is seen by many as a powerful inducement for many young females to turn to prostitution. Learning about sex, sexual acts, the male and female bodies, and the pleasures of orgasm — and getting paid for it — can make leaving the business much harder than entering it.[66] A similar addiction can be found in the sex industry itself — where the bright lights, excitement, dizzying pace, easy money, fast sex, independence, and adventure often can become to a girl prostitute what heroin is to a junkie.

Girl Prostitution and Mental Illness

Many teenage female prostitutes suffer from various emotional and psychological problems. For some, these problems were present before they entered prostitution. For others, the problems began after they entered the business. Studies show that 10 to 20 percent of teen prostitutes have been in psychiatric hospitals.[67] Half of them have been hospitalized on more than one occasion.

Adolescent prostitutes, already at a disadvantage in the world of sex-exploitation, typically are saddled with feelings of helplessness, worthlessness, low self-esteem, and depression. Often these feelings are brought on by lives of emptiness and despair and by being abandoned, unloved, or unwanted. As many as half the girl prostitutes have attempted suicide.[68] Others may have attempted it, in effect, simply by living their high-risk lifestyles, including regular sexual contacts that could lead to HIV infection.

Researchers show that many girl prostitutes are runaways and carry with them a host of emotional disorders often brought on by being sexually or physically abused.[69] Many of these teen prostitutes may not even be aware of their emotional problems or may attribute them to the wrong causes. Unfortunately, few of these girls seek professional help; and once they are out on the streets, it rarely comes looking for them.

Determinants in Girl Prostitution

Studies on the prostitution of adolescent females have found that the determinants or motivations for becoming a prostitute generally fall into three categories: (1) psychoanalytic, (2) situational, and (3) economic.

Psychoanalytical research has associated female teenage prostitution with such mental disorders as schizophrenia, depression, and emotional deprivation.[70] Situational studies have focused on the relationship between girl prostitution and child abuse and neglect, incest, molestation, rape, early sexual experiences, and other situational determinants.[71] The economically motivated factors in girl prostitution have been given the most attention. A number of studies have identified economic deprivation and incentives as key influences in teenage prostitution. James concluded, "The apparent reason for prostitution among adolescents is for economic survival and to meet other needs."[72] Most girl prostitutes have admitted in surveys that money and material items are the most common reasons for entering prostitution.[73]

Since most girl prostitutes tend to be runaways or throwaways, selling their bodies almost becomes a necessity for getting food, shelter, drugs, and the basic necessities of life. Few young prostitutes — often school dropouts with no significant work experience — can realistically expect to find legitimate, well-paying employment. This situation is put in its proper context by a former girl prostitute and street kid, who complained: "There's no doors open to us.... How are you going to be able to hold down a job if you have no high school diploma, if you're not able to take a shower every day, if you don't have clean clothes to wear to work?"[74]

Chapter 12

Runaway and Throwaway Girls

The relationship between runaways or throwaways and juvenile prostitution has been clearly established in the literature.[1] Most runaway and throwaway juveniles are female. Many come from abusive and/or dysfunctional homes. Others leave home for perceived greater independence, thrills, excitement, or adventure. Some are literally thrown out of the home for reasons ranging from punishment for disrespect to simple abandonment. Whatever the reason, these runaway or throwaway girls must often resort to selling their bodies for food, shelter, drugs, and survival on the streets across America. With this prostitution comes many risks, including AIDS and murder. Few homeless girls can escape life on the streets without serious emotional and physical implications.

The Magnitude of Girl Runaways and Throwaways

Most evidence suggests that the problem of girls who leave home is staggering. It is estimated that anywhere from several hundred thousand to over 2 million children run away from or are thrown out of their homes each year in the United States.[2] Of these, it is believed that as many as 60 percent may be female.[3] More than half the youths who run away are recidivists, having left home at least three times.[4] Approximately 300,000 runaways are described as "hard core" street kids, who run away repeatedly.[5] Studies reveal that over two-thirds of all runaway girls end up as prostitutes.[6]

Table 12-1 Female Arrest Trends for Running Away,
1986–1995[a]

1986	1995	Percent Change	1991	1995	Percent Change	1994	1995	Percent Change
66,469	101,657	+52.9	65,313	76,688	+17.4	105,743	104,098	-1.6

[a]Includes data for the three trend periods noted. Figures are based on arrest trends and may differ from data mentioned for only 1995.

Source: Adapted from U.S. Department of Justice, Federal Bureau of Investigation, *Crime in the United States: Uniform Crime Reports 1995* (Washington, D.C.: Government Printing Office, 1996), pp. 213, 215, 217.

ARREST DATA ON FEMALE RUNAWAYS

The best official measurement of girl runaways is arrest statistics. Runaways is a status offense, applicable only to persons under age 18. In the *Uniform Crime Reports* (*UCR*), a collection of crime data nationwide, the offense of runaways is defined as "limited to juveniles taken into protective custody under provisions of local statutes."[7] According to the *UCR*, there were 108,830 girls arrested as runaways in the United States in 1995.[8] By comparison, only 504 females under the age of 18 were arrested in 1995 for prostitution and commercialized vice.[9] This wide disparity is generally regarded as indicative of varying laws towards running away and prostitution (for example, some girl prostitutes are arrested for violating loitering laws), as well as differential enforcement of the law.

Girls are arrested more often as runaways than boys. In 1995, the female-male ratio of arrests for running away was 1.3 girl arrests for every boy arrested.[10] This differential may be partly the result of more boy runaways being arrested under other offenses such as suspicion or curfew and loitering law violations.[11]

ARREST TRENDS FOR GIRL RUNAWAYS

The number of girls leaving home as runaways is on the rise, if arrest trends are any indication. As seen in Table 12-1, between 1986 and 1995, arrests of females under the age of 18 for running away rose by almost 53 percent. For the period 1991–95, arrests grew by over 17 percent. For the one-year trend 1994–1995, there was a slight drop in arrests of runaway females at just under 2 percent. However, it is the long-term trends that are of concern, since they compare figures over a more meaningful stretch of time. Thus, they can tell us with greater accuracy about the patterns and characteristics of runaway girls.

Figure 12-1 Arrests of Girl Runaways, by Age, 1995

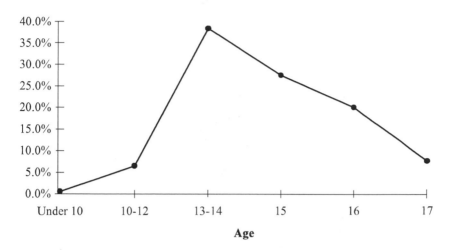

Source: Adapted from U.S. Department of Justice, Federal Bureau of Investigation, *Crime in the United States: Uniform Crime Reports 1995* (Washington, D.C.: Government Printing Office, 1996), pp. 222.

AGE AND GIRLS WHO RUN AWAY

The majority of runaway girls are between the ages of 13 and 16. Figure 12-1 shows the ages of girls arrested as runaways in 1995. Less than 7 percent of the arrests were of girls age 12 and under. Over 85 percent of those arrested fell between the ages of 13 and 16. Over 25 percent of all arrests occurred at age 15, declining steadily for ages 16 and 17. This drop in the arrests of older teens is believed to reflect a loosening of parental control as adolescents approach adulthood.

Similar findings on the age patterns of runaways are reflected in J. A. Bechtel's investigation of juvenile runaways.[12] Over 81 percent of the girl runaways were ages 13 to 16, with 27 percent age 15.

RACE AND RUNAWAYS

Most runaway youths are white, though black teens tend to be overrepresented in runaway data. The *UCR* reported that nearly 77 percent of the juveniles arrested in 1995 as runaways were white (see Figure 12-2). Nineteen percent of those arrested were black. Juveniles of Asian descent accounted for just over 3 percent of the arrests, and Native American youths composed less than 1 percent of the arrestees.

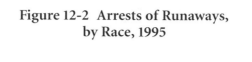

Figure 12-2 Arrests of Runaways,
by Race, 1995

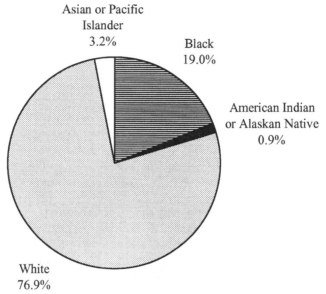

Source: Derived from U.S. Department of Justice, Federal Bureau of Investigation, *Crime in the United States: Uniform Crime Reports 1995* (Washington, D.C.: Government Printing Office, 1996), pp. 227.

In spite of the relatively low totals of arrests among racial minorities, some studies have found a high rate of minority representation among girl runaways and prostitutes in red-light districts and central cities.[13]

RUNAWAY YOUTHS AND COMMUNITY SIZE

Girl runaways are by and large a product of cities and suburbs. Table 12-2 lists community types and rates in which runaways were arrested in 1995. More than seven in ten runaway juveniles came from cities; nearly 25 percent were from suburban counties. Less than 6 percent of the youths ran away from homes in rural counties. The highest rate of arrests came in cities with populations between 50,000 and 249,999. The rate of arrest of city runaways was nearly twice that of runaways from rural communities. These figures may reflect, in part, the greater visibility of runaways in cities and suburbs, as well as variance in police practice and manpower.

Social Class and Runaways

Social class has been shown to play an important role for teenagers who run away from home — though this importance has varied from study to study. In James Hildebrand's study of runaways, he found that the "vast majority" were from the middle class.[14] A poor home environment and school problems were the dominant factors in running away. Similarly, in a study of suburban runaways, Robert Shellow found that over half were middle-class and working-class youths.[15] Twenty-eight percent of the runaways came from lower-class families, and 15 percent ran away from upper-middle-class homes. In her study of runaway girls, Louise Homer concluded that most of her sample were from lower- and lower-middle-class families.[16] Seventy percent of the runaways came from families receiving welfare. Some studies indicate, however, that the rate of runaways is equally distributed across the socioeconomic class strata.[17]

Characterizing the Girl Runaway

What are the dynamic forces that typically reflect girl runaways? Are there certain psychological or physiological anomalies common to female adolescents who leave home? Studies of runaway and homeless girls have identified the following characteristics:

- Seventy percent are white.
- One in five are black.
- Most are between 13 and 16 years of age.
- They come from white-collar and blue-collar families.
- Twenty-five percent of runaways were born to mothers under 17 years of age.
- More than half were victims of sexual or physical abuse.
- Seventy percent use or abuse drugs or alcohol.
- One in four female runaways have been raped.
- Thirty-six percent have been pregnant.
- Eighty percent have serious psychological or behavioral problems.
- A majority will resort to prostitution and street life.
- All face a high risk of HIV infection, violence, and other dangers associated with child prostitution and runaways.[18]

Many runaway girls have a variety of emotional disorders, ranging from depression to schizophrenia. In a study of runaways in youth shelters, Carol Canton and David Shaffer identified 41 percent of the runaways as depressed and antisocial, 30 percent as depressed, and 18 percent as antisocial.[19] Fifty percent had attempted or seriously considered suicide. Another study that compared runaways and nonrunaways concluded that 85 percent of the runaways were clinically depressed and 21 percent had serious mental illness.[20] The runaways

Table 12-2 Number and Rate of Runaway Arrests, by Community Type, 1995

	Total	Total cities	Counties		Suburban area[a]
			Suburban counties	Rural counties	
	(9,498 agencies; population 196,440,000)	(6,541 cities; population 132,932,000)	(1,039 agencies; population 43,729,000)	(1,918 agencies; population 19,780,000)	(4,680 agencies; population 82,984,000)
Runaways	189,696	134,752	44,658	10,286	78,090
Rate[d]	96.6	101.42	102.1	52.0	94.1

Cities

	Group I	Group II	Group III	Group IV	Group V	Group VI
	(53 cities, 250,000 and over; population 38,820,000)	(135 cities, 100,000 to 249,999; population 19,956,000)	(310 cities, 50,000 to 99,999; population 21,040,000)	(543 cities, 25,000 to 49,999; population 18,755,000)	(1,222 cities, 10,000 to 24,999; population 19,338,000)	(4,278 cities, under 10,000; population 15,023,000)
Runaways	34,075	24,415	25,613	18,619	18,704	13,326
Rate[d]	87.8	122.3	121.7	99.3	96.7	88.7

[a]Population figures were rounded to the nearest thousand. All rates were calculated before rounding.
[b]Includes only suburban county law enforcement agencies.
[c]Includes suburban city and county law enforcement agencies within metropolitan areas; excludes central cities. Suburban cities and counties are also included in other groups.
[d]Rate is per 100,000 population.

Source: Adapted from U.S. Department of Justice, Federal Bureau of Investigation, *Crime in the United States: Uniform Crime Reports 1995* (Washington, D.C.: Government Printing Office, 1996), pp. 211.

were four times as likely as nonrunaways to develop emotional problems and to have been victims of sexual abuse.

Typologies of Girl Runaways

Runaway girls can typically be divided into two types: (1) *preteen and early-teen runaways* and (2) *later-teen runaways*. Preteen and early-teen runaway girls are often characterized as "junior adventurers seeking some form of action."[21] Later-teen girl runaways tend to leave home to "establish themselves as adults."[22] In both categories, running away is a reflection of precipitating determinants such as sexual molestation, abuse, and neglect.

C. J. English characterized runaway girls based on their commitment to leave home (and stay away) and their reasons for running away. He grouped them into four types: (1) floaters, (2) runaways, (3) splitters, and (4) hard-road freaks:

- *Floaters*: girls who run away for a short period of time, usually just until things "cool off"
- *Runaways*: girls who are away from home for weeks or months, often due to a destructive family crisis or a problem the runaway is unable to share with others
- *Splitters*: girls who are pleasure-seekers; they run away to gain status among their peers
- *Hard-road freaks*: girls who leave home permanently; they reject conformity for street life, usually due to severe family situations[23]

A "hard-road freak" girl who ran away from an abusive home at age 12, never to return, recalled her initiation into the world of street life and child prostitution: "I was young, and men were after young women. The younger the better.... I watched everybody killing themselves. I watched one girl slit her wrists, another girl OD on the needle."[24]

Rat Packers

Many runaways, described as *rat packers*, have left home for life on the streets. According to police, rat packers are incorrigible teenagers who resist authority, often banning together for days, weeks, or months away from home, "rat packing."[25] These youths tend to be rebellious, are resentful of parents, school officials, or other authority figures, and are against the "establishment." Some come from abusive homes; others suffer from learning disabilities. In some instances, they live with friends, neighbors, relatives; other times they are homeless.

Rat packers are largely suburban adolescents. It is estimated that more than 30,000 troubled teens run away from the middle, upper-middle, and upper classes every year.[26] One observer noted that rat packers "glory in anarchy and destruction," often stealing what they want or need, using and abusing alcohol and drugs, and committing petty crimes or "childish pranks."[27]

Throwaways

A growing number of homeless children are apparently being put out of the house involuntarily — or forced onto the streets by parents, guardians, or others in the home. These children are often referred to as *throwaways* or "push-outs." In many instances they left home because of intolerable conditions (such as sexual abuse) that effectively forced them to flee. Throwaway girls and boys reflect a hidden population of runaway youths, since they are rarely reported as missing by parents or family. The Youth Development Bureau estimated that 30 to 35 percent of the runaways in the United States were in fact driven from home.[28] A similar observation was made by the National Network of Runaway and Youth Services, which estimated that 40 percent of the nation's 1.5 million homeless teens were throwaways.[29] Carolyn Males and Julie Raskin contend that since throwaway kids "crash" wherever they can, it is virtually impossible to know precisely how many there are.[30]

Throwaways are typically suburban youths who leave home due to family financial problems, incorrigibility, sexual identity issues, promiscuity, drug abuse, and/or parent-child disagreements. K. C. Brown argued that whereas national attention is focused on missing children abducted from loving homes, throwaway children continue to slip through the cracks and are especially vulnerable to prostitution, pornography, and substance abuse. "These are the children most preyed upon and exploited, the children most likely to be lying in John and Jane Doe graves all over the United States, unidentified because no one has reported them missing."[31]

Why Girls Run Away from Home

Girls who run away from home do so for a variety of reasons. Child sexual abuse and physical abuse are often at the core of a girl's decision to leave home. The National Network of Runaway and Youth Services estimated that 70 percent of the runaways in youth shelters have been sexually molested or abused.[32] One study of girl runaway prostitutes found that "at least" 90 percent were victims of "severe" child abuse.[33] These girls were subjected to "lots of incest, lots of alcoholism, lots of physical assault, lots of sexual battering," explained Ann Hayman, creator of the Mary Magdalene Project in Los Angeles.[34]

There are other reasons prompting girls to run away from home. According to one author who wrote about juvenile prostitution: "The children who run look for companionship, friendship, and approval from those they meet. Many such youths are easy marks for gangs, drug pushers, and pimps. Runaways often sell drugs or their bodies, and steal to support themselves."[35]

Some girl runaway adventurers court the imagined thrills of the runaway youth, combining precocity, promiscuity, immaturity, rebellion, and independence for a life out on their own. One social scientist stated, "The rule for runaway girls everywhere is often 'ball for bed'—meaning that implicit in an offer of lodging is the expectation of sexual intercourse."[36] One study of girl runaways found that the girls' initial objectives were to "acquire a place to sleep and then look for adventure—get a crash pad and some kicks."[37]

Other factors motivating girls to leave home include the following:

• A bad home environment
• Broken home (absence of one or both parents)
• School problems
• Substance abuse (by runaway or others in household)
• Sexual issues (such as pregnancy)
• Emotional problems
• Mental illness
• Rebellion
• Independence
• Romance or love interest
• Lures (for example, on the Internet)
• Peer pressure[38]

The Dark Realities of Street Life for Girl Runaways

In spite of the initial excitement and intrigue that many girls experience when running away to a new life of freedom and adventure, the reality is that they will face danger and adversity at every turn. Most girl runaways leave home with little money or direction and quickly find themselves homeless and literally living on the streets, in alleys, or on park benches. Many will turn to prostitution for food and shelter—often encouraged by men and other females ensconced in the world of child prostitution. "Runaway girls, scared and alone, are welcomed by pimps who watch for them as they arrive at bus and train stations," said the author of a *Psychology Today* article entitled "Coming of Age on City Streets." "They offer them a roof over their heads, a 'caring adult,' clothes, makeup and promises of love and belonging."[39]

What typically follows is often an unstable, perilous path from status

offender to juvenile delinquent to prostitute to drug addict to child victim —
and, in many cases, to adult female prostitute and criminal. These girl runaways commonly engage in petty crimes (and even serious crimes), substance
abuse, and abuse of their bodies and minds. Many are often arrested, jailed,
or incarcerated. Some die before they reach adulthood. June Bucy, who works
with runaways, noted the high mortality rate for runaway girls, adding that
they often "suffer from malnutrition, venereal disease, a high incidence of suicide, and are frequently sexually exploited."[40]

Runaway Girls and AIDS

Undoubtedly the most serious hazard that runaway and homeless girls
face is exposure to the AIDS virus. The high-risk factors are everywhere. "They
have sex with strangers. They use intravenous drugs or love somebody who
does.... Girls may have lovers who earn a living that way. Some try to practice
safe sex 'if the john doesn't object.'"[41]

Many believe that runaway prostitutes will figure prominently in the next
wave of the AIDS epidemic. Patricia Hersch recently wrote about the correlation between AIDS and runaways: "If geography is destiny, runaway and homeless kids gravitate to the very locations around the country where the risk is
greatest.... Often their immune systems are already compromised by repeated
exposure to infections.... Sex more than anything puts runaway kids at risk
for AIDS.... Their bodies usually become the currency of exchange.... There
is ... an epidemic of exposure, and many runaway kids, years hence, may pay
horribly for the events of their troubled youth."[42]

It is estimated that possibly hundreds of thousands of teen runaways are
actively involved in high-risk behavior for exposure to HIV and AIDS infection. According to an AIDS specialist at the Covenant House runaway shelter
in New York City, an estimated 40 percent of the runaway, homeless teens may
carry the AIDS virus.[43] See Chapter 5 for a more detailed examination of the
relationship between girl runaways, female prostitution, and HIV/AIDS exposure.

Runaway and Homeless Youth Act

The crisis of runaway and homeless adolescents in this country and the
frequent association with child prostitution, child pornography, substance
abuse, and delinquency led to the passage of the Runaway and Homeless Youth
Act of 1978 (RHYA).[44] The act made grants available to states, localities, and
nonprofit organizations for runaway shelters. Amended in 1980, the RHYA
recognized that many "runaways" are, in fact, "throwaways," and it clarified

the "requirements of runaway houses with respect to runaway and missing children as well as their families, and called for the development of model programs designed to help chronic runaway youths."[45] See Chapter 19 for more on the RHYA and other legislation involving adolescent runaways and prostitutes.

Chapter 13

Pimps and Girl Prostitution

The word *pimp* (defined in the dictionary as "a man who procures clients for a prostitute") almost immediately conjures up stereotypical images. They are often depicted in Hollywood productions as African-American men wearing flashy clothes, hats, and jewelry and driving a Cadillac or other large status symbol car. Whereas many of the more visible streetwalkers' pimps may fit the mold, the reality is that most pimps are white. This seems particularly likely when one considers the many types of prostitution operations — such as massage parlors, escort services, brothels, and strip clubs — in which the owners, managers, and "businessmen" are largely white males. There are also female pimps or madams. Heidi Fleiss, called "The Hollywood Madam," is one such notable example. What all pimps have in common is the psychological power they hold over a stable of females, enabling the pimps to earn a good (sometimes great) living at the expense and exploitation of the girls and women selling sexual favors.

The Pimp's Role in a Girl's Entry into Prostitution

The role of a pimp in recruiting females into prostitution has diminished somewhat in recent years, particularly among adult prostitutes, who are "less likely to accept the arrangement" of selling sex and turning over most of their earnings to men on the sidelines.[1] Also, prostitution services have expanded into a range of opportunities for females, allowing them to more easily circumvent the traditional street-level pimp. However, for teenage prostitutes, pimps continue to play an important role in their entry into and continuation

100

in the profession. The vast majority of girl prostitutes are streetwalkers.[2] Studies reveal that as many as nine in ten girl prostitutes entered the business through the charm and coercion of a pimp or ultimately became involved with one.[3] One study reported that almost every streetwalker questioned had some association with a pimp.[4]

In many instances, another prostitute under a pimp's direction will recruit a girl. One in five adolescent female prostitutes entered the business by becoming friends with other runaways and young prostitutes.[5] In rare cases, the "pimp" or the influence for becoming a prostitute may be a mother, a sister, or a male relative already in the business.[6]

There is some debate as to how many teenage girls are literally forced into the business. Some believe that most girl prostitutes were compelled to enter prostitution through direct or indirect physical or mental coercion. However, most evidence suggests that relatively few girls are actually abducted and enslaved as prostitutes. One study found that only 5 percent of the adolescent female prostitutes were forced into selling their bodies by a pimp's threats and intimidation.[7] These findings were corroborated in studies by Jennifer James[8] and Dorothy Bracey.[9]

So how does a pimp successfully recruit a girl into prostitution? The pimp generally uses charm, attention, affection, generosity, looks, drugs, and skills to seduce a gullible, vulnerable, starry-eyed girl. Often she is a runaway from an abusive home and has never known the type of kindness, love, and affection the pimp seems to lavish her with. In the article "Pimped," Deborah Jones describes the typical scenario for winning a girl over and turning her out: "It often starts with romance. Seduced at malls and in schoolyards, courted with restaurant meals and expensive gifts, the girls eventually find themselves cut off from their families and being asked to 'return a favor.' They are all, after all, very young. But the pimps also choose their targets well — girls from broken homes, girls living on the streets, girls who are just, somehow, troubled."[10]

Pimps often scour bus and train stations, coffee shops, street corners, and anywhere else that runaway and wayward girls are likely to hang out. The pimp can usually spot them a mile away, since they are often frightened, hungry, tired, dressed for the road, and actually looking for someone to come to their rescue. "The kids that are stable and know what their lives are about will tell these guys to hit the road," contends a police detective. "But kids who are vulnerable and hungry take up their offers of food, clothing, and a relationship, and once the girls are with them, they're the pimp's property."[11]

According to Joan Johnson in her research on the pimp-prostitute relationship, the pimp successfully uses the two most powerful human emotions to win the girl over: love and fear.[12] If he successfully plays these off against one another, through charm and false concern, the girl will respond like the child that she is — and take to the one person who seems to care and to offer her hope for a future and immediate security.

Types of Pimps

Contrary to popular belief, not all pimps are carbon copies of one another. Some are exposed for all to see. Some remain strictly behind the scenes in working their prostitutes. They can also vary considerably in their business acumen, money-making ability, and trouble with the law. Many are drug users and dealers. Some are gang members or associated with organized crime.[13]

Johnson described three classes of pimps: (1) the *popcorn pimp*, (2) the *player pimp*, and (3) the *Mack pimp*.[14] Popcorn pimps are seen as the least successful type of pimp. Working primarily with teenage prostitutes, they have little money and less roots. These pimps tend to be highly competitive with one another in recruiting girls, mostly runaways. They are the most violent toward their stable of girls and have a high turnover rate compared with more stable, successful pimps.

The player pimp is generally more successful, has a few prostitutes in his stable, and often has one "special" woman that he lives with. Players tend to be less violent than popcorn pimps, relying more on psychological persuasion to control their girls. According to an expert on the pimp hierarchy, a successful player or "mid-range" pimp can earn up to $200,000 annually.[15]

The Mack pimp is considered the upper class among pimps. He usually has a much larger number of prostitutes working for him and has one as his "lady." Mack pimps tend to combine street smarts with good business sense, investing profits in legitimate investments. This affords most of them a suburban lifestyle and a low profile — making them harder to reach and put out of business.

Criminologists believe the business of pimping itself is often passed from generation to generation.[16] The tricks of the trade are also learned from other pimps and prostitutes. Among the lower levels of pimps, there exists somewhat of a fraternity that, to some extent, encourages sharing and cooperation.

Keeping a Girl Prostitute in a Pimp's Stable

Aside from their charm, how do pimps manage to keep a girl from simply walking away at her leisure? There is, of course, the violence that many pimps will resort to if all else fails (or sometimes simply to demonstrate their willingness to be physical and to maintain the threat as a controlling device). Most pimps have devised other, more effective means of keeping women, short of damaging their property. Drug use is a common means of making girl prostitutes dependent, through addiction.[17] Pregnancy is also used to bind the girl to her pimp. The pimp will use the child as a pawn — often threatening to never relinquish *his* child to the girl — to maintain her loyalty.[18] Other common means for holding on to a prostitute include:

- Getting her to sell drugs or commit other crimes
- Changing her identity and cutting off ties with family or friends
- Psychologically manipulating her with humiliation and rejection, mixed with affection and false promises
- Making her jealous and thereby possessive and obsessive

Love is perhaps the strongest determinant the pimp uses to control a teen prostitute. If he can successfully convince her of his love, the pimp can convince her of almost anything — including that she should stay with him *and* that he needs other girls for sex, prostitution, and profit. Many girl prostitutes fall in love (or believe they are in love) with the idea of being loved by someone after often never experiencing love at home. Studies show, however, that this feeling of loving and being loved does not last forever. One study found that only 4 percent of the girl prostitutes said they loved their pimps.[19] For most girls, early love often gives way to hostile feelings, if not hatred.

Few girl prostitutes remain with a pimp very long. More than two-thirds switch from one pimp to another within a few months.[20] Ninety percent of teen prostitutes leave a pimp within a year's time.[21] During their early years in the business, prostitutes may have as many as four pimps before they settle for one pimp, continue prostituting on their own, or leave the business — in what literally becomes a cycle of prostitute-pimp dynamics.[22]

Pimp Violence Toward Girl Prostitutes

Most social scientists and researchers agree that violence is a part of any streetwalking prostitute's life. Much of it comes from the prostitute's pimp. A study of female prostitutes found that they were subjected to "extreme sexual, physical and psychological abuse" by pimps and johns. More than two-thirds of the streetwalkers reported being assaulted regularly by their pimps.[23] Statistics reveal that most female teen prostitutes routinely receive violent treatment from pimps.[24] This physical abuse can range from being hit with fists, slapped, whipped, burned, or even killed by a pimp. Some prostitutes have reported pimp-perpetrated "severe violence, torture and attempted murder."[25] The mortality rate for female prostitutes is 40 times the national average, according to the Department of Justice.[26]

Pimp violence directed at the girl prostitute is often unpredictable. The pimp may be "teaching her a lesson" for attempting to escape, for being disrespectful, or for not earning enough money. Or the pimp may be using her to set an example for other girls in the stable. In some cases, the pimp may be under the influence of drugs or alcohol. Other times the pimp acts strictly on a whim in exerting authority and domination over her.

A typical example of this violent relationship can be seen below:

In New York City, a girl's pimp kept her on the street six nights a week. She hated being a prostitute, but the pimp was the only person who had shown her any kindness. When she could stand it no longer and told him she had to quit, he broke her jaw. At the hospital where her jaw was wired shut, she was given pain pills and told to rest. But her pimp put her on the street the next night.

Later, she tried to commit suicide using the pills, but she vomited, breaking the wires in her jaw. Her pimp would not allow her to return to the hospital and sent her back on the street.... She turned herself in to the police.

When asked her age, she replied, "I'll be 15 tomorrow."[27]

Relatively few pimps ever get arrested or incarcerated for assaulting prostitutes. The victims often refuse to press charges out of fear, intimidation, love, or even self-blame for the beatings. Unfortunately, this ensures that the cycle of violence and teen prostitution will continue.

Pimps and Sexually Transmitted Diseases

Few pimps use condoms when engaging in sex with girls in their stable. Consequently, most teen prostitutes are regularly at risk for exposure to sexually transmitted diseases (STDs) such as gonorrhea and AIDS. This is particularly true when one considers that pimps are almost "never faithful to one girl, and they are notorious IV drug users."[28] It is unknown precisely how many pimps actually infect girl prostitutes with HIV/AIDS or other STDs; however, studies suggest that many female adolescent prostitutes have a lower risk of contracting STDs from johns than from their pimp lovers.[29] Other research has shown that the high-risk activities of multiple sexual partners, substance abuse, and IV drug use are closely related to AIDS and venereal infections.[30]

Chapter 14

The Dangers of
Child Sexual Abuse

Child prostitution carries with it many dangers for children across the country. In addition to the selling of sexual favors, adolescent prostitutes face abduction, sexual slavery, rape, pornography, violence from customers and pimps, sexually transmitted diseases such as AIDS, drug and alcohol abuse, and other threats to their safety, health, and well-being.

Sexual predators seek out young girls and boys for many sexual perversions that most people are unaware of. As a result, many will go to extremes to locate, lure, and/or kidnap children for prostitution and related sexual misuse. Though there are laws designed to discourage the sexual mistreatment of children and punish those responsible, many child sexual exploiters continue to prey on young children and teenagers for sexual purposes.

Child Abduction

The abducting of children has made front-page news since the 1970s, as a number of high-profile cases of child abduction have captured our attention. Child serial killers such as John Gacy and Wayne Williams were convicted of kidnapping and murdering dozens of children. Other children have been "snatched" by parents or other relatives in custody battles and divorce cases.

A number of children are believed to have been abducted for purposes of child prostitution and sexual slavery. Just how many children are actually kidnapped by strangers is open to debate. Some estimates are that as many as 150,000 juveniles are reported missing and are presumed kidnapped each year.[1] Others believe these figures to be grossly exaggerated.

105

The truth is, most child abductees are taken by relatives for purposes other than sexual misuse or exploitation. But there are children who are kidnapped and forced into prostitution or other sexual acts, both in this country and abroad.[2] Some of these children are listed as runaways; others have been thrown away. In some cases, the child is never reported as missing. More than 4,000 bodies of missing children are discovered annually.[3] Many more are feared dead, drugged, smuggled out of the country by slave traders, or kept prisoner by a kidnapper or a sex ring.[4] Some abducted children are believed to be forced to perform sex acts in child pornography films and literature.[5]

Two important pieces of legislation have been designed specifically to combat child abduction. In 1980, Congress passed the Parental Kidnapping Prevention Act, which allowed the Federal Parental Locator Service to aid in searching for kidnapped children.[6]

The Missing Children Act was enacted in 1982, enabling information on missing children to be entered into the FBI's National Crime Information Center computer.[7] Local police departments can tap into this database to assist in tracking down missing and abducted children anywhere in the country. The act also allowed for FBI intervention once it has been established that a missing child has been kidnapped.

These and other legislative responses to child abduction and child sexploitation will be more closely examined in Chapter 19.

Child Sexual Abuse

The relationship between child prostitution and child sexual abuse has been well established.[8] Most child prostitutes were sexually victimized by family members or others before entering prostitution. This has been shown to correlate with running away, prostitution, drug abuse, and the overall presence of children in the sex trade industry.[9] Child sexual abuse is defined by the Child Abuse Prevention and Treatment Act as "(a) the employment, use, persuasion, inducement, enticement, or coercion of any child to engage in, or assist any other person to engage in, any sexually explicit conduct or simulation of such conduct for the purposes of producing any visual depiction of such conduct, or (b) the rape, molestation, prostitution, or other such form of sexual exploitation of children, or incest with children."[10]

Estimates of child sexual abuse in large urban areas have been put at 4,000 cases each year,[11] with between 200,000 and 500,000 cases of sexual abuse of female children age 4 to 14 annually.[12] According to the National Committee for Prevention of Child Abuse (NCPCA), approximately 17 percent of all child abuse and neglect cases involve sexual abuse.[13] A National Child Abuse and Neglect Data System (NCANDS) report estimated that in 1991, 129,697 reports of child sexual abuse were substantiated or indicated following an investigation.[14]

Most child sex offenders are young, white, unmarried men.[15] Many are familiar with their victims. Sex offenders cross the socioeconomic ladder, though some studies have indicated a disproportionate representation of sex offenders among the poorly educated and the economically disadvantaged.[16]

Incest

A high percentage of girl prostitutes have been sexually molested, according to researchers. Estimates of incest — or sexual relations between family members — give rise to the severity of the problem. In the United States, estimates have ranged from tens of thousands of cases a year to well over one million cases annually.[17]

Mary Donaldson estimated that nearly one-third of all females in this country are victims of incest or molestation.[18] The Family Violence Research Program estimated that 5 to 15 percent of female juveniles have been molested by family members.[19]

Typically, the active aggressor of an incestuous relationship is a male; the passive victim is most often a female. It is estimated that 90 to 97 percent of all incest cases involve male perpetrators, with 85 percent of the victims female.[20] H. Stoenner found the female-male ratio of incest victims to be 10 to 1.[21] Female incest victims are often entering adolescence. The median age of a victim is 8.5, with most victims ranging in age from 5 to 16.[22]

Many female victims escape the incestuous relationship by running away — often into another world of sex abuse and exploitation: prostitution.[23]

Pedophilia

Pedophilia is another form of child molestation that often precedes child prostitution for many children. Believed by experts to be the most common form of child sexual abuse, pedophilia usually consists of "nonviolent sexual contact with a child including genital viewing or fondling, orogenital contact, penetration, and any other immoral or indecent behavior involving sexual activity between an adult and child."[24] It is estimated that as many as two million children are molested every year. An 18-month investigation of child molestation cases reported to child protection agencies revealed the following:

- Child molestation is more prevalent than child physical abuse.
- Female victims outnumbered male victims 10 to 1.
- The median age of a sexual molestation victim was 11.
- In 75 percent of the cases, the molester was not a stranger.
- The molesters were male in 97 percent of the cases.
- The molester's median age was 31.

• In more than 40 percent of the cases, the molestation occurred over a long
   period of time.
• Sixty percent of the victims were molested by force or threat of force.
• Two-thirds of the victims suffered some form of identifiable emotional disorder; 14 percent had become severely disturbed.[25]

Studies have found the pedophile to be frequently passive, immature, and
insecure about to his inability to engage in normal adult heterosexual relations.[26] J. M. Reinhardt advanced that some young or middle-aged pedophiles
molest children only after failure to achieve sexual satisfaction with adults.[27]
Older pedophiles, usually over 50, have been shown to molest juveniles because
of diminishing physical and mental abilities associated with the aging process.[28]

A number of organizations are seeking to abolish laws against pedophilia
and laws relating it to statutory rape, prostitution, and pornography statutes.
In Wales, England, the Paedophiliac Information Exchange (PIE) has been
organized for the express purpose of advocating consensual adult-child sexual
practices.[29] The Rene Guyon Society, based in California, claims to have 2,500
members who admit to having sexual relations with young children. The society's slogan is "Sex by the year eight or else it's too late."[30] Other politically
active pedophile groups include the Childhood Sexuality Circle, which boasts
more than 10,000 members.[31]

Exhibitionism

Exhibitionism ranks alongside pedophilia as one of the more common
forms of child sexual victimization. It refers to the "intentional, inappropri-
ate exposure of genitalia to either a woman or child."[32] Most exhibitionists are
male. Exhibitionism is seen as a compulsive behavior by a person to relieve
"unbearable anxiety."[33] J. L. Mathis contended that the exhibitionist is driven
by an uncontrollable force;[34] J. C. Coleman found exhibitionism to be associated with "personal immaturity (such as shyness, self-doubts about mas-
culinity, and feelings of inferiority) and interpersonal stress and acting out
(such as an inability to cope with an intense conflict)."[35]

Exhibitionists are most likely to expose themselves in parks, theaters, near
schools and playgrounds, and in cars. When targeting children, the perpetrator favors a group of children. It is estimated that anywhere from 20 to 50 percent of the victims of exhibitionists are children.[36] Though exhibitionism is
one of the most frequent sex offenses known to law enforcement, it is also one
of the least reported.[37] As a result, many children continue to be victims of
exhibitionists and the long-term effects, which may include becoming exhibitionists themselves or otherwise engaging in deviant sexual activity such as
prostitution.

Triolism

Triolism is a variation of exhibitionism, voyeurism, and prostitution in which the adult triolist receives sexual gratification by viewing others, as well as himself, in group sexual relations.[38] Triolism has been linked to child pornography as well.

Children are easily lured into triolism involvement. Triolists offer them money, drugs, or other items to participate in sexual acts. The typical pattern of triolism is described as follows: "To earn [her] extra money, the child gets others from among [her] friends to go to the offender's house or the back of his store and engage in acts, which are in themselves fun, while the pervert watches."[39] More study is needed on triolism in terms of its incidence and relationship to child victims.

Bestiality/Zooerastia

Although the terms *bestiality* and *zooerastia* are often used separately, both refer to the same sexual perversion: sexual intercourse between a human and an animal.[40] *Bestiality* is a legal term; *zooerastia* is a medical one. The practice is outlawed in most societies but still occurs. Men who engage in this act have been known to lure children into participating, often for pay. It is most often seen in rural areas, where many animals can be found. One study stated that 17 percent of the children practicing bestiality had experienced orgasm from contact with the animals.[41] Given its nature, bestiality/zooerastia involving juveniles is difficult to detect. Like other sex offenses against children, it is believed that many more minors may be exposed to this sexual perversion than statistics indicate.

Coprolagnia/Urolagnia

Another extreme sexual perversion associated with child molestation and prostitution is *coprolagnia* or *urolagnia*. This involves sexual gratification by "smelling, eating, throwing, or handling excrement, urine, or other filth."[42] Richard von Krafft-Ebing described the coprolagnia/urolagnia pathological person as "driven by an irresistible urge to touch or swallow feces, sputum, nasal mucus, earwax, or menstrual blood."[43]

Surprisingly, this has been found to be one of the more commonly encountered sex crimes for law enforcement.[44] The strong relationship between coprolagnia/urolagnia and the sexual victimization of children has been documented in several cases.[45] Robert Morneau and Robert Rockwell made an interesting observation regarding the correlation between coprolagnia/urolagnia and child molestation:

An officer who is booking a suspect for any crime and discovers excrement on his person (many times in dried form) should realize, at the very minimum, he may have a child molester on his hands....

Just as a child molester might be recognized from his interest in filth, anyone who is arrested as the result of a complaint that he is a child molester should be interviewed about unrelated cases where coprolagnia or urolagnia were part of the offense.[46]

Necrophilia

Necrophilia refers to a desire to have sexual relations with the dead. Many deceased missing, runaway, overdosed, and prostitute children are at risk for being violated by a necrophiliac, usually male.[47] Researchers have identified four primary types of necrophilia offenders: (1) the *true necrophiliac*, (2) the *sadonecrophiliac*, (3) the *sadomasochistic necrophiliac*, and (4) the *necrofetishist*.[48] Because these types can often overlap, it is difficult for law enforcement to discover the necrophilia offender or understand his motivations.

Necrophiliacs are often morticians, ambulance attendants, or others working with or exposed to the dead. One frightening example of necrophilia can be seen in a criminal investigation report in which a man with a history of sexual perversions is being questioned in relation to the sexual assault and murder of a young female:

> He admitted he had worked years before as a mortician's assistant ... fascinated by the bodies, especially those of young girls.... The mortician's vehicle was pressed into service.... The man described how he became aroused when driving back into town because of the screams and crying of the injured and dying children he was transporting.
>
> That night, working late and alone in the mortuary, he was seized with a compulsion to have intercourse with one young girl who was mutilated and, since additional wounds would not likely be noticed, he cut her stomach open at some point so he could see his penis down inside her.[49]

An important factor in necrophilia appears to be the complete passivity of the female, allowing the necrophiliac to do as he pleases without resistance or fear of discovery or reprisal. "Defenseless, helplessness, and decomposition of the victim are crucial in carrying out necrophilia."[50] For some necrophiliacs, the perversion is a reflection of religious fanaticism. Justification for their delusional, irrational behavior is often "found in the commands of the Lord, which reached them in clear language ordering the brutal violation."[51]

Ritualistic Sexual Abuse

The sexual misuse of children involving ritualism or satanism is on the rise in the United States. It is estimated that 1 to 5 percent of all child sex abuse cases may involve some form of religious, supernatural, or magic ritualistic or satanic practices.[52] In many instances, the victims of ritualistic sexual abuse are runaways, child prostitutes, and children who may have been sold into sexual slavery by parents. Three kinds of ritualistic child sexual abuse have been identified:

- *Pseudo-ritualistic*: sexual abuse is the primary goal.
- *Cult-based*: the sexual abuse is secondary to a larger goal.
- *Psychopathological*: there is a single perpetrator.[53]

Ritualistic sexual abusers can include the following:

- Organized groups, including cults, communes, and families
- National and international organizations with local and regional affiliates
- People who practice ritualism or satanism for fun, friends, curiosity, or sexual experimentation, while often abusing drugs and/or alcohol
- Mentally unbalanced individuals

Many groups practicing ritualism or satanism are highly structured and may involve a child victim's own parents or siblings, as well as their "cult parents" in their indoctrination. "Children may be taken from natural parents and placed in the care of other group members as a means of ensuring continued group involvement by natural parents."[54]

Ritualistic sexual abuse of children often includes other sex-related perversions such as drinking of blood, coprolagnia, incest, bestiality, triolism, and necrophilia. Substance abuse is also prevalent in the majority of cases involving ritualistic child sex abuse.

There are no national statistics or professional networks on ritualistic abuse. However, in Los Angeles, the Resource and Education Network on Ritualistic Abuse (RENRA) focuses on gathering and sharing information regarding this disturbing form of child sexual exploitation and maltreatment.[55]

The Effects of Child Sexual Abuse

The effects of child sexual abuse, including child prostitution, can be devastating to the child victim. Researchers have identified a variety of physical and psychological effects of child sexual victimization.[56] The scars can often last a lifetime. With the interruption of normal, healthy development, sexually abused children are often "unable to cope emotionally, intellectually, and/or physically with sexual stimulation and responsiveness, regardless of whether the child finds the experience emotionally satisfying, erotically pleasurable, or negative in some fashion."[57]

Most child sex abuse victims experience feelings of guilt, rage, betrayal, worthlessness, and withdrawal—"all of which have been shown to manifest themselves in both inwardly self-destructive behavior and outwardly socially aberrant behavior."[58] One study reported that the psychological scarring and emotional stress of child sexual abuse and sexploitation typically lead to substance abuse as a way to escape the memories, as well as to become numb to current circumstances, such as being a girl runaway or prostitute.[59] The physical effects of child sexual victimization can include "lacerations to the genitals, sexually transmitted diseases, pregnancy, internal injuries, broken bones, and even death."[60]

A strong correlation has been established as well between the sexual abuse of children and juvenile delinquency, domestic violence, and juvenile sex offenses.[61] The implications of child prostitution as it relates to child pornography will be addressed in Chapter 16.

Part IV

Other Dimensions of Prostitution and the Sex Trade Industry

Chapter 15

Pornography
and Female Prostitution

The relationship between pornography, female prostitution, and violence against and oppression of women has been debated for decades. Although no universal consensus has been reached, evidence supports the view that there are some correlates among prostitution, pornography,[1] and antisocial behavior, as well as a direct relationship between female prostitution and female participation in pornography.[2] The extent of these interrelationships is not yet fully known.

Similar research by social scientists, criminologists, feminists, and others has focused on the relationship between child prostitution and child pornography (see Chapter 22).[3] Generally speaking, there is greater evidence for this adverse association of child sexploitation. Both child prostitution and child pornography are prohibited and are invariably connected through an underground network of adult suppliers and male sexual deviants. The result is that many children are drawn into one or the other, if not both, as runaways, child prostitutes, indentured sex slaves, and even models.

There is little dispute that prostitution and pornography portray females as male sex objects, often in degrading and/or violent terms. This is disquieting and calls for more study on the cause-and-effect association between the two, as well as on the further implications for society as a whole and the female population in particular.

Defining Pornography

The term *pornography* has its historical roots in female prostitution. Pornography derives from the Greek word *pornographos*, which comes from

115

porne, meaning prostitute or female captive, and *graphein*, which means to write — hence, writings about prostitution and prostitutes.[4] In modern times, the definition of pornography has widened to encompass the multitude of ever expanding ways in which sexually explicit material can be produced, including pornographic literature, movies, videos, photographs, live shows, and computer pornography.

There is no universal definition of pornography, adding to the debate and sometimes confusion over its potential harm or harmlessness as free speech. The dictionary defines *pornography* as "writings, pictures, films, or other materials that are meant to stimulate erotic feelings by describing or portraying sexual activity." Philosopher Helen Longino's definition of pornography is material that "explicitly represents or describes degrading and abusive sexual behavior so as to endorse and/or recommend the behavior as described."[5] According to the *Academic American Encyclopedia*, "pornography, or obscenity, is any material, pictures, films, printed matter, or devices dealing with sexual poses or acts considered indecent by the public."[6]

Pornography is often associated by definition with *obscenity*, which is defined as "something condemnatory, offensive, indecent, disgusting, or lewd to prevailing concepts of decency." However, not everything that is obscene is pornographic; conversely, not all pornography is viewed as obscenity. For the purposes of this chapter, *pornography* is defined as: "any sexually explicit and/or titillating arousing written, photographic, pictorial, computer, or live depiction of women or children as objects for commercial exploitation, including acts of prostitution or other illicit sexual performances; or which depicts sexual abuse, degradation, or humiliation of subjects; and is offensive in its sexual content or acts to the population at large."

The Pornography Industry

Pornography is big business in the United States, taking in an estimated $6 billion annually.[7] It is estimated that in 1992 alone, 1,600 new pornographic videos were produced in this country, with 500 million rentals.[8] The major players in the porn business are the female models, actors, or "porn stars" and the mostly male photographers, producers, distributors, and advertisers. The sources for dispensing pornography are more diverse than ever and include adult theaters, strip clubs, cable TV, video stores, bookstores, on-line services such as the Internet, and phone companies. Even network television, in its attempt to compete with cable and motion pictures, has gone as far as the censors will allow in displaying seminude women and sexual violence against women. The television show *NYPD Blue,* which often portrays partial nudity (mostly of women's breasts and buttocks), has broken new ground in bringing to the small screen what many consider soft porn.

By its very nature, pornography is seen by many authorities as an industry that has long supported itself through "systematically eroticizing violence against women by producing and marketing images of men humiliating, battering, and murdering women for sexual pleasure.... Pornography is about power imbalances using sex as a weapon to subjugate women. In pornography, the theme is assailant vs. victim."[9] Frances Patai, organizer for Women Against Pornography, states: "Pornography objectifies women by caricaturing and reducing them to a sum of their sexual parts and functions — devoid of sensibilities and intelligence.... Objectifying the sexual anatomy of women renders them inferior and nonhuman, thus providing the psychological foundation for committing violence against them."[10]

Unfortunately, pornography consumers have an endless range of choices in the highly competitive marketplace, with millions upon millions of dollars at stake at any given time. Hence, it is unlikely that the pornography industry will go out of business anytime soon — nor will the controversy over its relationship to female prostitution and male antisocial behavior toward females.

Commissions on Pornography and Its Effects on Antisocial Behavior

In an effort to control smut and study the causal relationship between pornography and antisocial behavior toward females, two national commissions were established during the 1970s and 1980s. The first, the Presidential Commission on Obscenity and Pornography, concluded in 1970: "Empirical research designed to clarify the question has found no evidence to date that exposure to explicit sexual materials plays a significant role in the causation of delinquency or criminal behavior among youths or adults. The Commission cannot conclude that exposure to erotic materials is a factor in the causation of sex crime or sex delinquency."[11] These findings were reached in spite of the dissent of several commission members, who saw a connection between pornography and the word *harm*. Commissioner Charles Keating, Jr. (who was later convicted of fraud in the Lincoln Savings and Loan collapse) called the majority report "shocking and anarchistic."[12]

Fifteen years later, in 1985, a second commission, the Attorney General's Commission on Pornography, reached a starkly different conclusion in its task of determining "the nature, extent, and impact on society of pornography in the United States, and to make specific recommendations ... concerning more effective ways in which the spread of pornography could be contained, consistent with constitutional guarantees."[13] The commission concluded that there was a correlation between certain types of pornography and sexual violence and abuse toward women, adding that exposure to even nonviolent sexually explicit material "bears some causal relationship to the level of sexual violence."[14]

The commission's report read in part:

> When clinical and experimental research has focused particularly on sexually violent material, the conclusions have been nearly unanimous. In both clinical and experimental settings, exposure to sexually violent materials has indicated an increase in the likelihood of aggression.... The research ... shows a causal relationship between exposure to material of this type and aggressive behavior towards women.... The assumption that increased aggressive behavior toward women is causally related ... to increased sexual violence is significantly supported by the clinical evidence, as well as by much of the less scientific evidence.[15]

The commission called for a nationwide crackdown on the purveyors of hard-core pornography. Among its recommendations were amending federal obscenity laws for distributing obscene materials through interstate commerce and enacting legislation to prohibit transmitting obscene material by phone or similar common carrier.[16]

Though the commission's report was not without its share of critics, because of the vast data used most experts agreed that its findings and recommendations "clearly justify the conclusion that there is at least some relationship between the pornography industry and the victimization of women."[17]

Pornography and Violence Against Females

Researchers have established a significant correlation between pornography and violence against females, including those in the sex-for-sale business.[18] In *Take Back the Night: Women on Pornography*, Laura Lederer argued, "Pornography is the ideology of a culture which promotes and condones rape, woman battering, and other crimes against women."[19] One study of 100 abused wives found that 15 percent reported that their abusive husbands "seemed to experience sexual arousal" after viewing hard-core pornography, "since the demand for sexual intercourse immediately followed the assault."[20]

Other studies have focused on the correlation between pornography and sex crimes. Female prostitutes — already in a high-risk lifestyle involving illicit sex, physical assaults, and often substance abuse — are particularly susceptible to customer, pimp, or stranger rape as part of the sex industry cycle of victimization.[21] In a study of rape victims, Pauline Bart contended: "I didn't start out being against pornography; but if you're a rape researcher, it becomes clear that there is a direct link. Violent pornography is like an advertisement for rape.... Men are not born thinking women enjoy rape and torture.... They learn from pornography."[22] In their study of mass-circulation sex magazines and the incidence of rape, Larry Baron and Murray Straus found that "rape increases in direct proportion to the readership of sex magazines."[23] Neil Malamuth, co-editor of *Pornography and Sexual Aggression*, predicted, "In a culture that celebrates rape, the lives of millions of women will be affected."[24]

Further support for associating sex crimes and pornography can be seen in a public lecture entitled "Does Pornographic Literature Incite Sexual Assault?" The speaker, a detective for the Michigan State Police, cited "numerous cases where the assailants had immersed themselves in pornographic films or pictures and then gone out and committed sex crimes. These crimes included rape, sodomy, and even the bizarre erotic crime of piquerism (piercing with a knife till blood flows, a kind of sexual torture). In some cases the attacker admitted that the urge to rape or torture erotically came over him while reading an obscene picture magazine or attending a movie showing rape and erotic torture."[25]

Female Prostitution and Pornography

Some studies have shown a direct link between female prostitutes and pornography. The Los Angeles Police Department found a strong connection between the "clustering of adult entertainment establishments in Hollywood and an increase in the incidence of rape and other violent crimes."[26] Ironically, the department also found that prostitution in the Hollywood adult entertainment district had increased at a rate 15 times the city average over a recent six-year period.[27]

The Task Force on Organized Crime found a tripartite relationship between prostitution, pornography, and substance abuse. "The young actors in pornographic films often perform for drugs rather than for money, then are forced into prostitution" to support drug habits.[28] Female prostitution and the sexploitation industry have also been shown to correlate with other criminal activity, such as organized crime and drug dealing, as well as with sexually transmitted diseases, promiscuity, and child sexual abuse.[29]

Feminism, Prostitution, and Pornography

Many feminists have long associated prostitution, pornography, and the sex industry itself with the subjugation, subordination, and exploitation of females, as well as with gender and cultural biases with respect to social roles. Writer Laurie Shrage argued that prostitution "epitomizes and perpetuates pernicious patriarchal beliefs and values, and therefore, is both damaging to the women who sell sex and, as an organized social practice, to all women in our society.... Since commercial sex, unlike marriage, is not reformable, feminists should seek to undermine the beliefs and values which underlie our acceptance.

Indeed, one way to do this is to outwardly oppose prostitution itself."[30] She believes that the same principles apply to the pornography industry.

Reflecting the "abolitionist view" toward pornography and the social subordination of females to males under a patriarchy system of inequality, law professor Catherine MacKinnon stated, "Pornography is one of the ways in which the system of dominance and submission is maintained, a system whose underlying dynamic depends on the sexual objectification of women."[31] According to writer Alice Leuchtag, MacKinnon "places the dehumanization of women along a continuum of female submission — from visual appropriation of the female in pornography, to physical appropriation in prostitute sex, to forced sex in rape, to sexual murder."[32]

Responding to the question "What do men want?" MacKinnon wrote: "Pornography provides an answer.... What men want is: women bound, women battered, women tortured, women humiliated, women degraded and defiled, women killed ... women sexually accessible, have-able, there for them, wanting to be taken and used."[33]

Not all feminists see prostitution and pornography as offensive, sexist, or unacceptable. Some feminists have taken a stance supporting prostitution and pornography, viewing these as "career choices" or a type of "empowerment for women."[34] But Leuchtag argues, on behalf of feminist writers such as MacKinnon and Shrage, "Overall, women who work in these areas are exploited and demeaned ... their civil rights are frequently trampled upon, and ... they face severe physical and psychological risk."[35]

These writers and others like them favor altering or abolishing "the institutions of prostitution and pornography within the constitutional framework of law."[36] Some feminists regard this as the biggest challenge the women's movement will face heading into the twenty-first century. The task will indeed be daunting. Recent attempts to pass antipornography laws in Indianapolis and Minneapolis were promptly declared unconstitutional. Furthermore, stiff challenges by others will be made to decriminalize or legalize prostitution, pornography, and related sex industry occupations and preoccupations. See Chapter 20 for more discussion on this issue.

Chapter 16

Child Prostitution
and Child Pornography

Child pornography was described by one expert on child sexploitation as "the most inhuman of crimes. For pleasure and profit, pornographers have murdered the childhood of a million girls and boys, victims who must live with the dreadful memories of their experience."[1] Many would apply the same words to child prostitution. Both are part of the sex industry's sexual exploitation of children and are rooted in age-old beliefs and traditions that regard children in terms of sex objects and marketable commodities.[2] It is generally believed that the modern era of child pornography began in China during the mid-1400s with the sex manual *The Admirable Discourses of the Plain Girl*, in which sexual intercourse and other sexual acts involving children were graphically described.[3]

Often referred to as "kiddie porn" and "chicken porn," child pornography is defined as "photographs, videos, books, magazines, and motion pictures that depict children in sexually explicit acts with other children, adults, animals, and/or foreign objects."[4] Added to this is the most recent means of displaying child pornography—the Internet. Since keeping child porn out of the vast world of cyberspace is virtually impossible, this may represent the greatest threat to child pornography laws and the protection of children from smut.

Victims in child pornography are subjected to every form of abuse, perversion, and sexual exploitation—including rape, sadism, bestiality, pedophilia, triolism, torture, and even murder. One magazine vividly depicts adults in various sex acts with toddlers. At least one audiotape, accompanied by graphic narrative description, records the screams of a young girl being raped.[5]

Although child pornography is illegal in the United States, most criminologists and child sexploitation experts concur that current laws and law enforcement are gravely inadequate to halt the flow and availability of child porn and to apprehend child pornographers.

The Extent of Child Pornography

By most indications, child pornography is a multibillion-dollar business worldwide. In Germany, for example, it is estimated that annual sales of child porn exceed $250 million, with the number of consumers somewhere between 30,000 and 40,000.[6] The biggest market for child pornography is the United States, where an estimated $6 billion a year is taken in.[7] Eighty-five percent of worldwide sales of child pornography are in the United States.[8] In Los Angeles alone, it is estimated that 30,000 children are sexually exploited by child pornographers annually.[9] Child pornography accounts for approximately 7 percent of the pornography industry in this country.[10]

Many of the kiddie porn films and magazines come from abroad, from countries such as Denmark, Switzerland, Germany, and Sweden. One recent study found that at least 264 different magazines depicting sexual acts involving children are produced and distributed in the United States each month.[11] A magazine of sexually explicit pictures of children can be produced for as little as 50 cents and sold for twenty times that much.[12] The profit margin may be even higher when transmitting child porn via online services.

In spite of tough antipornography laws, increased crackdowns on child pornographers by law enforcement agencies, and efforts at greater community awareness of the problem and purveyors, child porn continues to flourish. Recent examples of its severity can be seen as follows:

- A woman was alleged to have made $500,000 annually by supplying 80 percent of the child pornography market.
- Houston police raided a warehouse full of child pornographic materials including 15,000 color slides of [children] engaged in [sexual] acts, more than 1,000 magazines and paperbacks, and over 1,000 reels of film.
- A child porn consumer was arrested in a police raid. Confiscated was a scrapbook containing articles about child rapes and murders. Included were photographs of young girls.[13]

Child pornographers have little difficulty recruiting willing participants. The pool of susceptible child victims includes runaways, throwaways, teen prostitutes, children from broken homes, homeless youth, drug-addicted children, and relatives or neighborhood youths looking for quick money, excitement, or adventure. These children are typically induced through money, food, drugs, shelter, gifts, trips, and friendship.

Some children are forced into child pornography as abducted sex slaves or are conned into indentured sexual servitude. These victims are often enslaved through intimidation, drugs, beatings, torture, or blackmail. (See also Chapter 22.)

CHILD PORNOGRAPHERS AND SEXUAL EXPLOITERS OF CHILDREN

Who are the people that exploit children as sellers and buyers of child pornography? They are almost always men. They come from all walks of life and may or may not have children of their own. Many are child molesters and pedophiles. Others consider themselves businessmen with a profitable target group. "The men who support this industry do so to rationalize and seek justification for their perverted and deviant mentality, whereas the pornographers who bring children into this seedy world are primarily interested in capitalizing monetarily from the sickness of disturbed, immature pedophiles who receive their only sexual satisfaction with children."[14]

The FBI's pedophile profile describes typical child pornographers or exploiters as men who are "intelligent enough to recognize they have a problem" yet who somehow justify in their minds that "what they're doing is right."[15] One FBI agent explained the mindset of the pedophile: "Pedophilia is a way of life. They believe there's nothing wrong with it, so naturally they're looking for other individuals who support their thinking."[16]

The most powerful allies of pedophiles and other consumers of kiddie porn are groups such as the Rene Guyon Society and the North American Man-Boy Love Association. These groups openly support child pornography and consensual sexual relations between juveniles and adults (see also Chapter 14). Despite the existence of such groups and affiliate chapters across the United States, law enforcement is often powerless to prevent or stop their activities or halt their membership "without an allegation or a reason to conduct" an investigation.[17]

THE RELATIONSHIP BETWEEN CHILD PORNOGRAPHY AND CHILD PROSTITUTION

There is a strong correlation between child pornography and child prostitution in the juvenile sex industry.[18] Many of the same dynamics apply in the sexual exploitation of children. Most have been sexually and physically abused, come from dysfunctional families, are runaways or throwaways, or are seeking independence and sex-related thrills. Substance abuse is virtually always a component of child sexual exploitation and victimization. Pornographers often use runaway teen prostitutes in child pornographic literature and films. Conversely, many juvenile prostitutes make extra cash by moonlighting in child porn flicks or photographs. One study found that almost one in three adolescent prostitutes interviewed admitted to participating in child pornography.[19]

The association between child prostitution and child pornography can also be seen through white slavery. Some children are forced into prostitution and pornography as sexual slaves or indentured sexual servants.[20] Though this practice is not as common in the United States as in other countries, such as Thailand and India, it does exist and may be growing as more illegal alien, young female prostitutes are smuggled in by child traffickers and "sex mobsters" for purposes of prostitution and pornography.[21]

Children caught up in this dual world of sexual exploitation are often victims of sexual assaults, sexual perversions, sexually transmitted diseases, and inescapable memories of sexual misuse and bodies that have been compromised, brutalized, and left forever tarnished.

THE LAW AND CHILD PORNOGRAPHY

Before 1978, there was little federal or state legislation that specifically related to the sexual misuse and exploitation of children. Public outcry against child pornography, teen prostitution, and other sexual exploitation of children led to a series of congressional hearings in the late 1970s. Consequently, Congress enacted the Protection of Children Against Sexual Exploitation Act of 1978.[22] The act was designed to stop the production and dissemination of child pornography by prohibiting the transportation across state lines of juveniles for purposes of sexual exploitation.

The federal legislation provided punishment and stiff penalties against people who use, employ, or persuade minors (defined as persons under 16 years of age) to participate in sexually explicit print materials or visual productions. Penalties include a fine of up to $10,000 for a first offense and up to ten years in prison.

Since 1978, 48 states have designed legislation to combat child pornography.[23] In 1993, President Bill Clinton instructed the attorney general to draft new, stricter laws against child pornography. This was in response to an action of the Justice Department, which changed "its interpretation of hard-core pornography in a Supreme Court case that involved videos of young girls posing seductively."[24] In 1995, the president signed the child sex crime bill, increasing the penalties for child prostitution and child pornography.[25]

The government has also sought to protect children from smut or "patently offensive" material on the Internet. The Communications Decency Act was signed into law by President Clinton in 1996, making it a crime for anyone who "by means of a telecommunications device knowingly makes, creates or solicits, and initiates the transmission of any comment, request, suggestion, proposal, image or other communication which is obscene or indecent, knowing that the recipient of the communication is under 18 years of age."[26] The act further held that any person using "interactive computer services to display in a manner available to a person under 18, any comment, request, suggestion, proposal, image or other communication that, in context, depicts or describes, in terms patently offensive as measured by contemporary community standards, sexual or excretory activities or organs could receive up to two years' imprisonment and a $250,000 fine."[27]

A three-judge federal court in Philadelphia quickly blocked enforcement of the Communications Decency Act and the government's attempt to regulate indecent material in cyberspace, arguing that the act violated the Internet's First Amendment right to free speech.[28] In June 1997, the Supreme Court affirmed the lower court ruling, declaring the law unconstitutional in that it infringed upon communication between adults.

The laws as related to prostitution, the sex industry, and child sexploitation will be more closely examined in Chapter 19.

Chapter 17

Customers of
Female Prostitutes

Most of us think of the world of prostitution largely in terms of the female prostitute, rather than her male counterpart or male client. This imbalance in perception is often reflected in arrest and conviction statistics. Females involved in the sex-for-sale industry are routinely brought into the criminal justice system at a significantly higher rate than male participants in the prostitution business.[1] A double standard can also be seen in attitudes regarding prostitution, depending on whether the involved person is female or male. Female prostitutes tend to incur the greater wrath even of other females over their male "johns," or customers. This leniency that men have long enjoyed in soliciting or pimping for prostitutes has generally allowed them far more freedom, without censure or punishment, to pay for sex at their leisure at the expense of the women and girls who service them.

Exposing the Prostitutes' Clients

Prostitution would not exist were it not for the males who pay for their sexual favors. Recently some clients of female prostitutes have made headline news, causing the public (and researchers) to take a harsher look at the people to whom prostitutes sell sexual favors. Oddly enough, the light has been cast on both high-class call girls' clients and streetwalkers' johns. During the trial of the "Hollywood Madam," Heidi Fleiss, actor Charlie Sheen revealed that he had spent $53,000 for sex with Fleiss's call girls. Another actor, Hugh Grant, paid only $60 for oral sex with a streetwalking prostitute in the front seat of his white BMW.[2] Other notable examples are listed below:

- In Des Moines, Iowa, the River Band Neighborhood Association started sending "Dear John" letters to men seen soliciting prostitutes in the neighborhood.
- In Broward County, Florida, a deputy sheriff solicited 107 prominent businessmen to have sexual relations with his wife for $150 an hour.
- In Santa Ana, California, hundreds of johns were involved in a prostitution ring. They paid $250 to $350 an hour for sexual favors.
- In West Hartford, Connecticut, a "stylish" escort service was raided by police. Put on public display was the ledger listing the names of call girls' clients.[3]

Because of these and other less well known cases, efforts have been made to level the playing field by making more customers accountable for their violations of prostitution laws. This has done little to curtail male solicitation of prostitutes, however. Even the deadly threat of AIDS has failed to control male aggression and desire with respect to prostitution. Many believe only prostitutes themselves can stem the tide. But this may be an impossible task, given the prostitution syndrome of money, drugs, pimps, abuse, and psychological manipulation that binds so many females to the profession.

The Extent of Prostitutes' Customers

How many johns seek the sexual services of female prostitutes? There are few studies to give an answer to this question. Most experts agree that a significant number of men (the vast majority of prostitutes' customers) are or have been involved with a prostitute for sexual relations. An estimated 20 percent of all males in the United States have solicited a prostitute at some stage in their life.[4] In a recent *Playboy* survey, one in five of the men admitted to paying for sex within the past five years.[5] Other researchers have suggested that as many as one-third of all men have gone to a prostitute.[6] Furthermore, it is believed that most johns are repeat offenders, paying for sexual services multiple times with multiple prostitutes.[7]

Arrest statistics fail to provide an adequate measurement of customers of prostitutes. In 1995, there were 31,573 arrests of males for prostitution and commercialized vice in the United States.[8] The data listed in the *Uniform Crime Reports* does not distinguish between male johns and male prostitutes or pimps. Other evidence suggests that the vast majority of these arrests are for male prostitution.[9]

Researchers have found that only two male clients are arrested for every eight female prostitutes arrested.[10] An example of this disparity can be seen in arrest figures in Portland, Oregon, for prostitution-related charges. There were 402 arrests for prostitution in 1995, compared with 18 for pimping and 10 for procuring or soliciting a prostitute.[11] Some male johns are arrested under suspicion of solicitation. Even in this category, there were fewer than 7,000 arrests nationwide in 1995.[12] Since arrests for suspicion are not broken down by offense, many of these were likely for crimes other than prostitution-related offenses.

Types of Male Customers

Who are the males who solicit prostitutes? They are men as well as teenage boys. Prostitutes' clients are white, black, Hispanic, Asian, and every other race or ethnicity. They tend to cross the socioeconomic spectrum. Rich, middle-class, and lower-class men all hire prostitutes. The occupational status of customers varies as well — including doctors, lawyers, congressmen, servicemen, teachers, waiters, and the unemployed. Some are addicts, others are wife abusers, and others are regular church attendees.

Most male clients of prostitutes tend to be in their 30s, 40s, and 50s but can be much younger or older.[13] They are often married. One call girl prostitute claimed that 90 percent of her clients were married.[14] Many are also single or have girlfriends. Some are bisexual, others homosexual (and solicit male prostitutes as well).

Many customers of prostitutes are pedophiles (soliciting child prostitutes), child molesters, rapists, abusers, or substance abusers; many seek various sexual perversions such as fellatio, anal sex, bestial sex, triolism, and ritual sex.[15] Others enjoy danger, variety, adventure, and freedom from commitment. "Some men crave the excitement, thrill and risk of what they perceive to be down and dirty sex," explained writer Susan Bakos.[16]

Most men are dishonest about their involvement with prostitutes — either to wives and lovers or to themselves. Therefore, their significant others are lulled into a false sense of trust. According to one john, an executive in his mid–40s: "My wife hasn't a clue. Her mind doesn't work that way. She thinks sex has to be meaningful all the time. Sometimes I don't want to be a nice, sensitive guy…. Her love and her need to talk about her feelings and mine can get kind of oppressive."[17]

In the book *The Comfort of Sin*, Richard Goodall classified male customers in eight categories:

- Men deprived of sexual gratification or regular sexual relations
- Young men who are shy and/or inexperienced sexually
- Men who are lonely
- Unlucky men (including unattractive, blind, or deformed)
- Occupational johns (for example, sailors)
- Deviant men (such as exhibitionists, sadomasochists, and sexual perverts)
- Menopausal men (spouses of menopausal women whose sexual interest has diminished)
- Castrated men (men under psychological pressure because of modern women's availability and ascendancy)[18]

A final classification of the prostitutes' male clients might be the *therapeutically motivated john*. This male seeks out prostitutes for therapeutic needs (to provide an outlet for venting problems or frustrations to and receive in return a sympathetic and somewhat impersonal listening ear) as much as for — if not more than for — sexual favors.[19]

Reasons Men Pay for Sex

Why do men solicit and procure prostitutes? Contrary to popular belief, the reason rarely has to do with the john's physical appearance or ability to attract nonprostitutes. Researcher Susan Bakos wrote in her article on prostitution: "Based on interviews I conducted with call girls and prostitutes, I concluded that the men most likely to use prostitutes are not losers who can't get a woman any other way, but married men, often attractive and successful, traveling on business."[20] These conclusions were echoed by writer Esther Davidowitz, who noted: "These men are not unique.... It's not just the old, the weird and the perverted who visit prostitutes. And it's not only cheap, drug-addicted and dim-witted women who go into the business."[21]

All types of males visit prostitutes, for reasons ranging from simple to complex. Experts on the phenomenon of soliciting prostitutes for sexual favors have found that the reasons typically include the following:

- *Oral sex*, which most johns favor over intercourse with prostitutes
- *Sex*, often for variety, experimentation, or adventure
- *A need for power and control*, which may be unavailable or impractical elsewhere
- *The fear of intimacy* and/or emotional involvement
- *The madonna-whore notion* of the good girl (often the wife) and the bad girl (the prostitute)
- *Preservation of the marriage*, by seeing a prostitute rather than having a "real" affair or getting a divorce
- *The danger and thrill* of the "adventure of prostitution" and the calculated risk of getting caught
- *Kinky or unnatural sex acts*, including sadomasochistic sex, anal sex, and coprolagnia
- *Building self-esteem*, through being treated well, pampered, and listened to by a prostitute who is nonjudgmental and positive-oriented[22]

According to a four-year study of prostitutes and their clients, the most important reasons men had for visiting prostitutes had to do with the women being, in effect, "paraprofessional therapists."[23] The men often found that the experience raised their self-esteem and self-awareness, eased burdens of home or the job, and restored confidence in their own sexuality.

Violence and Johns

Every prostitute faces the possibility of encountering a violent john. Studies show that virtually all prostitutes have been assaulted physically or sexually by a client at some point during their prostitution career.[24] Most have multiple experiences with violent customers. One study found that 70 percent of the prostitutes were raped repeatedly by johns, for an average of 31 sexual assaults per year.[25] The study also reported that 65 percent of the female prostitutes were the victims of repeated client abuse or beatings.

Customer violence is particularly common among younger streetwalking prostitutes because of their size, naiveté, vulnerability, and exposure to high-crime locations.[26] The risks of violence at the hands of johns is also a reflection of the overall perils that prostitutes face in a dangerous, high-risk sex trade industry, often accompanied by street crime, drugs, AIDS, gangs, and customers who are also caught in the crossfire.

On the other end of the spectrum, customers can also be victimized, by prostitute violence. One study found that half the prostitutes robbed their johns regularly.[27] Other research has found that many females carry knives and/or guns to use against clients for robberies of or self-defense against violent johns.[28] Some prostitutes are violent to customers due to drug addiction or to orders from pimps who want to steal the johns' money or drugs. Almost all female prostitutes disdain their customers, whom they regard as mere objects to be taken advantage of at every opportunity — including the use of violence and aggression.

AIDS and Clients of Prostitutes

In spite of the strong association between prostitution and HIV/AIDS infection, most prostitutes' clients prefer unprotected sex. One streetwalker notes, "Many men today offer hookers more money to have sex without a condom."[29] There are no logical explanations for why johns would put themselves (and their wives, lovers, and children) at risk by having unprotected sex. Many may fancy themselves as invincible or may think they "know" the prostitute as "safe." Others may feel the risks simply come with the territory; some may have a fatalistic view of prostitutes and AIDS.

Remarkably, the risk of a customer contracting AIDS from a prostitute appears to be relatively low. One of the few studies of johns and AIDS found that only about 2 percent of the sample group tested HIV-positive.[30] Half of these men carried additional risk factors, such as being IV drug users and/or engaging in homosexual acts. The other half had no apparent risk factors, apart from being with a prostitute. One study of prostitute-customer contacts found that 75 percent of these were limited to oral sex.[31] The implication was that this placed johns at a lower risk for HIV infection than female prostitutes, many of whom were found to be crack addicts (increasing their risk for AIDS exposure through lacerations of the mouth) and IV drug users.[32]

Some studies have found that clients of prostitutes face a high risk of HIV infection due to being caught up in the typical sex-for-sale dynamics: drinking, drugs, unprotected sex, and multiple partners.[33]

Health Hazard Implications for Johns and Their Partners

In addition to the risk of AIDS, men who pay for sex expose themselves to many of the same health hazards that prostitutes face: assaults, robberies, drug addiction, and even death. There are no national studies on the extent of these dangers for clients of prostitutes. However, the nature of the sex trade industry suggests that most regular johns have experienced one or more health-related woes at some point as a result of their procuring of prostitutes.[34]

Customers of prostitutes also put their spouses and girlfriends at risk for HIV infection, STDs, and other health hazards, including cancer.[35] A recent study found that women are 5 to 11 times more likely to develop cervical cancer if their husbands frequent prostitutes or have multiple sex partners.[36] The risk of cervical cancer was 8 times greater for wives of men who frequented prostitutes than for women whose husbands did not go to prostitutes. An expert on HPV (human papilloma virus), to which cervical cancer is directly linked, stated: "HPV is a very common type of virus. It has been known for some time that it places women at a higher risk of cervical cancer. The message from studies like this is that men should stay home."[37]

Laws Against Soliciting/Procuring Prostitutes

Although there are currently laws in every state making it illegal to solicit or procure prostitutes, until recently they have rarely been enforced — and certainly not to the degree that female prostitutes have been subjected to arrest and jail time. However, new efforts in some cities have been aimed squarely at the customers of prostitutes in an attempt to contain the sex-for-sale trade at the local level. Car-seizure laws, which allow police to impound the vehicle of a john arrested for prostitution-related charges, have been adopted in some cities such as Portland, Oregon, and Baltimore, Maryland.[38] These laws essentially "recognize that johns degrade not only women who are prostitutes but also others by assuming that any females in a given area are for sale."[39]

Since the civil seizure ordinance was enacted in Portland in 1989, police have seized more than 1,700 vehicles of men charged with soliciting prostitutes, according to the Portland Police Bureau.[40] In addition to losing their cars, suspected johns are excluded from all "prostitution free" zones for 90 days. If convicted, the johns are excluded from these zones for an additional year. If a john is caught propositioning a prostitute in one of these zones after being convicted, he is arrested and charged with trespassing, usually resulting in a fine.

Other cities and communities have enacted laws or measures to "publicize and shame would-be johns by publishing their names or pictures and stepping up arrests."[41] Laws such as car-seizure have been challenged in court on the grounds of being unconstitutional.[42] The Portland ordinance, however, was upheld in a circuit court.[43]

The long-term effectiveness of such laws is as yet unknown. In most cases, impounded vehicles are eventually returned to the owners. And prostitution continues to rise in some cities and towns, in spite of such would-be deterrents. However, there are indications that these tough measures have at least caused many prostitutes' potential clients to take notice, if not stop them in their tracks altogether. Regarding the effectiveness of car-seizure laws, one Portland police spokesman said: "It's been effective when we've done frequent missions against johns. When the word gets out it's good."[44]

U.S. Military Clients of Prostitutes Abroad

The U.S. military has long been a major player in the Third World sex trade industry. Historically, female prostitutes (as well as other women and girls) have been considered "part of the spoils of war — and foreign women of color are viewed by many in the military as theirs for the taking — even in the absence of armed conflict."[45] The economically motivated relationship between American soldiers and Third World prostitutes, particularly in Thailand, has its roots in a 1967 agreement between the U.S. and Thailand governments. "Thai ports would be the way-station for soldiers on leave from the Vietnam war."[46] The Thai government provided American troops with "rest and recreation" services, which included "government-sponsored" selling of sexual favors by Thai prostitutes.[47]

U.S. servicemen continue to exploit foreign prostitutes in Thailand, the Philippines, South Korea, and elsewhere around the world, particularly in Asia. One expert on international prostitution claimed, "Where the [U.S.] military has established bases, prostitution economics have grown up around them — that is, economics based on the prostitution of a nation's women to the American occupying forces."[48]

In some cases, U.S. soldiers conspire with "flesh" traders or Asian crime syndicates in places such as Korea to marry Asian prostitutes and bring them back to the United States. The soldiers are paid $5,000 to $10,000 for their trouble in the bogus marriage, in which the brides enter this country as legal citizens, and an equal sum for a divorce.[49] The women and girls are then forced into brothels in cities such as Detroit and Houston, where they must repay "marriage fees and plane fares" through prostitution services or indentured sex slavery.[50]

Most nations have been extremely reluctant to prosecute U.S. servicemen for prostitution-related charges. For example, from 1980 to 1990, 199 U.S. servicemen in Olangapo City in the Philippines faced sex-crime charges. As of this writing, "all but one of the cases were dismissed or are still pending."[51]

Furthermore, the U.S. military has traditionally stood solidly behind the soldiers accused of sex crimes, including prostitution. The U.S. Navy, for instance, "has been known to give accused servicemen certificates to 'prove' they were on duty when a crime occurred. Another method is to ship an accused serviceman out of the country before a case can be filed in court."[52] Should these maneuvers fail, "U.S. tax dollars, through the foreign claims fund, are often used to pay off the victims of rape, sexual abuse, and other assaults by servicemen."[53]

Some efforts are being taken by the U.S. military to "shape its servicemen's sexuality; to determine the location of bars, brothels, and massage parlors; to structure women's economic opportunities; to affect wives, entertainment, and public health."[54] And given that many of the sexually exploited foreign prostitutes of U.S. servicemen are female minors, American laws have been strengthened to make prosecuting the offenders easier. As part of the 1994 crime bill (which included a provision prohibiting the transport of children under 18 for purposes of prostitution or sexual acts), an amendment to the Mann Act made it illegal for "U.S. citizens and permanent-resident aliens to travel abroad to engage in sexual acts with minors."[55] Under U.S. law, Americans can now be prosecuted for sexually exploiting juveniles in foreign countries. It remains to be seen if the U.S. military will comply with these new provisions and effect real changes in the sexual behavior of its military personnel stationed abroad.

Chapter 18

Male Prostitution

Compared with female prostitution, the prostitution of males has received relatively little attention from researchers. Even less study has been done on the relationship between AIDS and male prostitutes, though many associate HIV and AIDS with the gay lifestyle and male prostitution. Like females who sell their bodies, male prostitutes typically have been victimized sexually, are runaways or throwaways, use and/or abuse drugs and alcohol, and face a life on the streets fraught with perils. Unlike female prostitutes, most male prostitutes are on their own, are less likely to be arrested, and are not likely to return home once they enter the dark world of prostitution. Many will die before ever getting a chance to escape the homosexual sex industry.

The Extent of Male Prostitution

It is unknown just how many male prostitutes there are in the United States. Some researchers believe the number to be at least equal to the number of female prostitutes.[1] In the book *For Love or Money: Boy Prostitution in America*, Robin Lloyd estimated that there were 300,000 male prostitutes under the age of 16 in this country.[2] Other evidence suggests that the vast majority of male prostitutes are over 18, indicating the magnitude of male prostitution.[3]

ARREST STATISTICS

Arrest data on male prostitutes can provide some perspective on juvenile-versus-adult male prostitution (as well as on male-verses-female prostitute arrests). It can also give us arrest trends, which may be used to interpret both the visibility and patterns of male prostitutes and the police enforcement of

Figure 18-1 Male Arrests for Prostitution and Commercialized Vice, by Age, 1995

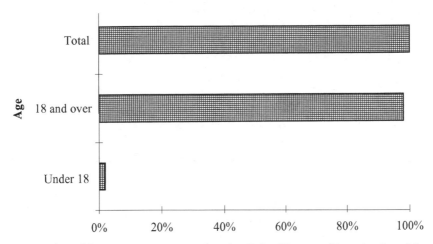

Source: Adapted from U.S. Department of Justice, Federal Bureau of Investigation, *Crime in the United States: Uniform Crime Reports 1995* (Washington, D.C.: Government Printing Office, 1996), p. 220.

prostitution laws. According to the *Uniform Crime Reports (UCR)*, 31,573 males were arrested for prostitution and commercialized vice in the United States in 1995 (compared with 49,491 arrests of females).[4] More than 98 percent of the males arrested were age 18 and over, as shown in Figure 18-1. The low arrest figures for males under 18 could reflect the fact that many boy prostitutes are arrested as runaways and/or on other charges. Over one in three arrestees were ages 24 to 34. Nearly 43 percent of all males arrested for prostitution and commercialized vice fell into this age range.[5]

Most men arrested for prostitution are white. Nearly 61 percent of the arrestees for prostitution and commercialized vice in 1995 were white.[6] Almost 37 percent of those arrested were black, whereas Native Americans and Asians accounted for slightly over 2 percent of all arrests for prostitution.

Male prostitutes are more likely to face arrest in cities, followed by the suburbs and rural communities.[7] City arrests of men for prostitution and commercialized vice were more than 13 times greater than arrests in suburban counties for prostitution in 1995.

Arrest trends in Table 18-1 reveal some inconsistencies in male arrests for prostitution. Over the period between 1986 and 1995, male arrests for prostitution and commercialized vice declined by 7.5 percent. However, an increase in arrests of nearly 2 percent was reflected between 1991 and 1995, whereas arrests remained virtually unchanged from 1994 to 1995.

Table 18-1 Male Arrest Trends for Prostitution
and Commercialized Vice, 1986-1995[a]

1994	1995	Percent Change	1991	1995	Percent Change	1986	1995	Percent Change
3,1343	31,241	-0.3	25,243	25,694	+1.8	31,959	29,576	-7.5

[a]Based on arrest trends data from the three time periods listed, which may differ from arrest data noted for only 1995.

Source: Adapted from U.S. Department of Justice, Federal Bureau of Investigation, *Crime in the United States: Uniform Crime Reports 1995* (Washington, D.C.: Government Printing Office, 1996), pp. 213, 215, 217.

Overall, arrest statistics only hint at the true scope of male prostitution. Its less visible nature, compared with female streetwalkers, makes arrest more difficult. See Chapter 1 for other shortcomings of official data.

Types of Male Prostitutes

● A number of types of male prostitutes have been established by researchers. S. Caukins and N. Coombs identified four types of male prostitutes: street hustlers, bar hustlers, call boys, and kept boys.[8] They advanced that a "gay sex market thrives in every big city ... a profit oriented street corner college for the recruiting, training, and selling of boys and men to older, affluent homosexuals."[9] In a psychosocial study, male prostitutes were categorized as follows:

• *Street hustlers*: often drifters, sometimes supporting a family through prostitution
• *Bar hustlers*: drifters, supporting a wife or children
• *Call boys*: often companions for upscale johns for social occasions such as dinner or the theater
• *Kept boys*: houseboys who perform various nonsexual domestic chores[10]

● In their study of male prostitutes and IV drug use, Dan Waldorf and Sheigla Murphy divided prostitutes into two general classifications: (1) *hustlers* and (2) *call men*.[11] Hustlers found customers in typical cruising places for male prostitution — arcades, adult bookstores, theaters, and gay bars. The researchers subclassified hustlers into three types:

• *Trade hustlers*: often heterosexual or bisexual males who sell their bodies for money; rarely do they admit to being gay or enjoying sexual relations with male johns

- *Drag queen hustlers*: transvestites and transsexuals, specializing in oral sex; They typically ply their trade in known gay red-light districts
- *Youth hustlers*: young, acknowledged homosexual males who appear naive and innocent; they are often fairly experienced in a range of sexual relations

Call men do not reflect erotic styles but rather the ways in which they locate customers as well as the kinds of sexual services they offer. These male prostitutes are subdivided into four groups:

- *Call book men*: often self-identified as gay or bisexual. They tend to acquire clients from a call book or have regular customers. *Drag queen call girls* are transvestites working from a call book.
- *Models and escorts*: men who find johns through advertising in general or special-interest publications. They often establish a network of regular clients and may also use a call book.
- *Erotic masseurs*: men who seek new customers through advertisements while maintaining regular clients. Most are certified by licensed massage schools and combine massages with sexual services, often for lower fees than other call men.
- *Porn industry stars*: the upper class or elite among male prostitutes, including erotic dancers and actors in pornographic movies. Clients (including females) are typically solicited at work and are serviced elsewhere. These men receive the highest pay in the male sex industry.[12]

Dynamics of Male Prostitution

Similar to female prostitutes, male prostitutes tend to come from every conceivable background, including being "delinquent school dropouts to well educated, refined college students; they come from inner city projects and middle class suburbs; from completely disintegrated families and from effective loving families."[13] Equally often, male prostitutes have been found to enjoy being in the sex-for-sale business, to merely tolerate it, and to abhor what they do.[14] Some will end up homeless, drug addicted, or incarcerated, whereas others will thrive in the world of big business and prosperity.[15]

Most male prostitutes are runaways and have experienced various sexual and physical abuses, as well as pathologies. One study found that two-thirds of full-time male prostitutes were runaways.[16] For those whose first sexual experience was with a male, more than half reported being seduced, and two-thirds were paid for sexual favors. Another study of male prostitution found that the average age for a prostitute's first homosexual experience was 9.6 years.[17] Three-fifths of the subjects recalled receiving some form of payment.

In a study examining age and socioeconomic status of male prostitutes, there was little to support the broken-home theories often associated with female prostitution.[18] However, male prostitutes' families were found to be larger than male nonprostitutes', as well as more dysfunctional (drug abuse and incestuous relations). Most male prostitutes had their first sexual encounter with a male who was at least five years older.[19]

The majority of male prostitutes do not label themselves as homosexual but see their sexual behavior as something done purely for the money or other payment.[20] In one study where almost 75 percent of the male prostitutes were judged to be homosexual, only 6 percent of the subjects defined themselves as gay.[21] However, another study reported that two-thirds of the male prostitutes identified themselves as homosexual or bisexual.[22]

Studies have found that most males who sell sexual favors tend to be self-destructive, have high levels of psychopathology, and are unstable, immature, and irresponsible.[23] Male prostitutes have also been shown to have a high rate of sexually transmitted diseases, drug addiction, and alcoholism.[24]

Gay customers of male prostitutes are typically reported to be middle-aged and physically unappealing. Most tend to seek "bizarre and unusual sex acts which would not meet with acceptance in conventional gay society."[25]

Male prostitutes and customers tend to have a "deep hatred" toward one another, according to authorities.[26] Both have to wrestle with conflicting emotions during their time together, often creating fantasies that are acted out in the course of the sexual encounter.[27]

Motivations for Male Prostitutes

Male prostitutes generally enter and remain in the sex-for-sale business for reasons that parallel those of female prostitutes:

- Need for a quick and easy way to make money
- Need for food and shelter
- Unemployment
- Desire for acceptance
- Drug or alcohol abuse/addiction
- Dysfunctional home life
- Rejection by parents
- Sexual identity issues
- Need for financial security
- Need for education (tuition paid)
- Desire for sexual experimentation
- Desire for adventure and thrills[28]

Virtually all male prostitutes are independent operators, with no pimps to take part or all of their earnings or to intimidate and manipulate them. Hence, their reasons for being in the business of prostitution are primarily self-serving

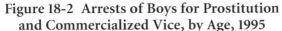

**Figure 18-2 Arrests of Boys for Prostitution
and Commercialized Vice, by Age, 1995**

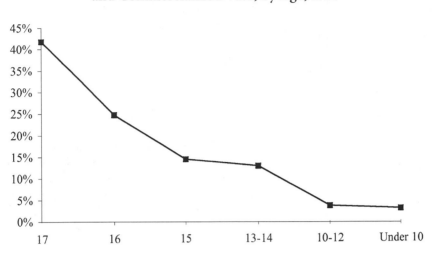

Source: Derived from U.S. Department of Justice, Federal Bureau of Investigation, *Crime
in the United States: Uniform Crime Reports 1995* (Washington, D.C.: Government Printing Office, 1996), p. 220.

(though strongly influenced by one or more of the aforementioned motivational
factors).

Boy Prostitution

Boy prostitution tends to differ somewhat from adult male prostitution.
There are believed to be hundreds of thousands of male prostitutes under the
age of 18.[29] Many adolescent male prostitutes are runaways and receive attention from law enforcement as runaways and prostitutes. The *UCR* reported that
there were 80,866 males under the age of 18 arrested for running away in the
United States in 1995.[30] This compares with only 540 male juveniles arrested
for prostitution and commercialized vice.[31] Boy runaways and prostitutes are
also arrested under such offenses as suspicion, curfew and loitering law violations, vagrancy, and alcohol and drug-related offenses.[32]

As seen in Figure 18-2, nearly 42 percent of all males under age 18 arrested
for prostitution and commercialized vice in 1995 were age 17. Almost one-quarter of those arrested were 16, with over 14 percent age 15. Nearly 13 percent of the
arrests were males ages 13 to 14; boys age 12 and under accounted for just over 6
percent of the male juvenile arrests for prostitution and commercialized vice.

Almost seven in ten boys arrested for prostitution-related charges in 1995 were 16 to 17 years old, reflecting the findings of other data on male adolescent prostitutes.[33]

❧ "CHICKENS" AND "CHICKEN HAWKS"

Boy prostitutes are often referred to on the streets as *chickens*; the homosexual men in search of boy prostitutes are called *chicken hawks* or *chicken queens*. These men are also known in law enforcement and psychiatry as pedophiles and child molesters (see Chapter 14). Much of the male adolescent prostitution occurs in large cities with a significant gay population. Young boys can also be found prostituting themselves in the ever-expanding suburbs and rural areas. A typical example of a chicken–chicken hawk encounter was recently described by a Baltimore police detective in the sex offenses unit:

> The boy will usually find a set of marble steps, sit, and observe passing cars. Eye contact is the key. The "chicken hawk" will stare at the boy he feels could be a "hustler." If a period of eye contact is made between both, the "chicken hawk" will still circle the block several times, making eye contact at each passing. Finally the "chicken hawk" will nod and, if the boy returns the nod, a deal is in the making. At times, the "chickens" would work as teams, usually two together. If the customer wanted two boys, he would use hand signals, indicating how many boys he wanted and how much he was paying.[34]

THE MEN WHO SEXUALLY EXPLOIT BOY PROSTITUTES

Although most pedophiles favor boy hustlers, many chicken hawks also seek out male prostitutes of any age. Some prefer chickens of a specific age or age range and "will not pick up any other boys who might be older or younger than he desires."[35] The following is a profile of the typical chicken hawk:

- Is often middle aged
- Relates to children well, usually better than to adults
- Regards the chicken as the sexual aggressor
- Is generally nonviolent
- Is often single but can be married
- Associates with other pedophiles and chicken hawks
- Often was sexually molested during childhood
- Pretends to be the boy prostitute's friend
- Is often a white-collar worker or professional[36]

CHARACTERISTICS OF THE ADOLESCENT MALE PROSTITUTE

The first national study of male juvenile prostitutes was conducted by the Urban and Rural Systems Association of San Francisco.[37] Its findings on the typical characteristics of boy prostitutes are listed below:

- Boy prostitutes sell their bodies primarily to survive financially, explore their sexuality, and/or make contact with gay men.
- Money is the most important motivation for male juveniles to become and remain prostitutes.
- The average age of the boy prostitute is 16.
- The vast majority of adolescent male prostitutes are runaways or throwaways.
- Most male juvenile prostitutes come from broken or dysfunctional homes.
- A high percentage of boy prostitutes have been sexually, physically, or emotionally abused.
- Many teenage prostitutes are high school dropouts or did poorly in school.
- Delinquency and criminal behavior are frequent among boy prostitutes.
- Pimps are practically nonexistent in the adolescent male prostitute subculture.
- Gay-identified boy prostitutes find the lifestyle initially exciting.

It is estimated that as many as half of all male juvenile prostitutes "are thrown out of their houses because of sexual identity issues."[38] The overwhelming majority of boys selling sex are streetwalkers. D. Kelly Weisberg found that 94 percent of her sample of boy prostitutes practiced their trade on the streets.[39] Nevertheless, there are boy brothels where young male prostitutes both live and work. These tend to be operated by owner-pimps, primarily for their profit. Joan Johnson refers to boy brothel prostitutes as being at the lowest level of the adolescent male prostitution hierarchy.[40]

CATEGORIES OF BOY PROSTITUTES

Like male prostitutes in general, boy prostitutes have been grouped into categories and subcategories by researchers. Weisberg identifies two distinct adolescent male prostitution subcultures: (1) the *peer-delinquent subculture* and (2) the *gay subculture*:

> For youth in the first subculture, prostitution is an integral aspect of delinquent street life. These adolescents engage indiscriminately in prostitution, drug dealing, panhandling, and petty criminal activity. They sell their sexual favors habitually as a way of making money, viewing prostitution as just one aspect of "hustling" — as the term is used to mean procuring more than one gives.
>
> Youth in the gay subculture engage in prostitution for different reasons. Prostitution is one outlet for their sexuality. They find in the gay male subculture a means of identification, and prostitution satisfies their needs for social interaction with gay persons and for sexual partners. Simultaneously, it provides a way of making money, since the purchase and sale of sexual activity is a product of the sexual mores of that community.[41]

Within these subcultures are several interchangeable subcategories, including the following:

- *Situational prostitutes*: male juveniles who engage in prostitution only in certain situations and who tend to regard prostitution as an occasional pastime
- *Habitual prostitutes*: adolescent males involved in inner-city street life, of which prostitution is an integral activity and that includes other criminal offenses such as drug dealing, robbery, and petty theft
- *Vocational prostitutes*: boys who regard juvenile prostitution as either a career or a stepping-stone to one and who see themselves as professionals
- *Avocational prostitutes*: vocational adolescent male prostitutes who see their prostitution as part-time employment[42]

In her study of adolescent prostitution, Johnson found that most male juvenile prostitutes are *street hustlers*—homosexual, heterosexual, and bisexual.[43] She wrote that many are aggressive, drug addicted, and physically unattractive. Other types described were the *transvestite boy prostitute* and the *upper-class adolescent male prostitute*. The latter male juvenile prostitute is often better looking, better dressed, older, higher class, and more self-confident than lower-class prostitutes.[44] Upper-class boy prostitutes, like their female counterparts, often work for escort services or have their own call boy service. Few ply their trade as street hustlers.

BOY PROSTITUTES AND SUBSTANCE ABUSE

Drug and alcohol use/abuse is common among boy prostitutes. The Huckleberry House Project found that 83 percent of the male prostitutes had tried marijuana and that 77 percent continued to smoke it.[45] Another study revealed that 29 percent of the teenage boy prostitutes regularly used hard drugs, whereas 42 percent were heavy drinkers or alcoholics.[46] In Weisberg's study, the reason most often given for using drugs was the enjoyment of "being high."[47]

LAW ENFORCEMENT AND MALE JUVENILE PROSTITUTION

Though studies have found adolescent male prostitutes to engage in other serious crimes more often than adolescent female prostitutes, the males are less likely to be arrested or incarcerated. In fact, although slightly more males under the age of 18 than females under 18 were arrested for prostitution and commercialized vice in 1995,[48] almost 28,000 more girls than boys were arrested as runaways—generally the forerunner and concurrent to juvenile prostitution.[49] D. Sweeney estimated that 70 percent of adolescent male prostitutes never come into contact with the criminal justice system.[50] Comparatively speaking, studies suggest that 75 percent of all adolescent female prostitutes have had some contact with the police, courts, or juvenile corrections.[51] When young male prostitutes are arrested, it is rarely for prostitution but rather for status offenses such as running away, loitering, and curfew violations, for petty offenses such as shoplifting, and for alcohol and drug-related violations of the law.

Most criminologists attribute the low rate of boy prostitute contact with law enforcement to the difficulty in identifying them, compared with girl prostitutes, who most often ply their trade as highly visible streetwalkers.[52] Laws also tend to be inconsistent from state to state or city to city regarding what undercover police officers can do or say when targeting male or female teen prostitutes. Young male prostitutes are generally more successful at circumventing police stings and entrapment than are young female streetwalking prostitutes.

Some studies have found that male juvenile prostitutes frequently come into contact with the law. For example, Weisberg reported a high incidence of teenage boy prostitutes involved with the criminal justice system.[53] Approximately two-thirds of the boys sampled had been arrested at least once, with prostitution-related offenses accounting for 33 percent of the arrests.

Male Prostitution and HIV/AIDS

Unlike the many studies focusing on the relationship between female prostitutes and HIV/AIDS, little research has been conducted on male prostitutes and the AIDS virus and its HIV precursor. Nevertheless, the existing data of the dynamics of male prostitution suggests that the risk of HIV/AIDS infection for male prostitutes is high.[54] This is attributed primarily to the knowledge of the two most common ways that HIV and AIDS are spread in the male prostitution subculture. One is the sharing, by IV drug users, of dirty needles and tainted blood. The other is the passing of AIDS-infected bodily fluids — usually through anal intercourse. With a high rate of IV drug use, homosexual relations, and multiple homosexual or bisexual partners, male prostitutes may be at a greater risk for exposure to the AIDS virus than female prostitutes.[55]

Two recent studies highlight the severity of the problem of HIV infection among male prostitutes. In a New York City study at a venereal clinic, 84 male prostitutes were tested for AIDS. Fifty-three percent of those engaging in homosexual prostitution were HIV-seropositive.[56] Of the prostitutes who serviced female customers only, 10 percent tested positive. The second study, conducted in Italy, HIV tested and compared 27 male prostitutes, 75 homosexual men, and 106 male IV drug users. Eleven percent of the male prostitutes tested positive, compared with 17 percent of the homosexual men and 49 percent of the IV drug addicts.[57] In both studies, the researchers concluded that male prostitutes were a high-risk population for contracting the AIDS virus.

Experts believe that male prostitutes and their male customers caught up in the high-risk lifestyle of prostitution, drugs, and paid frequent sex "may be, or could become, the major means through which HIV infection is passed into the general population."[58] Because a high proportion "of the clients of male prostitutes are family men from middle class communities ... male prostitutes may serve as an epidemiological bridge to females and children just as well as intravenous drug users."[59]

Chapter 19

Laws and Prostitution

Where do prostitutes and their clients stand in terms of laws and legal challenges in the United States? Presently there are laws against prostitution-related crimes — including solicitation, pandering, and procuring females (or males) for purposes of prostitution — in every state in the country.[1] Even in Nevada, where a limited amount of prostitution is legal, the practice is outlawed in most of the state.[2] However, the laws governing prostitution tend to be nonuniform, vague, and discriminatory. Female prostitutes operating at the lowest levels of the female prostitution subculture are typically the most susceptible to arrest, conviction, and incarceration.[3] Although male clients outnumber prostitutes, females who sell sexual favors are at least four times as likely to be arrested and charged with prostitution-related offenses as the men they service.[4]

These disturbing trends make it that much more difficult to control the institution of prostitution in the United States. Furthermore, efforts to legalize or decriminalize prostitution are adding to the complexity of trying to enforce existing laws and enact new ones.

Laws aimed at child prostitution and the sexual exploitation of children are generally taken more seriously on the local and national levels. However, even these laws leave room for tougher measures in dealing with pedophiles, pimps, pornographers, and others who sexually exploit children, as well as in more adequately addressing the problem of juveniles who sell sexual favors and are otherwise exploited by the sex trade industry.

Laws Against Prostitution

Prostitution is outlawed in 49 of the 50 states, with legal prostitution existing only in parts of Nevada. Antiprostitution laws vary from state to state, and

145

often from one violator to another as to how such laws are applied. Payment for sexual acts is strictly prohibited in 38 states.[5] Solicitation laws are enforced in 44 states and the District of Columbia.[6] In other states, prostitution is banned through vagrancy, curfew, and loitering statutes.[7]

Legally, prostitution itself (usually in the form of solicitation) is a misdemeanor, typically carrying a fine and up to 30 days in jail.[8] However, the charges and penalties can be more severe depending on the nature of the prostitution-related charges. For example, Heidi Fleiss's conviction for three counts of pandering resulted in a three-year state prison sentence, though the conviction was overturned due to jury misconduct. She was also convicted in federal court of prostitution-related charges of income tax evasion and money laundering of call girl profits, for which she received a 37-month sentence in federal prison.[9]

Laws Against Clients of Prostitutes

The men who pay for sexual favors are the least likely to be penalized for violating prostitution laws. However, recent legislation and community efforts have made it easier for law enforcement and antiprostitution activists to go after johns, in one way or another. Car-seizure laws in cities across the country, such as Baltimore and Portland, permit the police to confiscate vehicles of people caught soliciting or procuring prostitutes.[10] Other ordinances have enabled communities to publish in local newspapers or put on public display the names and/or photographs of prostitutes' clients.[11] These measures notwithstanding, male violators of prostitution-related offenses continue to evade harsher penalties, perpetuating the differential enforcement of the law and the cycle of sexual exploitation of females caught up in the sex-for-sale industry.

Legal Challenges to Prostitution Laws

Various legal attempts have been made to circumvent existing antiprostitution legislation. Most have been defeated. For example, in *Caesar's Health Club v. St. Louis County*, the issue of privacy in a massage parlor was argued before the Mission Court of Appeals. The court rejected the appeal, refusing "to apply the compelling state interest standards to protect the massage parlor because it could see no implicated 'fundamental right.'"[12] In another case, *Morgan v. City of Detroit*, an ordinance relating to "accosting and soliciting" was challenged by the claim that it prohibited consensual relations.[13] The court dismissed the notion that anyone solicited in a public setting would consent to a sex-for-sale offer.

Nevada's tough licensing requirements for escort services were challenged in *IDK, Inc. v. Clark County*.[14] The court, in upholding the requirements, held that "relationships" protected by the Fourteenth Amendment's due process clause apply only to the creation and sustaining of the family. It also rejected the escort service's "expressive association" right of the First Amendment, arguing that escort services "make no claim that expression is a significant or necessary component of their activities."[15]

In *Coyote v. Roberts*, the prostitution statutes of Rhode Island were challenged by the national prostitution organization called COYOTE (Call Off Your Old Tired Ethics).[16] In advocating sexual privacy, the suit maintained that in addition to outlawing paid sex, the laws prohibited consensual sexual relations without pay, such as extramarital sex acts and sexual perversions. Before a ruling came, the state's statute was amended, decriminalizing private consensual sexual relations between adults. Public solicitation for sexual acts between consenting adults continued to be illegal.

Car-seizure laws have also been challenged in court. An Oregon circuit court recently upheld the constitutionality of Portland's ordinance.[17] In 1996, in a Supreme Court case, the court ruled against a woman who sought to recover her share of the value of a car that she co-owned with her husband, after it was seized following his arrest for soliciting a prostitute.[18]

Although laws against prostitution-related offenses are rarely overturned, proponents of legalization and decriminalization of prostitution will continue to test the courts' resolve on the issues. At the same time, other laws are being enacted to further reduce the incidence of prostitution and to crack down on the males and females who engage in the sex-for-pay business.

Legal Prostitution

Prostitution is a legal profession in 12 rural counties in Nevada — the only state in the country where prostitution is not officially prohibited. Since 1971, strictly regulated legal brothels have been in existence in Nevada cities with fewer than 250,000 residents.[19] The Nevada Brothel Association oversees the regular testing of brothel prostitutes for AIDS and other sexually transmitted diseases. Studies have shown that brothel prostitutes have a lower rate of HIV infection than unregulated prostitutes.[20] Restrictions imposed on brothel prostitutes give them far less freedom than independent, or even pimp-controlled, prostitutes.[21]

Unofficial legal prostitution in the United States can be found in the hundreds of thousands of mostly unregulated escort services, massage parlors, and other fronts for prostitution that operate legally and often without interference from law enforcement agencies. Even many illegal prostitutes, such as streetwalkers and independent call girls, can ply their trade openly (or at least brazenly) with minimum risk of arrest or detention; the same can be said for many clients of prostitutes. Additionally, the weakness of current penalties for solicitation often encourage repeat offenses for most prostitutes and customers who are arrested.

Federal Laws Prohibiting Child Sexploitation

Since the 1970s, a number of important pieces of federal legislation have been enacted and centers established to protect children from the vices of the sex trade industry and to increase penalties for those who sexually exploit children: (1) Child Abuse Prevention and Treatment Act, (2) National Center on Child Abuse and Neglect, (3) National Child Abuse and Neglect Data System, (4) Juvenile Justice and Delinquency Prevention Act, (5) Runaway and Homeless Youth Act, (6) Missing Children Act, (7) National Center for Missing and Exploited Children, and (8) Protection of Children Against Sexual Exploitation Act.

CHILD ABUSE PREVENTION AND TREATMENT ACT

The Child Abuse Prevention and Treatment Act (P.L. 100-294) became law in 1974 and was amended in 1978 under the Child Abuse Prevention and Treatment and Adoption Reform Act (P.L. 95-266).[22] The act defined child abuse and neglect and provided for "(1) the establishment of a National Center on Child Abuse and Neglect, (2) increasing public awareness on child maltreatment, detection and reporting, (3) assisting states and local communities in developing more effective mechanisms for delivery of services to families, (4) providing training and technical assistance to state and local communities in dealing with the problem of child abuse and neglect, and (5) supporting research into causal and preventative measures in child victimization."[23]

To qualify for federal funds, states are required to meet several criteria, including a comprehensive definition of child abuse and neglect, specific child abuse reporting procedures, the investigation of reports of child abuse and neglect, and administrative procedures. Also required are the "confidentiality of records and the appointment of guardians for child victims involved in abuse or neglect judicial proceedings."[24]

NATIONAL CENTER ON CHILD ABUSE AND NEGLECT

The National Center on Child Abuse and Neglect (NCCAN) was established by P.L. 93-247 in 1974 and was reauthorized in 1988 under P.L. 100-294 (the Child Abuse Prevention, Adoption, and Family Services Act)[25] and the 1992 P.L. 100-295 (the Child Abuse, Domestic Violence, Adoption and Family Services Act).[26] As the federal agency in charge of child abuse and neglect concerns, the NCCAN administers grants to states and territories, local agencies, and organizations nationwide for research, service programs, and assistance for the identification, treatment, and prevention of child victimization in any form. Recent NCCAN funding included the following projects:

- Research on the impact of child abuse and neglect in neighborhoods
- A longitudinal study examining the antecedents and implications of neglect in high-risk groups of adolescents
- A project reviewing and synthesizing research on child maltreatment and recommending research needs in the future
- Improving services to drug- and alcohol-abusing youths, parents, and families
- The National Resource Center on Child Sexual Abuse[27]

Since 1975, NCCAN has funded more than 750 projects geared toward protecting children from child abuse, neglect, and sexual exploitation.[28]

NATIONAL CHILD ABUSE AND NEGLECT DATA SYSTEM

The National Child Abuse and Neglect Data System (NCANDS) was founded by NCCAN as part of the legislation enacted in 1988.[29] Through voluntary reporting, NCANDS collects nationwide data on child abuse and neglect from child protective services. It was designed to provide a comprehensive national database on the volume and nature of child abuse, neglect, and exploitation in order to assist policy-makers and child welfare professionals.

To achieve these objectives, NCANDS consists of two components:

- *Summary Data Component (SDC)*: A compilation of state child abuse and neglect statistics, including data on victims, offenders, and investigators
- *Detailed Case Data Component (DCDC)*: A compilation of case-level data to provide more detailed analysis of state data[30]

JUVENILE JUSTICE AND DELINQUENCY PREVENTION ACT

The Juvenile Justice and Delinquency Prevention Act was enacted in 1974 and amended in 1980.[31] Its purpose is to identify victimized or troubled juvenile status offenders and divert them from institutionalization. The act required (1) a comprehensive assessment of the effectiveness of the existing juvenile justice system, (2) the impetus for developing and implementing alternatives for delinquency prevention and diversion of status offenders from the criminal justice system, and (3) the use of juvenile justice system resources to deal more effectively with juvenile delinquents.

To receive federal delinquency funds, states must "provide within two years after submission of the plan that juveniles who are charged with or who have committed offenses that would not be criminal if committed by an adult, shall not be placed in juvenile detention or correctional facilities, but must be placed in shelter facilities."[32]

RUNAWAY AND HOMELESS YOUTH ACT

The Runaway and Homeless Youth Act (RHYA) was enacted in 1978.[33] Its purpose is to provide assistance to local organizations for operating temporary shelters for runaways. The act recognizes the severity and prevalence of runaway juveniles, as well as implications such as child prostitution and substance abuse, in making grants available for the establishment and maintenance of runaway shelters by states, localities, and nonprofit organizations.

The 1980 amendment of the RHYA included the following provisions:

• Recognition that many "runaways" are actually "throwaways," thereby forced out of the home
• Clarification of the requirement that shelter services be made available to families of runaway and homeless children
• Development of model programs aimed at helping chronic runaways[34]

MISSING CHILDREN ACT

The Missing Children Act, enacted in 1982, provides parents, guardians, or next-of-kin of missing children with the "confirmation" of an entry into the FBI's National Crime Information Center.[35] Many local law enforcement agencies now have access to the computer, assisting them in identifying and locating missing children, many of whom are runaways or child prostitutes or have been kidnapped. The act further allows for FBI intervention after proof that a minor has been abducted.

This legislation came on the heels of the 1980 Federal Parental Kidnapping Prevention Act, aimed at cracking down on parents or relatives who abduct children.[36] This act empowers the Federal Parental Locator Service to search for missing children, enforce custody rights, and prosecute child snatchers as a federal crime.

NATIONAL CENTER FOR MISSING AND EXPLOITED CHILDREN

The National Center for Missing and Exploited Children was established in 1984 in response to the increase in missing children and the relationship to child abuse and neglect, teen prostitution, child pornography, runaways, and delinquency.[37] The center serves as a central contact point for parents of missing children and people who may have seen them. Key features of the center include "providing assistance and expertise in education, legislation, public awareness, advocacy, improving the criminal justice system, and prevention of missing and exploited children."[38]

Further attention was drawn to the plight of missing children with the annual observance of National Missing Children's Day in the United States, beginning on May 25, 1984.

PROTECTION OF CHILDREN AGAINST SEXUAL EXPLOITATION ACT

The Protection of Children Against Sexual Exploitation Act of 1978 was designed to bridge the gaps existing in federal statutes aimed at protecting children from sexual exploitation and abuse.[39] The law hoped to halt the production and dissemination of child pornography by prohibiting the transportation of minors across state lines for purposes of sexual misuse and exploitation. Additionally, the legislation extended the federal government's ability to prosecute producers and distributors of child pornography.

> The law provides punishment for persons who use, employ, or persuade minors (defined as any persons under 16) to become involved in the production of visual or print materials that depict sexually explicit conduct if the producers know or have reasons to know that the materials will be transported in interstate, or foreign commerce, or mailed. Punishment is also specifically provided for parents, legal guardians, or other persons having custody or control of minors and who knowingly permit a minor to participate in the production of such material.[40]

The act further provided for stiff monetary penalties against those who sexually exploit children.

In 1995, President Clinton signed the child sex crime bill, increasing the penalties for child pornographers, those involved in child prostitution, and those transporting minors for the purpose of prostitution or sexual misuse.[41]

The sexual exploitation of minors abroad was also addressed as part of the 1994 crime bill. An amendment to the Mann Act made it a criminal offense for U.S. citizens and resident aliens to travel to other countries to engage in sexual activities with children.[42] This enables American pedophiles, pimps, and others to be prosecuted under U.S. laws for sexually exploiting persons under the age of 18 in foreign countries.

Protecting children from pornography on the Internet was the intent of the Communications Decency Act, enacted in 1996.[43] The act prohibited the online display of sexually explicit material that is accessible to minors; the crime is punishable by up to a two-year prison term and $250,000 fine. The law was struck down by a panel of federal judges in Philadelphia and New York, blocking enforcement of the act because it violates First Amendment rights of free speech.[44] The Supreme Court agreed that the law was unconstitutional, ruling in June 1997 that it restricted communication among adult users of the Internet.[45] The decision was the first Supreme Court ruling involving the Internet, World Wide Web, and "cyberspace." Many believe that the high court's ruling will leave millions of children at risk of sexual exploitation by online child pornographers.

State Legislation and the
Sexual Exploitation of Children

Before 1977, state legislation relating to child victimization and sexual exploitation was generally vague, nonuniform, inadequate, and in some cases, nonexistent. With the passage of significant federal laws to fight against the sexual maltreatment and exploitation of children, states were quick to follow. Today most states have enacted or strengthened laws, providing stiffer penalties for child molesters, abusers, pimps, pornographers, and others who sexually molest or exploit minors, including parents or guardians.[46] An example is a 1983 New York law prohibiting the "dissemination of child pornography regardless of whether the material is judged legally obscene."[47] The Supreme Court upheld its constitutionality, essentially upholding similar laws in 20 other states.[48]

States are also recognizing sexually exploited children, such as prostitutes, as victims rather than offenders, enacting "state criminal statutes that fail to punish adolescent prostitutes either by omitting any mention of sanctions or specifically excluding adolescents involved in prostitution from any liability."[49] A similar trend also exists in "civil legislation where in many states juvenile participation in prostitution is looked upon as a form of child abuse/sexual exploitation rather than delinquency."[50]

Chapter 20

Examining the Issues of Decriminalization and Legalization of Prostitution

Perhaps for as long as prostitution has been prohibited in most countries around the world, the arguments for and against decriminalizing or legalizing the world's oldest profession have been waged. Most agree that prostitution will continue to exist in one capacity or another whether it is illegal or not. Proponents and opponents of legal prostitution disagree on whether this would be in the best interests of the females (and males) who sell sexual favors, as well as in the best interests of society itself. In the United States, the debate has picked up steam in recent years as prostitution activists and organizations fight for rights and sexual privacy while antiprostitution forces are quick to point out the negative factors associated with the sex trade industry. With the complexities on both sides, the issue will continue to be fought over, with no clear-cut winner, well into the twenty-first century.

Defining Decriminalization and Legalization of Prostitution

Although decriminalization and legalization of prostitution are often linked together as though they have the same meaning, the two terms have different meanings and implications with respect to prostitution. In its purest sense, decriminalization means to remove the criminalization or criminal classification of an act, which in this instance is prostitution. It is unknown whether decriminalization of prostitution would mean the repeal of *all* prostitution-related statutes or just of certain ones in certain communities, cities, or states. Currently antiprostitution laws are inconsistently applied from jurisdiction to jurisdiction, suggesting that what may be considered a crime of prostitution in one city or town may not be in another and vice versa. If prostitution was completely decriminalized across the United States, it would no longer be a criminal offense to provide sexual favors for money — at least for adults. Undoubtedly, child prostitution would never receive a decriminalization stamp of approval from the government or the general public, due to the moral and social implications of the sexual abuse and exploitation of minors by adults for their sexual pleasures and perversions.

Legalization means that prostitution would likely be subject to government regulations and statutory laws — mandating everything from labor and safety practices and principles to taxation and licensing to mandatory testing for HIV/AIDS and sexually transmitted diseases. Prostitution would essentially become a *business* in the eyes of the government, much like the acting profession, the medical profession, or any other lawful enterprise that government regulates in some form or manner.

Like decriminalization, legalization of prostitution would not be an exact science — at least not immediately. For instance, would every prostitute be required to work out of a legally regulated brothel? Or could any prostitute work independently if she or he chose to? Would some aspects of the profession be subject to regulations while others remain illegal?

Again, legalized child prostitution would likely never become a reality because of morality issues and the sexploitation of minors. But this issue would still have to be dealt with if other forms of prostitution were decriminalized or legalized, potentially increasing the demand for illegal child prostitutes.

If adult prostitution is ever removed in part or total from the criminal statutes or is decriminalized, it will almost certainly as a consequence be at least partially regulated by the government — hence legalized.

Proponents of Decriminalization/ Legalization of Prostitution

PROSTITUTES' RIGHTS ORGANIZATIONS

The arguments for decriminalizing/legalizing prostitution come, not too surprisingly, mostly from women working in the profession. Prostitutes' rights organizations such as COYOTE (Call Off Your Old Tired Ethics) and PONY (Prostitutes of New York) are at the forefront of efforts to allow prostitutes more liberties to make an "honest" living just like any legal professionals, such as dancers, entertainers, doctors, lawyers, or even sex surrogates.[1] One major reason, they point out, for decriminalizing prostitution is to make it easier for prostitutes to report crimes against them — particularly sexual assaults. Most prostitutes regularly face the threat of rape in their profession. One study reported that prostitutes were raped on average 31 times per year.[2] Because prostitution itself is a crime subject to arrest and the indignities of the criminal justice system, few prostitutes ever report a violation. According to a study, only 4 percent of female prostitutes who are sexually assaulted ever report the crime.[3] Those that do report commonly complain that the police and prosecutors fail to take them seriously or to act on the accusation with the same urgency and professionalism they would if it had come from a more "respectable" woman.

COYOTE contends that decriminalization of prostitution (hence, repealing prostitution laws and removing pimps and purveyors from the picture) would eliminate this dilemma that prostitutes must go through with every assault by a customer or pimp. If prostitution work is a noncriminal enterprise, the industry "would be subject to standard labor and occupational safety regulations, and it would be easier for women to fight the abuses and crimes that accompany their work."[4]

The right to privacy is also high on the list in support of decriminalization/ legalization for prostitutes' organizations. "The government does not belong in my bedroom," insisted a strong advocate for prostitutes' rights.[5] Some cities apparently agree, at least in principle. San Francisco, for example, has appointed a task force to examine the possibility of decriminalizing prostitution.[6] In San Diego, a "citizens' group advocating prostitution-law reform" was formed.[7] COYOTE went after Rhode Island's prostitution laws, advocating the right to sexual privacy in *Coyote v. Roberts*.[8] The case caused the state to amend its statute to decriminalize private consensual sexual relations between adults.

Most prostitutes see decriminalization of prostitution as a matter of choice, similar to abortion. This is aptly summed up by a member of COYOTE and the National Organization of Women: "Sex work certainly isn't for everyone, but you have to give people the choice when it comes to their own bodies. Sex work can be dignified, honest, and honorable."[9]

Although prostitutes' rights groups favor decriminalization of prostitution, many are less supportive of legalization of prostitution, since "*legalization* is understood to mean decriminalization accompanied by strict municipal regulation of prostitution."[10] Many high-class prostitutes (and many lower-class prostitutes as well) entered the business because of the independence attached to it, and most are fearful of the prospect of this being taken away with legalizing the profession. One call girl writer explained:

> Legalization — unlike decriminalization — would probably mean that prostitutes could not act like independent business people. We'd have to work in a specific district, kick back part of our fees to the city or state, and register as prostitutes — which could go on a woman's public record and affect her ability to travel, get health insurance or an apartment, and

keep custody of her children. A lot of us would worry that the city would do a lousy job of running these establishments and we'd be faced with a "sex factory" situation.[11]

THE COSTS OF ILLEGAL PROSTITUTION

Many advocates of decriminalization/legalization of prostitution believe that it would significantly lower the enormous costs associated with enforcing prostitution laws. In 1992, for example, there were nearly 9,000 arraignments for prostitution in New York City, at an estimated cost of $1,200 per person (from the arrest to arraignment).[12] This added up to in excess of $10 million that was spent to "harass streetwalkers by jailing them, churning them through the courts, and then turning them back out onto the streets."[13] Some prostitutes have been arrested, at taxpayers' expense, over 30 times in a year.[14] A recent survey of operating costs in major U.S. cities found that the cities spent on average $12 million per year battling prostitution.[15] The writer, Julie Pearl, reported that the study "focused on sixteen of the nation's largest cities, in which only 28 percent of reported violent crimes resulted in arrest. On average, police in these cities made as many arrests for prostitution as for all violent offenses."[16]

> Opponents of law enforcement spending on attempting to control prostitution point to the absurd economy of enforcing sex laws. San Francisco employs 12 vice squad officers who do nothing but arrest street prostitutes. It costs significantly more than $5 million to process the nearly 5000 cases they added to a bulging court roster. Critics suggest the money and effort should have been used to solve the 91 murders, 292 rapes, and 6624 robberies committed during the same period. As if misuse of these resources wasn't enough, Bay bulldogs now confiscate condoms during street busts, terming them "an act of furtherance" — evidence of alleged prostitution. In fact, this only interferes with the practice of safe sex.[17]

Because prostitution is already illegal but usually consensual, few prostitutes or johns ever report the illegality of their sex acts to police. Hence, law enforcement must often go to the consensual offenders through various means of "deceit and trickery" to enforce prostitution statutes and create opportunities to spend more "crime"-allocated funds. The following is an example of what many see as costly entrapment of suspected prostitutes and clients by police:

> Honolulu police paid private citizens to pick up prostitutes in their cars, have sex with them and then drive them to nearby police cars for arrest.... In San Francisco, the police have wired rooms in the city's leading hotels to make videotapes of prostitutes servicing their customers.... Eight Fairfax County, Virginia, police officers rented two $88-a-night Holiday Inn rooms, purchased an ample supply of liquor and then [hired] a professional

stripper for a bachelor party. The stripper came, stripped, and was busted for indecent exposure.... Police justified the sting operation by claiming it was necessary to fight prostitution. But the department had made only 11 arrests on prostitution charges in the previous year — all with similar sting operations.[18]

The view of many decriminalization/legalization advocates is that decriminalizing prostitution would make it far easier for police and law enforcement management to redirect these resources into fighting more serious, violent crime and criminals, as well as other types of sex crimes such as child molestation and child pornography.

LEGAL PROSTITUTION AND HIV/AIDS

Some supporters of the legalization of prostitution point toward the correlation between legal brothel prostitution in Nevada and a low rate of HIV infection, compared with the rate of unregulated prostitutes. A study of brothel workers, incarcerated streetwalkers, and HIV revealed that whereas none of the brothel prostitutes tested HIV-positive, 6 percent of the unregulated streetwalkers were HIV infected.[19] Studies of prostitutes in New Jersey and New York found that 57 percent and 35 percent of the prostitutes tested positive for the AIDS virus.[20]

Decriminalization and legalization proponents attribute the low incidence of HIV exposure among brothel female prostitutes to the strict regulations, requiring regular testing of prostitutes for sexually transmitted diseases. Conversely, they blame higher rates of infection among unregulated prostitutes on the lack of regulations and health safeguards.

Legal prostitution in western European countries such as Germany and the Netherlands is believed by many social scientists to be a model for the legalization/decriminalization of prostitution. In Hamburg, for example, "streetwalkers are sanctioned in certain well-defined areas and prostitutes must undergo frequent health checks. Women with contagious diseases are strictly prohibited from plying their trade."[21]

Legal prostitution is also believed by many to be the way to provide safer conditions for prostitutes, as well as to reduce other crimes often associated with prostitution. Critics, however, dispute the significance of legal prostitution in controlling street crime. Moreover, they argue that the potential problems of legalized prostitution (such as corruption and discrimination) outweigh any positive areas. The logistics of the legalization of streetwalking prostitution in the United States would be a nightmare, they claim, particularly given the high percentage of teenage streetwalkers. Separating legalized adult prostitutes from illegal child prostitutes would be only one major problem to solve.

OTHER REASONS FOR DECRIMINALIZING/ LEGALIZING PROSTITUTION

Exponents for the decriminalization/legalization of prostitution have argued that prostitution as a criminal offense has transformed "local police officers into de facto car thieves ... under local asset-forfeiture laws," in which suspected johns' vehicles are seized.[22] Others maintain that antiprostitution laws lead to unnecessary and often dangerous police chases (by car and on foot), blatant disrespect for the law (sometimes by policemen who double as johns), and basically unenforceable laws for what many see as a "victimless" crime.

Further arguments in favor of the decriminalization/legalization of prostitution include the following:

- Would reduce violent crimes against women and children
- Would lower the rate of street crimes, including drug abuse and drug dealing
- Would result in a lower incidence of sexually transmitted diseases
- Would lower the rate of abortion and illegitimate children
- Would lead to a decline in pornography
- Would confine prostitution to brothels or particular areas
- Would lower the incidence of divorce and extramarital affairs[23]

Opponents of Decriminalization/ Legalization of Prostitution

Those opposed to decriminalizing/legalizing prostitution include criminologists, sociologists, feminists, "social and religious conservatives who object to prostitution on moral grounds and neighborhood groups worried about street prostitution's effects on safety and property values."[24] By and large, these forces have successfully rebuffed most serious attempts to decriminalize/legalize prostitution in this country.

MORAL AND RELIGIOUS OPPOSITION

Strong opposition to decriminalizing/legalizing prostitution comes from moralists and religious leaders who see prostitution as a morally wrong, sinful, un–Christian, spiritual and physical weakness. In his examination of prostitution in the 1990s, Richard Goodall summarized these arguments as follows:

> *The moralist arguments*: To give official recognition to what prostitutes do would amount to the codification of a double standard in human relations and would encourage promiscuity. More particularly, if a prostitute and/or a brothel were to be taxed, the State would be deriving income from an immoral activity.

The religious arguments: There is a sanctity in human sexual relations which is perverted by sexual activity with prostitutes; promiscuity is sin.[25]

Supporters of moral and/or religious perspectives against decriminalizing prostitution come in all denominations, classes, races, and demographic groups. In many instances, they also cross over into social, political, or legal opposition to the decriminalization or legalization of prostitution.

FEMINIST OPPOSITION

Feminists tend to oppose decriminalizing prostitution because many view the sex industry itself as "mechanisms of sexual objectification" and women's "social subordination," "inherently degrading," and "decontextualizing women's choices."[26] Goodall summed up the feminist arguments against decriminalization/legalization: "It is beneath the dignity of women to be treated as a chattel that can be bought and sold, women should not be a slave to man."[27]

Some feminists seek nothing less than the abolishment of prostitution. Feminist and ex-prostitute Evelina Giobbe, the founder of Women Hurt in Systems of Prostitution Engagement in Revolt (WHISPER), stated: "Prostitution is unwanted sex by definition. We don't think it can be reformed."[28] Other feminists, such as Laurie Shrage and Jane Anthony, concur, arguing that abolishing the institution of prostitution (as well as pornography) will offer the most compelling challenge for the women's movement into the next century.[29]

Some feminists have actually taken a proprostitution position, regarding prostitution as a "career choice" or form of "empowerment for women." In the words of one feminist prostitute: "For me, sex work happens to be the best alternative. It's better than being the president of someone else's company. It's better than being a secretary. It's the most honest work I can think of."[30]

THE REALITIES OF PROSTITUTION

Many critics of decriminalization/legalization of prostitution dismiss the notion of the prostitute as a "sexually free, consenting adult," arguing that the realities of the sex trade industry fail to support this view.[31] One opponent of decriminalization wrote that prostitution "hides the vast network of traffickers, organized crime syndicates, pimps, procurers and brothel keepers, as well as the customer demand that ultimately controls the trade."[32] Studies show that a high percentage of prostitutes have been sexually and physically abused during childhood, are frequently sexually and physically assaulted as prostitutes by pimps and customers, and have a high mortality rate.[33] These disturbing trends are seen as proof that few females in the sex business are there by their own free choice.

Most streetwalkers are essentially homeless, have a low income, and are often drug abusers who are controlled by pimps, drug suppliers, and customers.

Even prostitutes working for escort services or as independent call girls frequently face dire conditions including abuse, drugs, and dependency on customers to earn a living. The issue of freedom of choice must be weighed against the circumstances that make prostitution a necessity or addiction for many females.

The opposition to decriminalization/legalization of prostitution further points out that prostitutes in the United States and worldwide are typically society's "most vulnerable members, those least able to resist recruitment. They are those most displaced and disadvantaged in the job market: women, especially the poor; the working class; racial and ethnic minorities; mothers with young children to support; battered women fleeing abuse; refugees and illegal aliens."[34] A growing number of women are smuggled into this country as prostitutes or are forced into sexual slavery prostitution by criminal gangs and crime syndicates.[35]

Perhaps the strongest argument against decriminalizing prostitution is the large base of minors selling their bodies and sexual favors in the United States. Teenagers represent the greatest number of recruits into the sex trade industry. Removing the criminal status for adult prostitution would be an endorsement, in effect, for juvenile prostitution and the pimps that control them and pocket their earnings.

According to one article on worldwide prostitution, "faced with the difficulty of sorting out which women are prostitutes by choice and which are coerced," many officials find it easier to suggest that entering prostitution is implicit with free choice.[36] "The distinction between force and freedom ends in assigning blame to an already victimized woman for 'choosing' to accept prostitution in her circumstances."[37] This is challenged by Susan Hunter, representing the Council for Prostitution Alternatives, a social services agency for helping recovering prostitutes. She likens prostitutes to battered women. "When battered women ... repeatedly go back to the batterer, we do not take this as a legal consent to battering. A woman's acceptance of money in prostitution should not be taken as her agreement to prostitution. She may take the money ... because she has been socialized to believe this is her role in life. Just as battered women's actions now are understood in light of the effects of trauma and battered women's syndrome; prostituted women suffer psychologically in the aftermath of repeated physical and sexual assaults."[38]

CHILD PROSTITUTION

Calls for decriminalizing/legalizing prostitution are also rejected by many because of the substantial number of child prostitutes. It is estimated that there are well over one million teenage prostitutes in the United States, with as many as two-thirds female.[39] Children represent the most frequently recruited members — usually by pimps and organized (or unorganized) crime syndicates — into the sex-for-sale industry. According to sociologists, the average age for entering prostitution is 14.[40] The vast majority of teen prostitutes come from sexually, physically, or psychologically abusive homes, are runaways or throwaways, abuse drugs and alcohol, and are subject to the whims and sexual desires of customers and pimps.[41] They are also the most susceptible to violence, diseases, and exposure to the AIDS virus.[42]

Consequently, no child prostitute (even those entering the profession voluntarily) is in the business as a mature and able-bodied sex worker, cognizant of the risks even in a legitimate prostitution market. Few responsible proponents of decriminalization of prostitution would advocate decriminalizing child prostitution, making it difficult, if not impossible, to regulate and decriminalize effectively all prostitution.

THE DARK SIDE OF LEGAL BROTHELS

In spite of the plus factors associated with regulated legal brothels, opponents of legalizing/decriminalizing prostitution note that illegal prostitution continues to thrive in Nevada at casinos, conventions, and hotels because many prostitutes prefer "to avoid the isolation and control of the legal brothels."[43] Others favor working outside the stifling restriction of brothels; an independent prostitute can make "as much as $250 per one-hour session, reject a customer for any reason without risking management displeasure, and come and go as she pleases."[44]

According to an article on legal brothels, "behind the facade of a regulated industry, brothel prostitutes in Nevada are captive in conditions analogous to slavery."[45] Women are said to work as many as 12 hours a day, "even when ill, menstruating, or pregnant," with no right of refusal.[46] Although brothel prostitutes are routinely tested for sexually transmitted diseases, including HIV, their clients are not. Nor are clients restricted, per se, from having sex with unregulated prostitutes and contracting an STD to be potentially passed on to a brothel prostitute (who, if tested positive for a sexually transmitted disease or HIV, would lose her brothel job and possibly be forced back into street prostitution).

Legal brothels are also interconnected with illegal prostitution — paying finder's fees to procurers and pimps to bring in a steady supply of fresh prostitutes.[47] Critics contend that penalties and enforcement of legal brothel laws must be increased to get greater compliance from brothel owners, prostitutes, and pimps.

SAFE STREETS AND PROPERTY VALUES

Neighborhood groups have formed across the country to battle street prostitution and any possibilities of decriminalization/legalization. Their concerns rest primarily on the fears that prostitution — legal or not — will attract the worst elements of society, increasing crime and public safety, affecting their children's right to play in the neighborhood or walk to school unhindered, and decreasing property values. Researchers have found some merit in these concerns that the sex trade industry has an adverse effect on surrounding communities.[48]

However, it is not yet known if legal prostitution in this country would increase crime and the threat of crime and decrease property values or have the opposite effect — since legal prostitution is currently limited to brothels in a few rural communities in Nevada. Legalized prostitution in other countries has had mixed results (see Chapter 21).

Part V

Female Prostitution in Other Countries

Chapter 21

The Prostitution
of Women Worldwide

Outside of the United States, prostitution is legal in many countries including Australia, Japan, England, Brazil, Germany, and the Netherlands. In other countries it is tolerated and even encouraged in government-sponsored "*packaged sex tours.*" By most experts' estimations, female prostitution has become a worldwide epidemic as part of the global sex trade of flesh. Millions of women are actively involved in prostitution for economic survival, food, shelter, drugs, and even pleasure. However, an increasing number of women are entering prostitution involuntarily through deceit, coercion, kidnapping, or sexual slavery. It is estimated that 30 million women have been sold into prostitution since the mid–1970s.[1] The Human Rights Commission of Pakistan reported in 1991 that 200,000 Bangladeshi women were forced into prostitution that year in Pakistan alone.[2] Others estimate that as many as 500,000 women are smuggled by slave traffickers from developing countries to become prostitutes.[3]

Sociologists generally view this explosion in women's prostitution as "an unfortunate outgrowth of Third World poverty."[4] In her exposé on international prostitution, Alice Leuchtag warned: "*White slavery* and *indentured servitude* are not terms applicable only to a distant and benighted past; they are as applicable today as ever before.... And the poorer the country, the more likely it is that many of its girls and women find themselves trapped in a brothel life."[5]

Female prostitutes predominantly "cater to the sexual demands of military personnel on leave, tourists, businessmen or pedophiles from the U.S., Japan, and Western Europe. The demands of residents in the developed countries are often met by powerless people in less-developed nations."[6] For countless females, the consequences are lives as enslaved prostitutes, drug addicts, rape victims, crime victims, and sexual servants to men with a wide range of perverse and sadistic desires. Women prostitutes worldwide are also at great risk of developing AIDS and other sexually transmitted or intravenous-drug-transmitted diseases. Many believe the problem of prostituted women may already be too widespread and economically woven into many societies to be effectively contained.

Thailand

The international sexual exploitation of women is perhaps most conspicuous (or infamous) in Thailand. There are an estimated 500,000 female prostitutes in Thailand, with 200,000 in Bangkok alone.[7] In what many see as a government-backed prostitution business, Thailand's sex tour industry has become a $4-billion-a-year enterprise. "Sex-tour promoters feed the stereotype that Asian women are submissive and have a strong desire to please men.... A San Diego travel agency organized 'American Fantasy Tours,' which promised easy sex with Thai women who 'live in harmony with nature, fulfilling their mission to satisfy the needs of man.'"[8] In government literature, Thai cities are depicted in "glowing, exotic terms.... It is all part of the promotion of tourism among businessmen from Japan, Germany, Norway, Saudi Arabia, Holland, Australia, and the United States. Foreign johns, who feel safely anonymous away from home, are now among Thailand's leading sources of hard currency."[9]

Thailand's burgeoning sex trade of females is seen as intrinsically linked to two historical events. The first was an agreement in 1967 between the Thai and U.S. governments to provide American soldiers during the Vietnam War with a place to go for rest and "recreation." Soldiers quickly became "notorious for feeding the sex industry."[10] Second, in 1971, the World Bank recommended developing "mass tourism in Thailand as a way for the country to pay on its debts to the bank."[11] These economic initiatives resulted in the multi-billion-dollar-a-year multinational sex tour industry in Thailand, comprising a "network of cozy relations between banks, airlines, tour operators, hotels, and bar and brothel owners and agents, all of whom extract their profits from the bodies of pitifully underpaid village Thai female prostitutes."[12]

The official sanctioning of Thailand's sexploitation of women and girls can be found in the many Thai government officials, politicians, and police who "invest in the trade and grow rich from it."[13] Some officials are alleged to own "chains of brothels."[14] The Thai government's unofficial role as an international pimp is reflected in its dependency on female prostitution for a portion of its annual revenue.[15]

In spite of new U.S. laws to combat sexual exploitation of women abroad by Americans and in spite of a change in U.S. military policies regarding personnel's sexual practices, servicemen continue to exploit Thai prostitutes. For example, following the Gulf War, "boatloads of sailors" came onshore at Thailand's resort town of Pattaya, and "both Americans and Thais explicitly acknowledged that they were there for sex."[16]

Philippines

In the Philippines, like Thailand, the government was encouraged by international banks to promote tourism as the principal means of economic development. Thousands of Filipino women were regarded as a "natural resource" for sexual exploitation. During and after the war in Vietnam, "the American naval bases in the Philippines were notorious for feeding the sex industry, which is one of the reasons many Filipinos campaigned to close them."[17]

Sex tourism and prostitution in the Philippines had become critical to the country's economic survival by the mid–1980s. Activist groups campaigned for the government to eliminate sex tourism as an economic development strategy and, further, not to renew leases on two U.S. military bases. These were seen as responsible not only for a flourishing prostitution market around the bases but also for a growing amount of violence against Filipinos by U.S. servicemen. These efforts (along with, some would say, the eruption of the Mt. Pinatubo volcano) proved successful, and the bases were closed.

Raids on massage parlors, brothels, and bars in Manila's red-light district led to the arrests of hundreds of Filipino prostitutes, who were left without income and were provided no alternative employment or education. In what many feminists saw as sexist, relatively few prostitutes' customers or pimps were arrested. More pressure on the government to stop the sexual exploitation of women and children resulted in a law passed in 1993, in which pimps and clients could be imprisoned or deported.[18]

In spite of these efforts, the prostitution and exploitation of women and girls continues to flourish in the Philippines.

India

India has become one of the largest suppliers and buyers of female prostitutes in the global sex trade market. An estimated 10 million prostitutes live and ply their trade in India.[19] More than 100,000 female prostitutes are in Bombay, described as Asia's "largest sex bazaar."[20] According to human rights organizations, 90 percent of the women are indentured slaves, with perhaps half coming from Nepal.[21]

HIV infection among prostitutes in India has become a major catastrophe. It is estimated that 5 million Indians are HIV-positive.[22] With Bombay as the epicenter for the AIDS virus, some experts fear that as many as 10,000 infected Indian women will die each month by the turn of the century.[23]

Much of India's lucrative sex trade industry is run by organized crime, in cooperation with crooked politicians and police officials who exchange "blanket protection for cash payoffs and donations to campaign war chests. The corruption reaches the top rung of the ruling Congress party in New Delhi."[24]

The act of prostitution is technically legal in India. However, "brothel keeping, living off the earnings of a prostitute, [and] soliciting or seducing for the purposes of prostitution" are all criminal offenses and subject to severe penalties.[25] This has not seemed to deter those who peddle female flesh. The red-light district in Bombay, controlled by organized crime, is flourishing, and some believe it "may be the most perverse three square kilometers on earth."[26]

In his investigation of sexual slavery and political corruption in India, Robert Friedman described the cycle of servitude common for many female prostitutes:

> The girls' sole escape is Hindi movies — mawkish soap operas in which cops and politicians are inevitably shown as shifty villains who get their comeuppance in the final reel.... The movies cost a few rupees, or pennies, but the [prostitutes] never seem to have enough for a ticket. Though on average the girls see six customers a day, who pay between $1.10 and $2 per sex act, the madam gets the money up front. By the time [she] deducts for food, electricity and rent, as well as payment — with interest — on her purchase price, there is almost nothing left. So to pay for movies, clothes, makeup and extra food to supplement a bland diet of rice and dal, the girls have to borrow from moneylenders at an interest rate of up to 500 percent. They are perpetually in hock.[27]

Japan

As in a number of European and Asian countries, prostitution is not a crime in Japan (though pimping or profiting from prostitution is). Scores of women and schoolgirls are selling sex in cities such as Tokyo for money and the material items it buys.[28] Other females are being forced to become prostitutes by Yakuza-organized criminals. In the 1960s and 1970s, packaged sex tours took Japanese men to South Korea, Taiwan, Thailand, and the Philippines in search of prostitutes. In the 1980s, Japan's own sex tour industry began to flourish as Filipino and Thai prostitutes migrated, were kidnapped, or smuggled into the country. It is estimated that 70,000 Thai "hostesses" currently work as "indentured sex slaves" in bars usually controlled by the Yakuza.[29] The women "are sold by Thai brokers for an average of $14,000 each and resold to the clubs by Japanese brokers for about $30,000 — a sum they are obliged to work off, but rarely can."[30]

The Thai embassy in Tokyo repatriates approximately 250 of the women each month. However, Japanese authorities have been largely apathetic to the plight of the female prostitute slaves. There have been recorded instances of police, particularly in rural areas, returning escaped women to their Yakuza captors.[31] The recent murders of three madams, or *mama-sans*, by prostitutes seeking to escape drew greater attention to the worldwide problem of sexual slavery.[32]

Russia

With the breakup of the Soviet Union, "a new population of impoverished girls and women has been created and is grist for the mill of international organized prostitution."[33] Deregulation and privatization in Russia and other countries from the former Soviet bloc, along with rising inequality among social classes, have resulted in severe social and economic crises, including organized crime, poverty, and prostitution.[34] In Russia, more than 75 percent of the unemployed are women.[35] Many are well educated — lawyers, doctors, and teachers. Some are married with children. A large percentage have turned to prostitution as a means of survival, operating as streetwalkers in Moscow and other cities and controlled by the Russian Mafia and pimps. Other Russian women have become call girls as capitalism and a depressed economy clash, creating high-class prostitution in the former Soviet Union.

Many females from Russia and eastern Europe have become sexual pawns in the slave trade, fleeing to "fleshpots of the West."[36] Many are trained to become prostitutes for foreign clients. Thousands of women and girls have applied to places such as Aphrodite, Russia's "first licensed school of striptease," where a "tryout" means stripping down to their underwear before male judges and photographers.[37] The "graduates" are sent to such countries as Singapore, Germany, and Sweden, where they can earn up to $120 a night for up to a six-month tour of duty, with 15 percent of their earnings going to the school's director. Many of the women will remain abroad, working as prostitutes, confirming that such schools are merely fronts for "international organized prostitution."[38] Other Russian women are lured to foreign countries under the guise of high-paying jobs or perhaps marriage to a wealthy foreigner. Instead, they often find involuntary prostitution through coercion, language barriers, or economic necessity.

In the *Time* article "The Skin Trade," Margot Hornblower describes the sexploitation of many Russian prostitutes abroad: "In the puritanical Middle East, charter flights full of Russian women disembark weekly at Dubai's airport, ply their trade on 14-day visas and head home.... Scores of ads for 'entertainment services,' many boasting 'hot new Russians' riddle the Israeli papers.... In Tokyo, Russian girls are the latest addition to the menu in fancy 'hostess' bars.... Major Chinese cities now offer blond, blue-eyed Russian 'hostesses.'"[39]

Cuba

Once Cuba was a haven for a prostitution business that was "one of the mainstays of the Mafia-controlled gambling and tourist industry."[40] After the 1959 Cuban revolution, Fidel Castro abolished organized prostitution and shut down brothels in Havana, providing jobs and education for ex-prostitutes. In a 1992 speech, Castro declared that those who believe "the Cuban people will consent to see their country reduced once more to a U.S. satellite, a land of massive unemployment, poverty ... and prostitution ... are seriously deluded."[41]

However, Cuba — virtually isolated from the world community since the collapse of the former U.S.S.R.— is experiencing a new wave of prostitution, borne largely out of the severe economic and social hardships the country is facing. The prostitutes, called *jineteras*, are typically "middle class women — former teachers, former translators, women with university educations, who work the weekends and go back to their middle class neighborhoods in the morning. They are not prostitutes, they say, because they would not be doing this if the money earned at their day jobs could buy anything."[42]

In Cuba today, professionals stand to make far less than comparable professional people in the United States. The Cuban state pays its people in pesos, whereas stores accept only U.S. currency. A doctor working in Cuba earns the equivalent of about $3 a month, compared with a prostitute who can earn $50 in one night of work.[43] This imbalance has compelled many women, perhaps tens of thousands, to prostitute themselves to supplement other income. They rationalize that it is, "for the most part, a matter of eating or not eating."[44]

Many of these women ply their trade in posh hotels and swinging discos in Havana, "Castro's decaying capital." In the article "Havana at Midnight," Lynn Darling observed:

> They spill into the lobby, languid girls with golden ringlets, creamy mulattos with spindly arms and long legs, and big-breasted, big-assed black girls, their heads thrown back as if a harsh hand held them at the napes of their necks. The women wear neon-orange biking pants and black spike heels and ruffled off-the-shoulder shirts. They wear Daisy Mae-style checked shirts and tight spandex pants laddered with cutouts all the way up the sides, from ankle to waist. They wear shirred fifties-style conga dresses and black-and-white striped anything. Their hair is pulled back or swept up or cascading over one eye or erupting in frizzy fountains and dyed all manners of blond.[45]

Along with the *jineteras*, Cuba is also seeing a rise in streetwalkers, drug-addicted prostitutes, and child prostitutes. The men they service come from Mexico, Germany, Spain, the United States, Italy, and Canada, "though the women hate the Mexicans for their drunkenness and cheapness and laugh at the Canadians for their inhibitions."[46] Many johns come to Cuba on business. Others arrive as tourists for the "latest stop on the international sex tour."[47]

No one knows for certain what will happen once the Castro regime has ended. In the interim, prostitution in Cuba has proven, for an increasing number of Cuban women, to be a viable alternative to impoverishment.

The Netherlands

The Netherlands, particularly Amsterdam, is believed by some to be the model for legalized prostitution. In fact, the business of prostitution is not legal in Holland per se but is condoned in "toleration zones" in confined areas throughout the country. It is illegal to sell sex outside such zones or to pander prostitutes. An estimated 20,000 full-time prostitutes ply their trade in Holland.[48] Experts believe this number would be at least doubled if part-time prostitutes were included.

According to an article on prostitution in the Netherlands, Amsterdam's red-light district "with its overt and provocative window prostitution is one of the major tourist attractions of the Dutch capital."[49] The business of women's prostitution is seen as an "integrated and accepted" part of Amsterdam and other cities in Holland.

Less accepted but still a significant part of Holland's prostitution is the street-walking prostitute, along with "kerb-crawling cars" and the frequent drug use and dealing associated with the street profession.[50] Sex clubs or brothels — inexpensive and superexpensive — can also be found in the cities or in the countryside.

Social controls over prostitution in the Netherlands are seen as being weakened by the surge in prostitution since the 1970s, which involved drug addicts who turned to the profession to support habits. Further eroding such controls is the influx of foreign female prostitutes — many trafficked in by international criminals or immigrating on their own from Third World countries for a chance at a better life. Language and cultural barriers, along with illegal status, often force many of these women into sexual slavery, indentured servitude, and cheap prostitution.

The incidence of HIV and AIDS among prostitutes in Holland is relatively low. A 1985 testing of 84 Dutch prostitute non–drug users found that none tested HIV-seropositive.[51] The National Committee on AIDS Control has concluded that prostitution does not pose a significant threat in the spread of AIDS.[52] Nevertheless, *safe* sex was encouraged for prostitutes and nonprostitutes alike (see also Chapter 23).

Germany

In Germany, it is not unlawful to be a prostitute but it is illegal to live off a prostitute's earnings as a pimp or brothel owner. Legal prostitutes are required to have regular examinations for sexually transmitted diseases, including for HIV infection. Those given health clearance are allowed to work in "tolerated districts" for prostitution work. Communities that have less than 50,000 inhabitants are not required to accept legal prostitution; hence in some cities, prostitution may be officially prohibited.[53]

Most prostitutes in Germany pay income taxes, though their profession is not officially recognized as such. Thus prostitutes cannot pay directly for health insurance or a pension plan. It is estimated that there are 200,000 female prostitutes in Germany.[54] One-fourth of these women immigrated from the former Soviet bloc, often becoming sexual prisoners of white slavery. Many prostitutes working in German brothels are subjected to intimidation and violence by pimps and flesh-traders. Recently in Bautzen, Germany, for example, prostituted women "were beaten with bats and administered electric shocks."[55]

Drug abuse and alcohol abuse are high among German prostitutes. A study of Frankfurt prostitutes concluded that more than 56 percent of the women had been regular drinkers and irregular drug users by the age of 14.[56] The study found that the average age for entry into prostitution was 20. Two-thirds of the prostitutes stated that selling sexual favors was done primarily to support drug habits.

United Kingdom

Prostitution is controlled in the United Kingdom through a series of laws such as the 1751 Disorderly Houses Act, the 1956 Sexual Offenses Act, and the Public Order Act 1986, whose purposes are to "prevent serious nuisance to the public caused when prostitutes ply their trade in the streets; to discourage women from becoming prostitutes; and to penalize pimps, brothel-keepers and others who seek to encourage, control or exploit the prostitution of others' bodies for financial gain."[57] As in many European countries, a woman is not breaking the law by merely being a prostitute in the United Kingdom, but the laws are such that the government, in effect, prohibits all forms of prostitution.

The U.K. prostitution laws are aimed particularly at streetwalking prostitutes. The term *common prostitute* first appeared in British laws in the Metropolitan Police Act, which pejoratively related prostitution with *night-walkers*.[58] Today the term still appears in legislation, the belittling implication being that prostitutes are night-walkers or *kerb-crawlers* or vice versa. Streetwalkers in England and Wales are typically prosecuted under the 1959 Street Offenses Act, which states, "It shall be an offense for a common prostitute to loiter or solicit in a street or public place for the purposes of prostitution."[59] In Scotland, female and male prostitutes guilty of solicitation are governed by the 1982 Civic Government Act.[60]

Like the streetwalker in the United States, the streetwalker in Britain is considered the lowest form of prostitute and the most likely to be subject to arrest, violence, jailing, and discrimination by police and the public alike. Escort service prostitutes are regarded as the crème de la crème of the U.K. sex trade industry, catering to wealthy customers amid first-class hotels. "Some agencies organize women to work in the hotels of a particular city where a business conference is held."[61]

Though actual figures are scarce, it has been estimated that at least 2 million women are selling (or have sold at some point in their lives) sexual favors in Britain.[62] The bulk of these are brothel prostitutes — working in massage parlors, saunas, or private health clubs "in practically every reasonable-sized town and city across the country, whether in the guise of a private flat or house, or run on more commercial and professional lines."[63] Indoor prostitution is believed to be thriving in many British cities. In Bristol, for example, police estimate that there are over 40 massage parlors with an average "of five staff per business, giving a total of around 200 'parlor girls' in the city."[64]

A strong relationship exists between U.K. prostitutes and substance abuse, which drives many women into the sex business.[65] IV-drug-using prostitutes are particularly prominent in Scotland in such cities as Glasgow. According to researchers, 70 percent of the city's streetwalkers are IV drug addicts, injecting heroin, Temazepam, and Tengesic.[66] These prostitutes face an increased risk for HIV infection. In Edinburgh, which has the highest rate of HIV-seropositive IV drug addicts of all cities in Britain, a significant number of those addicts testing HIV-positive have been identified as prostitutes.[67]

France

Prostitution is a booming business in France, as in other European countries. An estimated 30,000 full-time prostitutes operate in France's sex-for-sale industry, with 95 percent involved with pimps.[68] Another 60,000 women are part-time prostitutes.[69] Some believe the actual figures are much higher.

The French laws against prostitution focus primarily on those who seek to earn a living off prostitutes and on public-order offenses related to prostitution. Penalties are generally lenient for prostitutes and more significant for pimps and procurers who, if convicted, can receive a stiff fine and up to ten years' imprisonment.[70]

Prostitutes in France are subject to taxation on their earnings and are also obligated to make annual tax declarations. The income generated from selling sex can be significant for the French government as well as for prostitutes. In Paris, a streetwalker can make as much as £3,800 a month, whereas a high-class call girl may earn up to £20,000 a month.[71]

Drug abuse, the risk of contracting AIDS, customer violence, and other characteristics of the trade are typically present among prostitutes in France.

Australia

Female prostitution has a long history "Down Under," often in conjunction with organized crime, alcohol, drugs, and demand. Public awareness of the Australian illicit sex trade grew considerably during the late 1960s and the Vietnam War, when Australia, like Thailand and the Philippines, became a place for rest, relaxation, and sex for American troops on leave.[72] The visibility of prostitution further heightened with the repeal of solicitation laws in the late 1970s.[73]

Legalized brothels have existed in Australia since the mid–1980s.[74] Both female prostitution and male prostitution are legal in some Australian states, with the minimum age for prostitutes to ply their trade legally set at 18. Local authorities tightly regulate brothel prostitution, applying "character tests" to brothel owners and managers and maintaining regular medical examinations of prostitutes, as well as monitoring brothels. Drug use by prostitutes is strictly prohibited. In New South Wales, over 60 percent of the prostitution business takes place in suburban brothels.[75]

Unregulated escort service agencies and massage parlors are also thriving enterprises in Australia. These are largely fronts for prostitution and, in that sense, are illegal yet tolerated. Streetwalking prostitution is also against the law but can be found in most major cities such as Sydney and Melbourne. A series of laws control Australian prostitution outside of and within red-light districts, "containment" zones, and legal brothels, including the Disorderly Houses Act 1943, the Crimes Act 1900, and the Summary Offenses Act 1988.[76] Where brothels are illegal, there are laws against owning or managing a brothel, working as a sitter or receptionist at a brothel or earning income from prostitution by any other means while not being a prostitute.

Studies have found that a relatively high rate of IV and non–IV drug use exists among female prostitutes in Australia. Almost 25 percent of the prostitutes surveyed at the Sydney Sexually Transmissible Disease (STD) Centre were IV drug users within the last five years, with 11 percent current IV drug addicts.[77] Other research showed an overdependency on non–IV drugs by many prostitutes for reasons that included reducing stress, relaxing, and coping with the pressures and demands of the profession.[78]

Condom use by brothel prostitutes in Australia increased considerably following an AIDS public-awareness campaign in 1987. A survey of brothel prostitutes in 1988 found that nearly 88 percent reported using condoms with customers.[79] Thirty-three percent of the women said they used condoms for all heterosexual relations they were involved in. However, Australian brothels employing large numbers of Thai prostitutes with a largely Asian clientele have been found to discourage the use of condoms,[80] resulting in a higher incidence of sexually transmitted diseases than for English-speaking female prostitutes.[81]

Although researchers note the potential for the spread of HIV by prostitutes, there have been no reported cases of AIDS in female prostitutes in Australia as of this writing (although some women who had worked as prostitutes tested HIV-seropositive).[82]

Women's Prostitution in Other Countries

The business of sexually exploiting women is flourishing in many other countries. Organized prostitution, sex tourism, and white slavery can be found in such countries as South Korea, Cambodia, Myanmar, Canada, Brazil, China, and South Vietnam. In Ho Chi Minh City, it has recently been reported that the number of prostitutes has increased from 10,000 to 50,000.[83] "Morocco has become a Mecca for Saudi sex tourists.... In Italy, Nigerian streetwalkers are flooding into Bologna, while in Belgium, the neon-bright windows of Antwerp's red-light district are filled with Ghanaians in lacy underwear. Around Miami, massage parlors owned by Cuban immigrants import prostitutes from Colombia, Nicaragua and Canada."[84]

This globalization of the sex trade industry has alarming implications for the women coerced, cajoled, or financially enticed into entering prostitution, as well as for the spread of the AIDS epidemic.

Chapter 22

Child Prostitution and Sexploitation Internationally

The proliferation of the sex trade industry globally has resulted in an increase in the prostitution and sexual exploitation of children. Millions of children — mostly girls, runaways, and homeless youth — are being targeted by flesh traders, pimps, gangs, organized crime syndicates, and promoters of tourism worldwide for a lucrative sex tourism business. "Many have been coerced into sexual servitude. Some, abducted by con men, are raped and psychologically pummeled into submission.... Their pimps lurk in cars in the shadows, calculating the night's take. But not all pimps are gangsters. Often it is the father who sits in the backup car or mother who negotiates the deal for her daughter."[1]

The growth of international prostitution not only is robbing its victims of innocence and any semblance of a normal life during or after prostitution but also is putting them at greater risk for exposure to crime, criminals, unfamiliar foreign countries and languages, and health problems including the AIDS virus. Although laws against prostitution vary considerably from country to country, most prohibit prostituting children, as well as profiting from it. However, the laws are differentially enforced. In some countries — or towns, cities, or districts within — enforcement is nonexistent. The result is countless children being sold or forced into the sex-for-sale trade with little or no law enforcement intervention or chance for escape.

The Extent of Child Prostitution Worldwide

Reliable statistics on the number of girl and boy prostitutes across the globe are hard, if not impossible, to come by. Varying definitions of child prostitution, forms of measurement, and government policies from country to country, along with the often unknown quantity of children working in brothels, massage parlors, and private residences, greatly hamper uncovering the extent of this branch of child sexploitation. A number of studies suggest that the magnitude of the problem of child prostitution worldwide is enormous.

UNICEF estimated that in Asia alone there are over one million minors enslaved as prostitutes.[2] According to sources such as End Child Prostitution in Asian Tourism (ECPAT), there are an estimated 800,000 child prostitutes in Thailand, 400,000 in India, and 60,000 in the Philippines.[3] Other estimates of global juvenile prostitution include up to 500,000 child prostitutes in Brazil[4] and 200,000 teenage prostitutes in Canada.[5] The chamber of commerce recently reported that the number of child prostitutes under age 14 in Bogota, Colombia, has quintupled in seven years.[6] In Moscow, over 1,000 youths are estimated to be in the sex-for-sale business.[7] In most cases, the actual number of child prostitutes tends to far exceed the estimates, indicating the significance of the problem.

The nature of child involvement in prostitution varies from one country to another. In Africa and Latin America, juvenile street prostitutes tend to ply their trade independently, whereas in Thailand and the Philippines, countries with strong sex tourism industries, child prostitutes are often recruited and enslaved to work in child brothels.[8] The worldwide growth of child prostitution is rapidly "emerging as a crucial issue for human rights and women's groups and has recently led to a debate in the European Parliament in Strasbourg, France."[9] Most experts agree that only strengthened cooperation between countries in the trafficking and exploitation of children and enactment of international laws against such practices can hope to stem the flow.

Canada

In Canada, tens of thousands of teenage girls are being recruited into street prostitution, in spite of laws against such action and in spite of nationwide police crackdowns on pimps and procurers.[10] According to Canadian authorities, the center of Canada's teenage prostitution trade is the Halifax area community of North Preston, where as many as 50 pimps actively pursue and compel girls into selling their bodies.[11] Decades of racial inequality for blacks, "bad schools and ostracism by the white community," spawned the pimping industry.[12] Today, in nearly every major Canadian city, "men from North Preston and three black communities adjacent to it own the rights to most corners on the hookers' strolls — and own the mostly white teenage girls working them."[13] Many of the pimps are related to or interrelated in Canada's child prostitution subculture.

An exposé on teenage prostitution and pimps in Canada noted:

No one knows how many teenage girls have been coerced into a life of prostitution by men from the Halifax area ... [or] how many thousands of Nova Scotia girls have been pimped throughout Canada and as far away as New York, Los Angeles and even, in one case, Naples, Italy.... Dozens of pimps have been jailed; scores of young women have given evidence of torture and confinement in cities across the country.... No one knows how many girls have died at the hands of pimps. Until recently, no one seemed to care.[14]

The vast majority of Canadian girl prostitutes are runaways from homes or foster homes.[15] A study of Winnipeg runaways found that 67 percent had run away from home at least five times.[16] Most had been abused sexually or physically.

Street life for most Canadian teen prostitutes means not only prostitution for pimps, food, and shelter, but also substance abuse (many were abusing drugs before entering the sex trade). A Toronto study of adolescent prostitutes found that 89 percent abuse alcohol and/or drugs.[17]

In an article on pimping in Canada, writer Deborah Jones depicts the sexual bondage of girl prostitutes and their drug-abusing pimps: "Through the windows comes a faint sound of traffic on the nearby highway. There, an occasional big luxury model with tinted windows goes by, heading for Montreal, Toronto, Calgary and Vancouver. Behind the smoked glass of some of these cars, men snort cocaine and fondle teenage girls. The girls are headed for a life of prostitution, torture and sometimes, death."[18]

Authorities believe that even with the arrest and incarceration of many pimps, many have already served their time, are due soon to be released, or will quickly be replaced by others. This led Jones to contend bleakly, "Canada's homegrown teen-pimping industry is still very much alive."[19] Alas, so too, is its prostitution of teenage girls.

Brazil

In Brazil, prostitution is not outlawed. However, only recently has the country become a mecca for the international child sex trade industry. Estimates of the number of children working as prostitutes in Brazil range from a 1993 government commission estimate of 500,000 to as many as 10 million.[20] Many believe the numbers will rise, fueled by tougher child prostitution laws in Asia against child sex tourism.

Many Brazilian child prostitutes are forced into the sex trade, often due to impoverishment and lack of education. Investigators in Rio "tell of girls as young as 9 being rented by destitute parents to neighborhood men. Poverty-stricken northeastern cities such as Recife are drawing organized sex tours from Europe. Everywhere in Brazil, as in Asia, there are reports of children being kidnapped and forced into prostitution or sold to pimps by their parents."[21]

It is estimated that 25,000 girls from impoverished families in Brazil, some as young as 9, have been forced into prostitution in remote Amazon gold mining camps.[22] "*Recruiters*," promising high earning jobs, fly in children and hand them to brothel owners. The girls become indentured sex slaves who must work to pay off plane fare, food, and shelter expenses. Attempts to escape often result in torture and/or death.[23]

Thousands, perhaps millions, of other Brazilian girls and boys (many who are runaways or homeless) independently sell their bodies to men, enticed by money, the "access to luxuries and their desire to escape a life that offers few opportunities."[24]

Because it is not illegal to be a prostitute in Brazil, authorities are nearly powerless to combat child prostitution. Customers can be charged with rape, but only if the prostitute is younger than 14, which is often difficult to prove with street children who have no families to identify them. Pimps who pander girls under 18 can be charged with exploiting minors. However, with police corruption, arrests and incarcerations are rare.

India

Child prostitution and sexual slavery are rampant in India. At least 400,000 underage prostitutes are believed to be actively involved in the country's sex bazaar.[25] Ninety percent of these prostitutes are indentured sex slaves.[26] Of Bombay's estimated 100,000 female prostitutes, 20 percent are under 18 years of age.[27] Girl prostitutes as young as 9 "can fetch up to 60,000 rupees, or $2,000, at auctions where Arabs from the Persian Gulf bid against Indian men who believe sleeping with a virgin cures gonorrhea and syphilis."[28]

Prostitution is legal in India; however, child prostitution and trafficking of females are strictly prohibited. Police and political corruption, along with a strong organized crime presence, make circumventing the law relatively easy for those involved in India's thriving juvenile flesh trade.

Indian girl prostitutes are at great risk to contract AIDS. According to Human Rights Watch, "India's red-light districts are the primary vector of its [AIDS] spread into the general population."[29] Bombay is described as the epicenter for India's AIDS epidemic, and young female prostitutes are caught in the throes of HIV infection.[30]

The sad conditions that girl prostitutes are forced to endure in India's sex slave industry are described in the following investigative report: "Dozens of sari-clad prostitutes sat on wooden benches that overlooked a half-moon-shaped interior courtyard. There were twenty-five metal cubicles, each with a pallet. The cubicles, where the girls perform their tricks and otherwise live, were no more than 3 feet by 6. In one of them, decorated with a montage of Hindu elephant gods and movie stars, a prostitute dozed while a toddler scooted across the floor sucking on a used condom."[31]

Thailand

There are nearly one million child prostitutes in Thailand.[32] Notorious for its international sex tourism industry and indentured sexual servitude, Thailand is one of the world's leading traffickers and sexual exploiters of girl prostitutes. Between 6.2 percent and 8.7 percent of the country's female population are estimated to be, or to have been, involved in prostitution.[33]

The relatively high earnings of Thai girl prostitutes can be significant not only for the Thailand economy but also for the families of the prostitutes. In a study of Thailand girl sex workers, the income of prostitutes was estimated to be 25 times "that attainable in other occupations. Entire families in the countryside are supported on the earnings of one daughter in Bangkok, and entire rural villages are made up of such families."[34] Many of these young female prostitutes are, in fact, indentured sex slaves, "typically recruited from rural families; the sum given to the parents representing several months' advance salary, with the rest to be remitted after a ten-month or one-year term.... This form of contract binds the sex worker to her job, the sense of family obligation overwhelming negative feelings about the work itself."[35]

The relationship between prostitution and girls in Thailand reflects youth, virginity, and the AIDS epidemic. "In the brothels serving local men, where there's a premium on extreme youth and virginity, a girl who has not yet menstruated brings a price that is more than sixty times the usual. Deflowering a virgin is said to increase virility, and fresh prepubescent crops are brought into the city for good luck at the Chinese new year. Very young girls, even if no longer virgins, are also believed likelier to be free of disease."[36] The evidence suggests otherwise, particularly with respect to HIV infection. It is estimated that 50 percent of the girl prostitutes in Thailand are HIV-positive.[37]

A typical example of a Thai girl sex slave prostitute in Thailand's prepubescent sex trade is shown in the following account: "Armine Sae Li, 14 ... was spirited away from northern Chiang Rai province at age 12 when child traffickers convinced her parents they would give her a good job in a beach resort restaurant. When she reached Phuket, a center for sex tourism, she was forced into prostitution in conditions of virtual slavery until she was released last December by Thai police. But they arrived too late; Armine has tested HIV positive and will die of AIDS."[38]

Japan

Teen prostitution is thriving in Japan, as in other Asian countries. However, sociologists believe that unlike places such as Thailand and India, where child prostitution is a product of poverty or coercion, in Japan the proliferation is a reflection of materialism. Being a prostitute is not against the law in

Japan. Teenage girl prostitution is especially rampant in Tokyo, where it is legal for adults to engage in sexual relations with juveniles over 12 "and where prostitution isn't punishable unless arranged by a pimp."[39]

Caught up in a materialistic world that encourages sex for pay, many Japanese girls have entered the business of their own volition. They refer to their clients as *papasan* and regard the prostitution as merely *enjo kosai*, or "financially supported dating." It is estimated that 8 percent of Japanese schoolgirls are in the sex-for-sale business; one-third of the girls attending schools not geared toward college are working as prostitutes.[40] "It seems that prostitution is the fashion for kids," observed a Tokyo police official. "Kids want brand-name clothes like *Chanel*; their friends have them, and their parents don't give them the money."[41] Prostitution thereby becomes a source of revenue.

Japanese authorities blame the rise in adolescent female prostitution on lax child prostitution laws, "permissive attitudes and the cheap cellular phones that make it easy for girls to arrange dates away from parents."[42] Where laws are violated against indecent activities with minors — with penalties of up to two years in prison and a $10,000 fine — the punishment is generally less severe. Tokyo's legislature is considering laws that would outlaw sex with juveniles; but opponents of tougher child sex laws — such as the Communist Party, teachers' unions, and mothers' groups — are challenging such moves as giving the police too much power or as shaming girls charged as prostitutes.[43]

At this time, AIDS does not appear to be a factor in the prostitution of Japanese girls. Reported cases of HIV infection are low in Japan; only 19 HIV-positive cases were reported among teenagers from 1994 to 1995.[44] Officials believe that the figures may be misleading due to unreported cases and the small number of juveniles being tested.

Other Countries and Child Prostitution

The globalization of girl and boy prostitution can be seen in countries throughout the world. In most instances, child prostitutes are bound by slavery, indentured servitude, or poverty. Other child prostitutes are runaways, throwaways, or substance abusers.

Examples of international sexploitation abound. Thousands of British girl prostitutes work the streets of London, Bradford, and other cities to please pimps, to get drugs, and to earn "money to live."[45] Russian girls ply their trade on the streets of Moscow and in the clubs in Tokyo or China, where they work as "hostesses."[46] In Prague, girl prostitutes are beaten or tortured into submission.[47] Cases of girls being sold into sexual slavery and brought to the United Arab Emirates and Oman have been reported;[48] in Bangladesh, 5,000 girls, ages ten and up, are estimated to work as prostitutes in one section of Dacca alone.[49]

Why Are Children Being Increasingly Sexually Exploited?

A number of reasons, often in conjunction, account for the rise in the sexual exploitation of children worldwide as prostitutes, sex slaves, and indentured sex servants. In general, these reasons include a "pernicious combination of Third World poverty, First World economic development policies, laws that permit international trafficking and indentured servitude, and worldwide patriarchal cultural norms that encourage male sexual prerogatives."[50] More specifically, the increase in child prostitution is primarily in response to the following conditions or circumstances: (1) the spread of HIV and AIDS, (2) a burgeoning sex tourism industry catering to pedophiles, procurers, pimps, and organized criminals; (3) the growth of the sex trade market, (4) impoverishment in underdeveloped countries, (5) the collapse of the Iron Curtain, and (6) drug use.

THE THREAT OF AIDS

The AIDS scare may be the biggest reason behind the increased demand for children for purposes of prostitution and sexual servitude. Because of the false sense of security that minors are less likely to be infected with HIV, girls as young as eight years old are being marketed to clients as "virgins, free of AIDS.... So there is a high price on virginity."[51] Consequently, customers "are willing to pay far more for very young girls or boys who are described as virgins or whose youth suggests innocence."[52]

Experts believe, however, that juvenile prostitutes pose a greater risk for customers and, conversely, are at a higher risk for becoming exposed to AIDS infection. The director of the World Health Organization's Collaborating Center for Sexually Transmitted Disease stated: "Both boys and girls are more vulnerable to infection because they are more prone to lesions and injuries in sexual intercourse. Imagine intercourse occurring millions of times under these conditions.... They are playing Russian roulette with their lives."[53]

SEX TOURISM

Sex tourism is seen by many countries as a way to generate increased revenue at the expense of native women and children. The success of packaged sex tours in countries such as Thailand — where young females are promoted to foreign businessmen as sexually ripe for the taking — has spawned similar sex tourism in other countries, including the Philippines, China, Vietnam, Laos, Cambodia, Brazil, and the Dominican Republic. This has provided a lucrative worldwide market for flesh peddlers of children, indentured child sex slaves, and child prostitutes. Government-sponsored or -tolerated sex tourism tied into economic policies makes it difficult for many countries to reject this form of international organized child prostitution.

THE SEX INDUSTRY

The ever broadening and increasingly profitable sex industry itself is believed by many to be the catalyst for the prostitution and exploitation of girls and boys. Increased demands for pornography, child pornography, peep shows, strip clubs, lap dancing, and other dimensions of the sex business have "normalized the open buying and selling of sex and have eroded taboos against sexual exploitation of children."[54] Noted a United Nations official: "We are losing all boundaries. More and more children are being sacrificed to the sex industry."[55]

THIRD WORLD POVERTY

Third World poverty has forced many women and children into prostitution as a means of economic survival. "Impoverished families no longer able to get by on subsistence farming turn to selling their female children to procurers. Lack of educational or job opportunities contributes to families' decisions to put their daughters on the market."[56] Many families are conned into giving children away. Often it is the promise of a well-paying job that will allow them to help support the family. Once a girl leaves home, she is often never seen or heard from again by relatives. Girls are quickly turned into child prostitutes and sex slaves, with little recourse. "Those who do not speak the language of the city or country where they wind up are particularly vulnerable and unable to extricate themselves from their situations."[57]

THE DISINTEGRATION OF COMMUNISM

With the collapse of the Soviet Union, a massive population of impoverished women and girls from eastern Europe emerged to be exploited sexually by slave traders, pimps, and tour promoters in other countries eager for new, vulnerable recruits into the international world of prostitution. In Russia alone, 75 percent of the unemployed are female.[58] "Many Russian and East European women and girls have experienced a great step backwards," read one article.[59] This has resulted in a huge exodus of "poverty-stricken East European [females], desperate to sell themselves for what rarely turns out to be the good life."[60]

According to a Prague vice squad detective: "The naiveté is unbelievable. The vision of earning hard currency blurs the girls' senses."[61] The many ways in which East Bloc girls are duped into selling sex at home and abroad, only to be forced into brothels or street prostitution, include such ruses as promised jobs as dancers or waitresses, invitations to complete schooling, and cons from international traffickers pretending to be marriage brokers. With the severely depressed economy of Russia and other eastern European countries, this sad cycle of economic distress and girl prostitution shows no sign of letting up.

DRUGS

The increase in drug use and abuse among children in undeveloped and affluent countries is also seen as being strongly related to the growth in juvenile prostitution worldwide.[62] As more girls and boys become addicted to drugs — often supplied by pimps, brothel owners or managers, procurers, sex merchants, and relatives — more are turning to or remaining in prostitution to support habits. Others are sexually enslaved into prostituting themselves in order to feed addictions and maintain loyalty to pimps, gangs, and flesh traders. The correlation between drugs and child prostitution has been well documented and is usually linked as well to child pornography and other dimensions of the sex trade industry.[63]

Chapter 23

AIDS and Female
Prostitution Globally

The globalization of female prostitution in its many forms — including streetwalkers, indentured sex slaves, and child prostitutes — has had a significant impact on the transmission of the AIDS virus. Though some studies have indicated that prostitutes are not spreading HIV infection at a greater rate than is the general public, the strong correlation between prostitution and HIV or AIDS exposure is well documented.[1] Most authorities on AIDS agree that the high-risk activities characteristically associated with female prostitution (in combination or separately) — activities such as multiple sex partners, multiple sexual contacts, intravenous drug use, substance abuse, and unsafe sex practices — put women and girls worldwide directly in the path of AIDS and its deadly consequences. When this is combined with an increasing international market for female and child prostitutes by men of all persuasions, who may be drug users or IV drug addicts, bisexual or active with multiple sex partners, HIV or AIDS infected, and uneducated in or unwilling to practice safe sex, it becomes clear that the implications for female prostitutes (as well as other women who may be sexually active with the same men) are alarming.

Nevertheless, there is still a paucity of conclusive evidence on the role that prostitution and prostitutes play in the transmission of HIV. Until more such studies are conducted, we can only rely on available data and common sense in recognizing the seriousness of the global link between AIDS and female prostitution.

What follows is the available research on HIV/AIDS and its adverse relationship with women and girl prostitutes around the world.

India

With its estimated 10 million prostitutes, India has been described as being "in the throes of an AIDS pandemic, and Bombay is the epicenter."[2] An estimated 5 million people in India are HIV infected, with predictions that as many as 20 million Indians will be HIV-positive by the year 2000.[3] Of these, it is believed that as many as 10,000 a month will die from AIDS, pulling "the country into a black hole of despair unlike anything seen in this century."[4]

The World Health Organization reported that one-third of Bombay's prostitutes tested HIV-positive;[5] Human Rights Watch estimated that more than half of the female prostitutes in Bombay are infected with the AIDS virus, making Indian prostitutes "one of the highest risk groups in the world."[6]

Whether or not the worst-case scenario will occur by the twenty-first century is debatable. However, the current mixture of sexual slavery, young female prostitutes, corruption, and neglect makes it a possibility that cannot be ignored.

Thailand

Since 1987, HIV infection has reached epidemic proportions among prostitutes in Thailand.[7] The Public Health Ministry reported that between 200,000 and 400,000 Thais are currently infected with the AIDS virus.[8] The Thai Red Cross estimated that one-third of all deaths in Thailand by the year 2000 may be attributed to AIDS.[9]

Prostitutes are at the "epicenter of the epidemic" of HIV infection in Thailand. In brothels, as many as four out of five prostitutes are carriers of the HIV virus.[10] It is estimated that 50 percent of all child prostitutes in the country are HIV-positive.[11] As in India and other Asian countries, the potent mix of the illicit sex trade, drugs, corruption, and organized crime in Thailand is fueling the adverse relationship between female prostitution and AIDS.

In a study of risk factors associated with HIV infection of female prostitutes in Khon Kaen in northeastern Thailand, the researchers found the risk for infection to be most significant when four variables were present: (1) previously working in an area with a high prevalence of HIV, (2) working in Khon Kaen for less than a month, (3) charging a low price for sexual favors, and (4) using injectable contraceptives.[12]

Vietnam

The rate of HIV infection in Vietnam has increased dramatically since 1990, when a single case of an infected person was known, to 1993, when 1,000 new cases were reported.[13] Estimates are that 570,000 of Vietnam's 72 million population could be infected with the AIDS virus by 1998.[14] Vietnamese prostitutes are believed to be the primary carriers of HIV and its spread, due to unsafe sex with customers and the low status of Asian women in general.[15]

Various U.S. agencies have joined the fight to halt the spread of AIDS in Vietnam. One Washington nonprofit organization, DKT International, deals with AIDS prevention and in 1994 distributed more than one million condoms in Vietnam.[16]

China

In China, the official number of people infected with the AIDS virus nearly doubled in 1995. Over 1,500 cases were reported, bringing the total to more than 3,300.[17] Public health officials believe the actual number of HIV-infected Chinese to be as high as 90,000 of the country's 1.2 billion population.[18] Prostitutes are seen as major carriers in the spread of the virus, though officially the government regards AIDS as a "disease carried by foreigners and the people they fraternize with."[19]

Brazil

Brazil has one of the highest incidences of AIDS, ranking fourth in worldwide cases.[20] An estimated 700,000 Brazilians are HIV infected, and 23,000 have full-blown AIDS.[21] The relationship between prostitution, IV drug use and sharing of needles, record unemployment, and poverty is cited as significant in the country's AIDS epidemic.[22]

Hospital costs for the growing AIDS-infected population in Brazil exceed $20,000 per year, according to an official at the University of the State of Rio de Janeiro.[23] The director of a São Paulo AIDS clinic ominously warned, "We've seen only the very beginning, and we're having trouble dealing with it already."[24]

Holland

In Holland, where prostitution is legalized, as many as 30,000 people are estimated to be HIV-seropositive.[25] Studies relating AIDS to prostitution in Holland have been inconsistent. A municipal health service of Amsterdam tested 84 Dutch (non-drug-using) prostitutes for the HIV antibody; none tested HIV-seropositive.[26] However, other studies involving drug using prostitutes have yielded different results. One such study found that 31 percent of the Dutch drug using prostitutes sampled tested HIV-seropositive.[27] This supports a number of researchers' findings that show a stronger relationship between prostitution and AIDS when drug use or IV drug use is a factor.[28]

Germany

AIDS cases among females in Germany have risen dramatically in recent years, nearly tripling between 1987 and 1988.[29] More than half these females were IV drug users. The vast majority of the AIDS-infected female prostitutes in Germany, which has legal prostitution, are IV drug addicts.[30] German prostitutes have also been found to have increased risk for exposure to HIV infection due to the high-risk activities of unprotected sex and the use of such mind-impairing drugs as heroin.[31]

Spain

As in many other European countries, prostitution is not a crime in Spain. The relationship between prostitution and AIDS in Spain has been the subject of a number of studies. In an HIV study of 2,172 prostitutes in nine provinces, it was found that nearly 10 percent tested positive for the HIV virus.[32] The highest rate of seroprevalence was for Madrid prostitutes. Twenty-six percent of these women were HIV-seropositive.[33] Of these, 38 percent were IV drug users. Another study found that 67 percent of IV-drug-injecting Madrid women prostitutes tested HIV-positive.[34] Other factors found to increase Spanish prostitutes' risk for HIV infection include being a streetwalker and an IV drug addict.[35]

Studies of HIV infection among non-drug-using prostitutes in Spain have yielded infection rates between 4 and 9 percent, with the risk of infection highest among female prostitutes in ports such as Barcelona and at highway intersections.[36] These higher infection rates are postulated to be due to greater contact with transient HIV-carrying customers such as sailors and long-distance truck drivers.

Africa

Africa has the highest rate of AIDS infection among females worldwide (though many believe Asia will soon surpass Africa in the number of HIV-infected females).[37] The high HIV infection rate of African prostitutes has been found to be related primarily to unsafe sexual practices; in contrast, in Europe and the United States, IV drug use and other high-risk activities may be even more influential to risk.[38]

AIDS was first reported in Africa as being transmitted through heterosexual relations. People with multiple sexual partners had an increased risk of infection. In East Africa, female prostitutes were found to "serve as a reservoir of infection."[39] A high percentage tested HIV-positive.[40]

In West Africa, fewer studies have been done on the relationship between prostitution and HIV rates of infection. One significant study was undertaken in 1986 in Ghana, where prostitution is illegal but openly conducted in some areas. The study involved two distinct classes of Ghanaian prostitutes: (1) home-based or low-class prostitutes and (2) high-class prostitutes.[41]

The latter group was subdivided into three levels. The top-level high-class prostitute was the most sophisticated, operating only from top international hotels and clubs. The second level was somewhat less sophisticated and operated out of hotels, discos, and nightclubs. The third level of high-class prostitutes was the largest — plying their trade in cheap bars and hotels. These women usually serviced several customers a day, with earnings averaging $5 per day.

Less than 1 percent of the prostitutes tested seropositive for HIV-1.[42] It was at this time that the first confirmed cases of AIDS among prostitutes began appearing in Ghana. Most of the infected were young women who had worked as prostitutes on the Ivory Coast and returned to Ghana for medical treatment.[43] The female-male ratio of HIV infection at the time was 11 to 1.[44]

Reports came in that Ghanaian prostitutes could be found in virtually every West African major capital or seaport. The majority of the women were part of the mass exodus from Ghana during the late 1970s and early 1980s due to the severe economic decline and political instability of the country. Experts believe these prostitutes became infected with the AIDS virus in neighboring French-speaking countries and passed it on to Ghanaian fishermen, traders, international businessmen, and others.[45] These customers then passed it on to other prostitutes, wives, and girlfriends, in a vicious cycle of exposure to HIV.

A second six-month study, educating West African prostitutes about AIDS and prevention and offering condoms and spermicides, was done in 1987.[46] The study was considered successful in changing prostitutes' attitudes on the use of condoms. Two-thirds of the prostitutes reported always using condoms. Only one case of HIV-1 infection was found.

It was concluded that more such intervention and education programs were needed throughout Africa (and elsewhere) to prevent the rapid spread of the AIDS virus by prostitutes.

United States

Insufficient studies have documented the relationship between HIV infection and female prostitution in the United States. Those studies that have been conducted do indicate that prostitutes face a significant risk for contracting the AIDS virus, with the risk increasing for IV drug users, drug and alcohol abusers, and streetwalking prostitutes.[47]

A study of IV-drug-using female streetwalkers found that 37 percent were HIV-positive.[48] Another study of streetwalkers and escort service prostitutes found an infection rate of 41 percent in the streetwalking prostitutes,[49] though none of the escort service workers tested positive.

Other researchers have painted a bleak picture for teenage prostitutes in the United States. At Covenant House in New York City, it is estimated that 15 percent of the runaway and prostituting youths passing through the shelter each year are HIV-positive.[50] More than 50 percent of the teenage girl prostitutes who turn tricks nightly are estimated to have been exposed to the AIDS virus.[51] Refer to Chapter 5 for a detailed examination of female prostitution and AIDS in this country.

Chapter 24

Responding to the Worldwide Tragedy of Female Prostitution

The international response to the increased misuse and sexual exploitation of women and girls in prostitution has generally been weak. Economies in Thailand, India, and Brazil depend too heavily on a sex tourism industry to be wholly committed to stamping out sex tours and sexual slavery. Other nations are committed in theory to reducing worldwide prostitution but in practice have been slow in instituting real reforms aimed at penalizing and prosecuting the men who pimp, pander, and solicit female prostitutes. Even countries without a sex tourism industry per se may have a vested interest in the sex trade industry politically, socially, or through other intrinsic ties.

Fortunately, there is some light at the end of the tunnel in combating the thriving sex industry.

Efforts to Combat the Sexual Exploitation of Women and Children

Some governments continue to ignore the plight of sexually exploited women and girls — many of them native prostitutes, others lured by sex tour promoters into the countries under false pretenses only to be turned into sex slave prostitutes to service men's sexual needs and fantasies. But with the global spread of the AIDS virus, often by female prostitutes and their johns, increased pressure has been placed on all countries to try to defuse what threatens to be

191

the world's greatest tragedy as increasing numbers of women and girls in the sex trade are placed at risk of exposure to the HIV virus. There are recent signs that many countries and their people are beginning to heed this threat and crack down on the sex-for-sale industry and those who profit and exploit females and children. In Pakistan, human rights lawyers have galvanized support against the organized criminals who have abducted 200,000 Bangladeshi females into prostitution in the country.[1] In Sri Lanka, Catholic priests have staged protests against prostitution and pedophilia, forcing authorities to step up efforts to combat the country's sex trade.[2] A Child Protection Code has recently been adopted in the Philippines to guard against child exploitation and abuse,[3] and in Manila, the mayor vowed to "eradicate prostitution," padlocking 300 clubs.[4]

Western countries have also begun to come down hard on the sex industry. Germany recently stiffened antitrafficking and prostitution laws,[5] as did Belgium.[6] France has made it more difficult to use its Minitel — a video-text telephone service — for child prostitution advertising.[7]

These efforts and others notwithstanding, many experts believe the task of stemming the flourishing sex trade industry will be daunting at best and impossible at worst. The prostitute victims, often unable to speak the native language, are reluctant to file charges against pimps, flesh traders, tour operators, brothel managers, or even rapist-clients because of fear of violence and/or deportation. Other prostitutes may be runaways or drug-addicts or psychologically manipulated so as to be dependent on their enslavers or pimps. Few males in the sex trade industry — whether procurer or customer — have any incentive (aside from AIDS) to exhibit self-control or disinclination to sexually exploit women and children, especially since most prostitution laws tend to more severely punish the victim than the offender.

Many authorities, facing the dilemma of differentiating voluntary prostitution versus forced prostitution, all too often take the approach that *all* female prostitutes are exhibiting free will when entering and remaining in the business. Noted one Swiss official, "We cannot reform the world's morals."[8]

Others are willing to try or, at the very least, to appeal to a collective sense of shame and decency. They advocate a humane, common recognition that female prostitutes, voluntary or not, are *all* being sexually exploited, should be put at the forefront of the AIDS crisis, and are entitled to be treated with dignity, respect, and consideration. What follows is a review of some of the most promising efforts at reducing the scope and consequences of prostituted women and girls globally.

THE UN 1949 CONVENTION FOR THE SUPPRESSION OF THE TRAFFIC IN PERSONS AND OF THE EXPLOITATION OF THE PROSTITUTION OF OTHERS

UNESCO has recently endorsed a proposal by antiprostitution activists to update the 1949 United Nations Convention for the Suppression of the Traffic in Persons and of the Exploitation of the Prostitution of Others.[9] The proposal would ban *all* sex-for-sale, rather than only forced prostitution. Most feminists support such a ban, positing that legalized prostitution, such as in Holland, Germany, and Australia, is little more than "an open door for traffickers."[10]

Many others regard such a tough measure as impractical and impossible to enforce. Some opponents of illicit prostitution favor decriminalization or legalization of prostitution as a better means to protect females' health, security, and earnings. Others feel that legalized prostitution is condoning the sexual exploitation of women (which, in effect, would trickle down to supporting girl prostitution).

It is doubtful that prostitution in all forms would ever be banned so that it would be enforceable across all nations. But debating the issues in a serious forum may be an important step in dealing with female sexual exploitation. Toward this end, a proposed UN Convention Against All Forms of Sexual Exploitation would explore the sex-for-sale industry, specifically targeting pimps, procurers, and johns and holding governments liable for their policies.[11]

U.S.-BASED COALITION AGAINST TRAFFICKING IN WOMEN

The U.S.-based Coalition Against Trafficking in Women is an organization concerned with combating the forces of white slavery and prostitution.[12] Its goals are to strengthen and enforce antitrafficking legislation and to create and enforce tougher laws against pimps and prostitutes' customers. Similar groups also exist in the United States and abroad, dedicated to fighting the forces that sexually exploit women.

Other efforts can be found around the United States. in response to the plight of women in prostitution. These include halfway houses, such as the Mary Magdalene Project in Los Angeles, for women who seek to leave prostitution and acquire new skills,[13] and other support, such as Joyce Wallace's Care-Van in New York City, which offers prostitutes free HIV tests and condoms as well as education on safe sex.[14]

END CHILD PROSTITUTION IN ASIAN TOURISM

One of the more impressive organizations in the fight against international child prostitution and sexual exploitation is ECPAT, or End Child Prostitution in Asian Tourism.[15] ECPAT was started by three Asian-based Christian organizations: the Asian Catholic Bishops' Conference, the Christian Conference of Asia, and the Ecumenical Coalition on Third World Tourism. Formed in response to the increasing influx of minors in the sex trade industry, ECPAT has become a leader in efforts to halt the prostitution of children.

With offices around the world, including four in the United States, and an extensive network of connections with religious, social, and women's organizations, ECPAT has been influential in strengthening prostitution laws in many countries. Australia, New Zealand, and Germany recently passed legislation similar to that recently enacted in the United States making it illegal to sexually abuse children in other countries.[16]

The Philippines and Thailand have also yielded to pressures from ECPAT and other child advocates to strengthen laws against child prostitution.[17] More and more foreign men who sexually abuse girls in Asia are being arrested, tried, and convicted to prison terms rather than encouraged to exploit children as sex tourists.

UN CONVENTION ON THE RIGHTS OF THE CHILD

A key tool in the protection of children from sexual predators is the United Nations Convention on the Rights of the Child.[18] This was adopted in 1989 by the UN and was ratified by 180 countries (the United States and 14 other countries have yet to ratify the convention). Representing an international coalition on children's rights, the convention obligates a government "to secure the well-being of its constituencies."[19]

According to Article 34, the countries signing the convention must work to prevent the "inducement or coercion of a child to engage in any unlawful sexual activity; the exploitative use of children in prostitution, or other unlawful sexual practices; the exploitative use of children in pornographic performance and materials."[20]

Yet in spite of this strongly worded commitment and the convention's broad acceptance, children continue to be exploited through prostitution, pornography, and other sex crimes, indicating that the problem of child sexploitation has not gone away and will require continued efforts.

TASK FORCE TO END CHILD EXPLOITATION IN THAILAND

In Thailand, which is notorious for its sex tours and government-sponsored organized prostitution, steps are being taken to reduce the involvement of children in prostitution. One such measure is the Task Force to End Child Exploitation in Thailand.[21] Consisting of a coalition representing 24 government and private agencies, the task force's aim is to expose connections between Europe and Bangkok's child sex trade industry. In one example, the task force set its sights on Lauda Air, an Australian-based airline, for "running a caricature in its in-flight magazine that allegedly promoted child sex tourism."[22]

The efforts appear to be working. Recently, 153 members of Britain's Parliament signed a motion requesting that Thailand take stronger action against sex tourism. Some suggested that the British might take stronger measures to protect Asian women and children from being sexually exploited by British men. According to one source, 83 percent of British tourists to the Philippines in 1991 were men (80 percent of all the visitors to the Philippines that year were male).[23] This underscores the need for stricter penalties worldwide against sexual predators and exploiters of females and minors.

PROJECT CHILD

Project Child was instituted in India in 1994 to provide day care for children of prostitutes.[24] The Swedish-funded day-care center offers two meals a day, clean clothes, and hot showers for children under seven. Forty percent of the children have tested positive for HIV.[25]

Although all the prostitutes are sex slaves, they are not encouraged by staff at Project Child to flee their captors, or *goondas*, because of the very real threat of bodily harm and because of the fact that, realistically, there are very few places they could escape to. Society has already turned its back on these women and their children.

Yet Project Child offers them some hope, if only compassion and understanding. Unfortunately, prospects are bleak. In a Project Child survey of 200 prostitutes in 1995, none wanted their own children to become prostitutes. Yet more than 95 percent of these children will wind up as sex slaves themselves.[26]

WORLD CONGRESS AGAINST COMMERCIAL SEXUAL EXPLOITATION OF CHILDREN

In a 1996 international conference, representatives of the World Congress Against Commercial Sexual Exploitation of Children called on governments worldwide to stop child prostitution and child pornography, as well as other forms of sexual exploitation of children.[27] Delegates from more than 120 countries vowed international cooperation, including adopting measures for tougher criminal sanctions against child sexual predators, pimps, traffickers, and clients of child sex workers. Participants were also urged to do more to halt child abuse and other forms of mistreatment of children.

As female prostitution and AIDS collide, with implications that are as frightening as they are tragic, one can only hope that the battle against sexual enslavement, prostitution, sex tourism, and other forms of sexual exploitation of women and girls never lets up — or at least not until every female is protected from the vicious cycle of victimization that prostitution entails. Given this unlikelihood, the commitment toward tougher legislation against pimps, slave traders, traffickers, tour promoters, customers, and other exploiters must continue, as also must research efforts that can shed new light on the problem and the dynamics of prostitution and the prostituting of women and girls.

Notes

PREFACE

    1. Cited in Richard Goodall, *The Comfort of Sin: Prostitutes and Prostitution in the 1990s* (Kent, England: Renaissance Books, 1995), p. 67.
    2. "U.N. Report Finds Increase in Violence Against Women," *Oregonian* (March 1, 1996), p. A4.
    3. Quoted in Margot Hornblower, "The Skin Trade," *Time* 141 (June 21, 1993), p. 47.

CHAPTER 1. DEFINING PROSTITUTES AND PROSTITUTION

    1. Harry Benjamin and R. E. L. Masters, *Prostitution and Morality* (New York: Julian Press, 1964), pp. 36, 161; Vern Bullough and Bonnie Bullough, *Women and Prostitution* (Buffalo, N.Y.: Prometheus, 1987), p. 27.
    2. Richard Goodall, *The Comfort of Sin: Prostitutes and Prostitution in the 1990s* (Kent, England: Renaissance Books, 1995), pp. 40–41.
    3. Bullough and Bullough, *Women and Prostitution*, p. 27.
    4. Benjamin and Masters, *Prostitution and Morality*, p. 36.
    5. *Ibid.*
    6. *Ibid.*, pp. 40–41.
    7. Ronald B. Flowers, *Children and Criminality: The Child as Victim and Perpetrator* (Westport, Conn.: Greenwood Press, 1986), p. 7.
    8. Ronald B. Flowers, *Women and Criminality: The Woman as Victim, Offender, and Practitioner* (Westport, Conn.: Greenwood Press, 1987), p. 120.
    9. Robert E. Faris, *Social Disorganization* (New York: Ronald Press, 1955).
    10. Marshall B. Clinard, *Sociology of Deviant Behavior* (New York: Holt, Rinehart and Winston, 1957), p. 249.
    11. Edwin M. Lemert, *Social Pathology* (New York: McGraw-Hill, 1951).
    12. Charles Winick and Paul M. Kinsie, *The Lively Commerce: Prostitution in the United States* (Chicago: Quadrangle Books, 1971), p. 3.

13. Paul J. Goldstein, *Prostitution and Drugs* (Lexington, Mass.: Lexington Books, 1979), p. 33.

14. Abraham Flexner, *Prostitution in Europe* (New York: Century, 1914), p. 11.

15. Goodall, *The Comfort of Sin*, p. 1.

16. Kate Millett, "Prostitution: A Quartet for Female Voices," in Vivian Gornick and Barbara K. Moran, eds., *Women in a Sexist Society* (New York: New American Library, 1971), p. 79.

17. *U.S. v. Bitty*, 208 U.S. 393, 401 (1908); Charles Rosenbleet and Barbara J. Pariente, "The Prostitution of the Criminal Law," *American Criminal Law Review* 11 (1973), p. 373.

18. Howard B. Woolston, *Prostitution in the United States* (New York: Century, 1921), p. 35.

19. *Ibid.*; Isabel Drummond, *The Sex Paradox* (New York: Putnam, 1953), p. 208.

20. *State v. Perry*, 249 Oregon 76, 81, 436, P.2d 252, 255 (1968); Rosenbleet and Pariente, "The Prostitution of the Criminal Law," p. 381.

21. Flowers, *Women and Criminality*, p. 120.

22. R. Barri Flowers, *Female Crime, Criminals and Cellmates: An Exploration of Female Criminality and Delinquency* (Jefferson, N.C.: McFarland, 1995), p. 101.

23. U.S. Department of Justice, Federal Bureau of Investigation, *Crime in the United States: Uniform Crime Reports 1995* (Washington, D.C.: Government Printing Office, 1996), p. 225.

24. Marilyn G. Haft, "Hustling for Rights," in Laura Crites, ed., *The Female Offender* (Lexington, Mass: Lexington Books, 1976), pp. 212–13.

25. Jennifer James, "The Prostitute as Victim," in Jane R. Chapman and Margaret Gates, eds., *The Victimization of Women* (Beverly Hills: Sage, 1978), p. 176.

26. "Offenders in the District of Columbia," *Report of the D.C. Commission on the Status of Women* (Washington, D.C.: Government Printing Office, 1972), p. 18.

27. Joan J. Johnson, *Teen Prostitution* (Danbury, Conn.: Franklin Watts, 1992), p. 35.

28. *Ibid.*

29. *Ibid.*

30. Cited in Margot Hornblower, "The Skin Trade." *Time* 141 (June 21, 1993), p. 45.

31. Susan Ladika, "Booming Slave Trade Lures Europeans." *Oregonian* (June 11, 1996), p. A1.

32. Hornblower, "The Skin Trade," p. 47; Susan Moran, "New World Havens of Oldest Profession," *Insight on the News* 9 (1993), p. 15.

33. Moran, "New World Havens," p. 15; Hornblower, "The Skin Trade," p. 47.

34. R. Barri Flowers, *The Victimization and Exploitation of Women and Children: A Study of Physical, Mental and Sexual Maltreatment in the United States* (Jefferson, N.C.: McFarland, 1994), p. 36.

CHAPTER 2. THE MAGNITUDE OF FEMALE PROSTITUTION

1. U.S. Department of Justice, Federal Bureau of Investigation, *Crime in the United States: Uniform Crime Reports 1995* (Washington, D.C.: Government Printing Office, 1996), p. 373.

2. *Ibid.*, p. 225.

3. *Ibid.*, p. 222.

4. Edwin W. Sutherland and Donald R. Cressey, *Criminology*, 10th ed. (Philadelphia: J. P. Lippincott, 1978), p. 29.

5. Charles H. Shireman and Frederic G. Reamer, *Rehabilitating Juvenile Justice* (New York: Columbia University Press, 1986), p. 20.

6. R. Barri Flowers, *Female Crime, Criminals and Cellmates: An Exploration of Female Criminality and Delinquency* (Jefferson, N.C.: McFarland, 1995), pp. 141, 149.

7. R. Barri Flowers, *The Adolescent Criminal: An Examination of Today's Juvenile Offender* (Jefferson, N.C.: McFarland, 1990), pp. 55–57.

8. Sam Meddis, "Teen Prostitution Rising, Study Says," *USA Today* (April 23, 1984), p. 3A.

9. Flowers, *Female Crime, Criminals and Cellmates*, p. 141.

10. "'Runaways,' 'Throwaways,' 'Bag Kids'— An Army of Drifter Teens," *U.S. News & World Report* (March 11, 1985), p. 53.

CHAPTER 3. TYPES OF PROSTITUTES

1. Harry Benjamin and R. E. L. Masters, *Prostitution and Morality* (New York: Julian Press, 1964).

2. Paul J. Goldstein, *Prostitution and Drugs* (Lexington, Mass.: Lexington Books, 1979), p. 34.

3. *Ibid.*, pp. 35–37.

4. Jennifer James, "Two Domains of Streetwalker Argot," *Anthropological Linguistics* 14 (1972): 174–75; Jennifer James, "Prostitutes and Prostitution," in Edward Sagarin and Fred Montanino, eds., *Deviants: Voluntary Actors in a Hostile World* (Morrison, N.J.: General Learning Press, 1977), pp. 390–91.

5. Barbara Goldsmith, "Women on the Edge: A Reporter at Large," *New Yorker* 69 (April 26, 1993), p. 66.

6. Cited in Linda Lee, "The World (and Underworld) of the Professional Call Girl," *New Woman* (January 1988), p. 61.

7. Adrian N. LeBlanc, "I'm a Shadow," *Seventeen* 52 (March 1993), p. 216.

8. Joan J. Johnson, *Teen Prostitution* (Danbury, Conn.: Franklin Watts, 1992), p. 109.

9. LeBlanc, "I'm a Shadow," p. 216.

10. R. Barri Flowers, *Female Crime, Criminals and Cellmates: An Exploration of Female Criminality and Delinquency* (Jefferson, N.C.: McFarland, 1995), p. 101. See also Sydney Barrows and William Novak, *Mayflower Madam: The Secret Life of Sydney Biddle Barrows* (New York: Arbor House, 1986).

11. Susan Moran, "New World Havens of Oldest Profession," *Insight on the News* 9 (1993), p. 14.

12. Goldsmith, "Women on the Edge," p. 74.

13. R. Barri Flowers, *The Adolescent Criminal: An Examination of Today's Juvenile Offender* (Jefferson, N.C.: McFarland, 1990), pp. 59–60; D. Kelly Weisberg, *Children of the Night: A Study of Adolescent Prostitution* (Lexington, Mass.: Lexington Books, 1985), pp. 117–19.

14. Flowers, *Female Crime, Criminals and Cellmates*, p. 153; Flowers, *The Adolescent Criminal*, p. 59.

15. Goldsmith, "Women on the Edge," p. 67; R. Barri Flowers, *The Victimization and Exploitation of Women and Children: A Study of Physical, Mental and Sexual Maltreatment in the United States* (Jefferson, N.C.: McFarland, 1994), pp. 83–85.

16. Flowers, *Female Crime, Criminals and Cellmates*, pp. 113–14; Flowers, *The Adolescent Criminal*, pp. 57–63.

17. Goldsmith, "Women on the Edge," p. 67; Flowers, *The Victimization and Exploitation of Women and Children*, pp. 81–85.

18. Robert Karen, "The World of the Middle Class Prostitute," *Cosmopolitan* 202 (January 1987), p. 205.

19. Kat Sunlove, "Putting a Price on Pain," *Harper's* 289 (August 1994), p. 20.

20. Flowers, *Female Crime, Criminals and Cellmates*, pp. 150–51.

21. Flowers, *The Adolescent Criminal*, p. 56; Jennifer James, *Entrance into Juvenile Prostitution* (Washington, D.C.: National Institute of Mental Health, 1980), p. 19.

22. Marilyn G. Haft, "Hustling for Rights," in Laura Crites, ed., *The Female Offender* (Lexington, Mass.: Lexington Books, 1976), p. 212.

23. *Ibid.*; R. Barri Flowers, *Women and Criminality: The Woman as Victim, Offender, and Practitioner* (Westport, Conn.: Greenwood Press, 1987), p. 129.

24. Haft, "Hustling for Rights," p. 129.

25. Cited in Goldsmith, "Women on the Edge," p. 65.

26. The Enablers, *Juvenile Prostitution in Minnesota: The Report of a Research Project* (St. Paul: The Enablers, 1978), p. 18.

27. Sparky Harlan, Luanne L. Rodgers, and Brian Slattery, *Male and Female Adolescent Prostitution: Huckleberry House Sexual Minority Youth Services Project* (Washington, D.C.: U.S. Department of Health and Human Services, 1981), p. 7.

28. *Ibid.*, p, 18; James, *Entrance into Juvenile Prostitution*, p. 19.

29. Flowers, *Female Crime, Criminals and Cellmates*, p. 151; Mimi H. Silbert, *Sexual Assault of Prostitutes: Phase One* (Washington, D.C.: National Institute of Mental Health, 1980), p. 10.

30. Cited in James Bovard, "Safeguard Public Health: Legalize Contractual Sex," *Insight on the News* 11 (1995), p. 20.

31. *Ibid.*

32. Laura Miller, "Prostitution," *Harper's Bazaar* 3400 (March 1995), pp. 208–10.

33. Anastasia Volkonsky, "Legalizing the 'Profession' Would Sanction the Abuse," *Insight on the News* 11 (February 1995), p. 21.

34. Miller, "Prostitution," p. 210.

35. Richard Goodall, *The Comfort of Sin: Prostitutes and Prostitution in the 1990s* (Kent, England: Renaissance Books, 1995), p. 201.

CHAPTER 4. THEORIES AND MOTIVATIONS REGARDING FEMALE PROSTITUTION

1. Cesare Lombroso and William Ferrero, *The Female Offender* (New York: Appleton, 1900).

2. Joy Pollock, "Early Theories of Female Criminality," in Lee H. Bowker, *Women, Crime, and the Criminal Justice System* (Lexington, Mass.: Lexington Books, 1978), p. 29.

3. See, for example, J. Cowie, B. Cowie, and E. Slater, *Delinquency in Girls* (London: Heinemann, 1968); R. Barri Flowers, *The Adolescent Criminal: An Examination of Today's Juvenile Offender* (Jefferson, N.C.: McFarland, 1990), p. 79.

4. Ronald B. Flowers, *Women and Criminality: The Woman as Victim, Offender, and Practitioner* (Westport, Conn.: Greenwood Press, 1987), p. 121; Sigmund Freud, *New Introductory Lectures in Psychoanalysis* (New York: W. W. Norton, 1933).

5. Flowers, *Women and Criminality*, p. 121; Freud, *New Introductory Lectures on Psychoanalysis*.

6. Flowers, *Women and Criminality*, p. 121.

7. Jennifer James, "Motivations for Entrance into Prostitution," in Laura Crites, ed., *The Female Offender* (Lexington, Mass.: Lexington Books, 1976), p. 190.

8. Ronald B. Flowers, *Children and Criminality: The Child as Victim and Perpetrator* (Westport, Conn.: Greenwood Press, 1986), pp. 81–83.

9. William I. Thomas, *Sex and Society: Studies in the Social Psychology of Sex* (Boston: Little, Brown, 1907); William I. Thomas, *The Unadjusted Girl: With Cases and Standpoint for Behavior Analysis* (New York: Harper and Row, 1923).

10. Pollock, "Early Theories of Female Criminality," p. 45.

11. *Ibid.*

12. Sheldon Glueck and Eleanor Glueck, *Five Hundred Delinquent Women* (New York: Alfred A. Knopf, 1934).

13. Otto Pollak, *The Criminality of Women* (Philadelphia: University of Philadelphia Press, 1950).

14. Pollock, "Early Theories of Female Criminality," p. 50.

15. Charles Winick and Paul M. Kinsie, *The Lively Commerce: Prostitution in the United States* (Chicago: Quadrangle Books, 1971).

16. Flowers, *Women and Criminality*, p. 121; Kingsley Davis, "The Sociology of Prostitution," *American Sociological Review* 2 (1937): 744–55.

17. Flowers, *Women and Criminality*, pp. 121–22; Davis, "The Sociology of Prostitution."

18. Edwin M. Lemert, *Social Pathology* (New York: McGraw-Hill, 1951), p. 237.

19. Robert E. Faris, *Social Disorganization* (New York: Ronald Press, 1955), p. 271.

20. Flowers, *Women and Criminality*, p. 122.

21. *Ibid.*; James, "Motivations for Entrance into Prostitution," p. 186. See also Norman Jackson, Richard O'Toole, and Gilbert Geis, "The Self-Image of the Prostitute," in John H. Gagnon and William Simon, eds., *Sexual Deviance* (New York: Harper and Row, 1967), p. 46.

22. Winick and Kinsie, *The Lively Commerce*, p. 271.

23. Lemert, *Social Pathology*.

24. James, "Motivations for Entrance into Prostitution," p. 194.

25. Joan J. Johnson, *Teen Prostitution* (Danbury, Conn.: Franklin Watts, 1992), pp. 102–3.

26. *Ibid.*, p. 103.

27. Rolaine Hochstein, "Prostitutes: Happy Hookers or Society's Victims?" *Glamour* 83 (May 1985), p. 187.

28. R. Barri Flowers, *Female Crime, Criminals and Cellmates: An Exploration of Female Criminality and Delinquency* (Jefferson, N.C.: McFarland, 1995), p. 113.

29. *Ibid.*, p. 120; Ronald B. Flowers, *Demographics and Criminality: The Characteristics of Crime in America* (Westport, Conn.: Greenwood Press, 1989), pp. 132–33; U.S. Department of Justice, National Institute of Justice, *Characteristics of Different Types of Drug-Involved Offenders* (Washington, D.C.: Government Printing Office, 1988), p. 21.

30. Cited in Flowers, *Female Crime, Criminals and Cellmates*, p. 120.

31. Barbara Goldsmith, "Women on the Edge: A Reporter at Large," *New Yorker* 69 (April 26, 1993), p. 65.

32. Anastasia Volkonsky, "Legalizing the 'Profession' Would Sanction the Abuse," *Insight on the News* 11 (1995): 20.

33. Cited in Johnson, *Teen Prostitution*, p. 97.

34. R. Barri Flowers, *The Victimization and Exploitation of Women and Children: A Study of Physical, Mental and Sexual Maltreatment in the United States* (Jefferson, N.C.: McFarland, 1994), p. 88.

35. *Ibid.*; Flowers, *Female Crime, Criminals and Cellmates*, pp. 148–56.

36. Quoted in Michael S. Serrill, "Defiling the Children," *Time* 141 (June 21, 1993), p. 53.

37. Flowers, *Female Crime, Criminals, and Cellmates*, p. 144.

38. Goldsmith, "Women on the Edge," pp. 65–66.

39. Sparky Harlan, Luanne L. Rodgers, and Brian Slattery, *Male and Female Adolescent Prostitution: Huckleberry House Sexual Minority Youth Services Project* (Washington, D.C.: U.S. Department of Health and Human Services, 1981), p. 21.

40. Mauran G. Crowley, "Female Runaway Behavior and Its Relationship to Prostitution," Master's thesis, Sam Houston State University, Institute of Contemporary Corrections and Behavioral Sciences, 1977, p. 63.

41. Harlan, Rodgers, and Slattery, *Male and Female Adolescent Prostitution*, p. 15.

42. Dorothy H. Bracey, *"Baby-Pros": Preliminary Profile of Juvenile Prostitutes* (New York: John Jay Press, 1979), p. 23.

43. "Prostitutes: The New Breed," *Newsweek* (July 12, 1971), p. 78.

44. Johnson, *Teen Prostitution*, pp. 105–6.

45. Jennifer James, *Entrance into Juvenile Prostitution: Progress Report, June 1978* (Washington, D.C.: National Institute of Mental Health, 1978).

46. Flowers, *Children and Criminality*, pp. 81–83; Flowers, *Female Crime, Criminals and Cellmates*, p. 76.

47. Cited in Johnson, *Teen Prostitution*, p. 131.

48. *Ibid.*

Chapter 5. AIDS and Female Prostitution

1. R. Barri Flowers, *Female Crime, Criminals and Cellmates: An Exploration of Female Criminality and Delinquency* (Jefferson, N.C.: McFarland, 1995), pp. 113–14; Linda Lee, "The World (and Underworld) of the Professional Call Girl," *New Woman* (January 1988), p. 62.

2. Barbara Goldsmith, "Women on the Edge: A Reporter at Large," *New Yorker* 69 (April 26, 1993), pp. 64–77.

3. *Ibid.*, p. 65; Martin A. Plant, "Sex Work, Alcohol, Drugs, and AIDS," in Martin A. Plant, ed., *AIDS, Drugs, and Prostitution* (London: Routledge, 1990), pp. 1–17.

4. Goldsmith, "Women on the Edge," p. 65.

5. *Ibid.*

6. Joan J. Johnson, *Teen Prostitution* (Danbury, Conn.: Franklin Watts, 1992), pp. 124–25.

7. Plant, "Sex Work, Alcohol, Drugs, and AIDS," pp. 2–11.

8. M. J. Rosenberg and J. M. Weiner, "Prostitution and AIDS: A Health Department Priority," *American Journal of Public Health* 78 (1988): 418–23.

9. *Ibid.*, p. 420.

10. R. Shilts, *And the Band Played On* (Harmondsworth, Middlesex: Penguin, 1987).

11. Paul J. Goldstein, *Prostitution and Drugs* (Lexington, Mass.: Lexington Books, 1979), p. 6.

12. *Ibid.*, p. 45.

13. D. Kelly Weisberg, *Children of the Night: A Study of Adolescent Prostitution* (Lexington, Mass.: Lexington Books, 1985), pp. 117–18.

14. *Ibid.*; E. McLeod, *Women Working: Prostitution Now* (London: Crown Helm, 1982).

15. Plant, "Sex Work, Alcohol, Drugs, and AIDS," p. 4.

16. *Ibid.*

17. E. M. Adlaf and R. G. Smart, "Risk-Taking and Drug Use Behavior: An Examination," *Drug and Alcohol Dependence* 11 (1983): 287–96.

18. Cited in R. Barri Flowers, *The Adolescent Criminal: An Examination of Today's Juvenile Offender* (Jefferson, N.C.: McFarland, 1990), p. 63.

19. Cited in Lee, "The World (and Underworld) of the Professional Call Girl," p. 62.

20. *Ibid.*

21. Goldsmith, "Women on the Edge," p. 65; Plant, "Sex Work, Alcohol, Drugs, and AIDS," p. 8.

22. W. R. Lange et al., "HIV Infection in Baltimore: Antibody Seroprevalence Rates Amongst Parenteral Drug Abusers and Prostitutes," *Maryland Medical Journal* 36 (1987): 757–61.

23. Flowers, *Female Crime, Criminals and Cellmates*, p. 118.

24. G. L. Smith and K. F. Smith, "Lack of HIV Infection and Condom Use in Licensed Prostitutes," *Lancet* 2 (1986): 1392.

25. Cited in James Bovard, "Safeguard Public Health: Legalize Contractual Sex," *Insight on the News* 11 (1995), p. 20.

26. *Ibid.*

27. Anastasia Volkonsky, "Legalizing the 'Profession' Would Sanction the Abuse," *Insight on the News* 11 (1995), p. 21.

28. Bovard, "Safeguard Public Health," p. 19.

29. Goldsmith, "Women on the Edge," p. 65.

30. Cited in *ibid.*, p. 74.

31. *Ibid.*

32. J. Van den Hoek et al., "Prevalence and Risk Factors of HIV Infections Among Drug Users and Drug-Using Prostitutes in Amsterdam," *AIDS* 2 (1987): 55–60.

33. A. M. Johnson, "Heterosexual Transmission of Human Immune Deficiency Virus," *British Medical Journal* 296 (1988): 1017–20.

34. Rosenberg and Weiner, "Prostitution and AIDS," p. 418.

35. John Zaccaro, Jr., "Children of the Night," *Woman's Day* (March 29, 1988), p. 137.

36. Patricia Hersch, "Coming of Age on City Streets," *Psychology Today* (January 1988), pp. 28–37.

37. Quoted in Johnson, *Teen Prostitution*, p. 125.

38. Cited in *ibid.*, p. 126.

39. Hersch, "Coming of Age on City Streets," p. 37.

40. *Ibid.*

41. *Ibid.*

42. Cited in Goldsmith, "Women on the Edge," p. 65.

43. Cited in Lee, "The World (and Underworld) of the Professional Call Girl," p. 62.

44. Flowers, *The Adolescent Criminal*, pp. 60–61.

45. Cited in Johnson, *Teen Prostitution*, p. 127.

46. P. Simon, E. Morse, and H. Osofsky, "Psychological Characteristics of a Sample of Male Street Prostitutes," *Archives of Sexual Behavior* 21 (1992).

47. See, for example, Dan Waldorf and Sheigla Murphy, "Intravenous Drug Use and Syringe-Sharing Practices of Call Men and Hustlers," in Martin A. Plant, ed., *AIDS, Drugs, and Prostitution* (London: Routledge, 1990), pp. 109–30.

48. Margaret Engel, "Many Prostitutes Found to Be AIDS Carriers," *Washington Post* (September 20, 1985), p. A1.

49. George Gallup, Jr., *The Gallup Poll Monthly*, no. 313 (October 1991), p. 73.

50. Richard Goodall, *The Comfort of Sin: Prostitutes and Prostitution in the 1990s* (Kent, England: Renaissance Books, 1995), p. 203.

51. Waldorf and Murphy, "Intravenous Drug Use and Syringe-Sharing Practices of Call Men and Hustlers," p. 125.

52. Cited in Goldsmith, "Women on the Edge," p. 65.

CHAPTER 6. THE SCOPE OF WOMEN'S PROSTITUTION

1. Cited in Alice Leuchtag, "Merchants of Flesh: International Prostitution and the War on Women's Rights," *The Humanist* 55,2 (1995), p. 11.

2. Margot Hornblower, "The Skin Trade," *Time* 141 (June 21, 1993), p. 48.

3. Cited in Leuchtag, "Merchants of Flesh," p. 11.

4. Robert I. Friedman, "India's Shame: Sexual Slavery and Political Corruption Are Leading to an AIDS Catastrophe," *The Nation* 262 (1996), p. 12.

5. Hornblower, "The Skin Trade," p. 45.

6. Friedman, "India's Shame," p. 12.

7. Cited in Leuchtag, "Merchants of Flesh," p. 13.

8. *Ibid.*

9. *Ibid.*, p. 14; Hornblower, "The Skin Trade," pp. 44–50; Lynn Darling, "Havana at Midnight," *Esquire* 123 (May 1995): pp. 96–104.

10. Hornblower, "The Skin Trade," p. 45.

11. Susan Ladika, "Booming Slave Trade Lures Europeans," *Oregonian* (June 11, 1996), p. A1.

12. Quoted in Hornblower, "The Skin Trade," p. 45.

13. R. Barri Flowers, *Female Crime, Criminals and Cellmates: An Exploration of Female Criminality and Delinquency* (Jefferson, N.C.: McFarland, 1995), p. 103.

14. *Ibid.*

15. U.S. Department of Justice, Federal Bureau of Investigation (FBI), *Crime in the United States: Uniform Crime Reports 1995* (Washington, D.C.: Government Printing Office, 1996), p. 222.

16. *Ibid.*, pp. 220, 222.

17. *Ibid.*, p. 225.

18. Cited in Laura Trujillo, "Escort Services Thriving Industry in Portland Area," *Oregonian* (June 7, 1996), p. B1.

19. Jennifer James, "The Prostitute as Victim," in June R. Chapman and Margaret Gates, eds., *The Victimization of Women* (Beverly Hills: Sage, 1978), p. 176.

20. Flowers, *Female Crime, Criminals and Cellmates*, p. 105; D. Kelly Weisberg, *Children of the Night: A Study of Adolescent Prostitution* (Lexington, Mass.: Lexington Books, 1985), pp. 124–28.

21. Flowers, *Female Crime, Criminals, and Cellmates*, pp. 107–14, 153–55.

22. *Ibid.*, pp. 120–21, 153, 166–67.

23. U.S. Department of Justice, FBI, *Crime in the United States*, pp. 215, 217.

24. Flowers, *Female Crime, Criminals and Cellmates*, p. 151.

25. Mimi H. Silbert, *Sexual Assault of Prostitutes: Phase One* (Washington, D.C.: National Institute of Mental Health, 1980), p. 10.

26. Marilyn G. Haft, "Hustling for Rights," in Laura Crites, ed., *The Female Offender* (Lexington, Mass.: Lexington Books, 1976), p. 212.

27. *Ibid.*

28. Cited in Barbara Goldsmith, "Women on the Edge: A Reporter at Large," *New Yorker* 69 (April 26, 1993), p. 65.

29. Flowers, *Female Crime, Criminals and Cellmates*, pp. 35, 150.

30. Ronald B. Flowers, *Women and Criminality: The Woman as Victim, Offender, and Practitioner* (Westport, Conn.: Greenwood Press, 1987), p. 77.

31. John Braithwaite, "The Myth of Social Class and Criminality Reconsidered," *American Sociological Review* 46 (1981): 36–57.

32. Flowers, *Female Crime, Criminals and Cellmates*, p. 150.

33. Silbert, *Sexual Assault of Prostitutes*, p. 15.

34. *Ibid.*; Weisberg, *Children of the Night*; Paul J. Goldstein, *Prostitution and Drugs* (Lexington, Mass.: Lexington Books, 1979), p. 45.

CHAPTER 7. STREETWALKING PROSTITUTES

1. Paul J. Goldstein, *Prostitution and Drugs* (Lexington, Mass.: Lexington Books, 1979), pp. 35–37.

2. Barbara Goldsmith, "Women on the Edge: A Reporter at Large," *New Yorker* 69 (April 26, 1993), p. 66.

3. Adrian N. LeBlanc, "I'm a Shadow," *Seventeen* 52 (March 1993), p. 214.

4. Cited in Linda Lee, "The World (and Underworld) of the Professional Call Girl," *New Woman* (January 1988), p. 61.

5. LeBlanc, "I'm a Shadow," p. 216.

6. Cited in Goldsmith, "Women on the Edge," p. 65.

7. LeBlanc, "I'm a Shadow," p. 214.

8. Quoted in *Ibid.*

9. *Ibid.*, p. 216.

10. R. Barri Flowers, *The Victimization and Exploitation of Women and Children: A Study of Physical, Mental and Sexual Maltreatment in the United States* (Jefferson, N.C.: McFarland, 1994), pp. 36–45.

11. *Ibid.*, pp. 41, 81–89.

12. Anastasia Volkonsky, "Legalizing the 'Profession' Would Sanction the Abuse," *Insight on the News* 11 (1995), p. 20.

13. Cited in *Ibid.*

14. Cited in Goldsmith, "Women on the Edge," pp. 65–66.

15. *Ibid.*

16. *Ibid.*, p. 66.

17. *Ibid.*

18. *Ibid.*

19. Jennifer James, "Two Domains of Streetwalker Argot," *Anthropological Linguistics* 14 (1972): 174–75.

20. Joan J. Johnson, *Teen Prostitution* (Danbury, Conn.: Franklin Watts, 1992), p. 75.

21. *Ibid.*, p. 78.

22. Quoted in Deborah Jones, "Pimped," *Chatelaine* 67 (November 1994), p. 111.

23. Johnson, *Teen Prostitution*, p. 86.

24. Quoted in Jones, "Pimped," p. 112.

25. Lee H. Bowker, *Women, Crime, and the Criminal Justice System* (Lexington, Mass.: Lexington Books, 1978), p. 155; Jennifer James, "Prostitute-Pimp Relationships," *Medical Aspects of Human Sexuality* 7 (1973): 147–63.

26. Bowker, *Women, Crime, and the Criminal Justice System*, p. 155.

27. Quoted in Rolaine Hochstein, "Prostitutes: Happy Hookers or Society's Victims?" *Glamour* 83 (May 1985), p. 184.

28. Jennifer James, "Prostitutes and Prostitution," in Edward Sagarin and Fred Montanino, eds., *Deviants: Voluntary Actors in a Hostile World* (Morrison, N.J.: General Learning Press, 1977), pp. 390–91.

29. Cited in LeBlanc, "I'm a Shadow," p. 214.

30. R. Barri Flowers, *Female Crime, Criminals and Cellmates: An Exploration of Female Criminality and Delinquency* (Jefferson, N.C.: McFarland, 1995), pp. 107, 120.

31. LeBlanc, "I'm a Shadow," p. 214.

32. *Ibid.*, p. 217.

33. *Ibid.*

34. Flowers, *Female Crime, Criminals and Cellmates*, p. 113.

35. *Ibid.*

36. Cited in Goldsmith, "Women on the Edge," p. 74.

37. Cited in Lee, "The World (and Underworld) of the Professional Call Girl," p. 62.

38. Goldsmith, "Women on the Edge," p. 65.

39. W. R. Lange, F. R. Snyder, D. Lozovsky, V. Kaistha, A. Kaczaniuk, and J. H. Jaffe, "HIV Infection in Baltimore: Antibody Seroprevalence Rates Amongst Parenteral Drug Abusers and Prostitutes," *Maryland Medical Journal* 36 (1987): 757–61.

40. Flowers, *Female Crime, Criminals and Cellmates*, pp. 105, 120.

CHAPTER 8. CALL GIRL PROSTITUTES

1. Linda Lee, "The World (and Underworld) of the Professional Call Girl," *New Woman* (January 1988), p. 61. See also Barbara Ignoto, *Confessions of a Part-Time Call Girl* (New York: Dell, 1986).

2. Quoted in Joan J. Johnson, *Teen Prostitution* (Danbury, Conn.: Franklin Watts, 1992), pp. 109–10.

3. Quoted in Lee, "The World (and Underworld) of the Professional Call Girl," p. 61. See also Sydney Barrows and William Novak, *Mayflower Madam: The Secret Life of Sydney Biddle Barrows* (New York: Arbor House, 1986).

4. Quoted in Lee, "The World (and Underworld) of the Professional Call Girl," p. 61.

5. Adrian N. LeBlanc, "I'm a Shadow," *Seventeen* 52 (March 1993), p. 216.

6. R. Barri Flowers, *Female Crime, Criminals and Cellmates: An Exploration of Female Criminality and Delinquency* (Jefferson, N.C.: McFarland, 1995), p. 110.

7. *Ibid.*, p. 101.

8. "Ring of 150 Call Girls Broken Up, SF Cops Say," *Sacramento Bee* (August 24, 1983), p. A5.

9. Susan Joffe, "I Was a Heidi Fleiss Girl," *Cosmopolitan* 217 (December 1994), p. 200.

10. Paul J. Goldstein, *Prostitution and Drugs* (Lexington, Mass.: Lexington Books, 1979), p. 45.

11. Coramae R. Mann, "White Collar Prostitution," unpublished paper, 1974.

12. Joffe, "I Was a Heidi Fleiss Girl," p. 200.

13. Quoted in Robert Karen, "The World of the Middle Class Prostitute," *Cosmopolitan* 202 (January 1987), p. 207. See also Norma J. Almodovar, *Cop to Call Girl: Why I Left the LAPD to Make an Honest Living as a Beverly Hills Prostitute* (New York: Simon and Schuster, 1993).

14. Joffe, "I Was a Heidi Fleiss Girl," p. 199.

15. Lynn Hirschberg, "Heidi Does Hollywood," *Vanity Fair* 57 (February 1994): 88–92.

16. Karen, "The World of the Middle Class Prostitute," p. 205.

17. *Ibid.*

18. Olivia Perkins, "I Am a High-Class Call Girl," *Cosmopolitan* 215 (October 1993), p. 96.

19. Quoted in Karen, "The World of the Middle Class Prostitute," p. 206.

20. Quoted in *ibid.*, p. 205.

21. *Ibid.*, p. 206.

22. *Ibid.*, p. 207.

23. Freda Adler, *Sisters in Crime: The Rise of the New Female Criminal* (New York: McGraw-Hill, 1975), p. 73.

24. Mann, "White Collar Prostitution."

25. J. Exner, J. Wylie, A. Leura, and T. Parill, "Some Psychological Characteristics of Prostitutes," *Journal of Personality Assessment* 41 (1977), p. 483.

26. Cited in Lee, "The World (and Underworld) of the Professional Call Girl," p. 62.

27. Harold Greenwald, *The Elegant Prostitute: A Social and Psychoanalytic Study* (New York: Walker and Co., 1970).

28. *Ibid.*

29. *Ibid.*, p. 242; Lee H. Bowker, *Women, Crime, and the Criminal Justice System* (Lexington, Mass.: Lexington Books, 1978), pp. 151–52.

30. James H. Bryan, "Apprenticeship in Prostitution," *Social Problems* 12 (1965): 287–97; James H. Bryan, "Occupational Ideologies and Individual Attitudes of Call Girls," *Social Problems* 13 (1966): 441–50.

31. Bowker, *Women, Crime, and the Criminal Justice System*, p. 152.

32. Bryan, "Occupational Ideologies and Individual Attitudes of Call Girls," pp. 441–50.

33. Quoted in Lee, "The World (and Underworld) of the Professional Call Girl," p. 63.

34. M. Stein, *Lovers, Friends, Slaves...* (New York: Berkeley, 1974), pp. 1–2, 317, 320.

35. *Ibid.*, p. 317.

36. Karen E. Rosenblum, "Female Deviance and the Female Sex Role: A Preliminary Investigation," *British Journal of Sociology* 26 (1975): 173–78.

37. Stein, *Lovers, Friends, Slaves...*, p. 22.

38. *Ibid.*, p. 21.

39. Cited in R. Barri Flowers, *The Adolescent Criminal: An Examination of Today's Juvenile Offender* (Jefferson, N.C.: McFarland, 1990), p. 63.

40. Cited in Lee, "The World (and Underworld) of the Professional Call Girl," p. 62.

CHAPTER 9. DRUGS, CRIME, AND VICTIMIZATION

1. R. Barri Flowers, *Female Crime, Criminals and Cellmates: An Exploration of Female Criminality and Delinquency* (Jefferson, N.C.: McFarland, 1995), pp. 108, 110, 115, 120, 153.

2. *Ibid.*, p. 165.

3. *Ibid.*, pp. 116, 153.

4. *Ibid.*, p. 121.

5. *Ibid.*, pp. 110, 153; Paul J. Goldstein, *Prostitution and Drugs* (Lexington, Mass.: Lexington Books, 1979), pp. 6, 45, 117–18.

6. Flowers, *Female Crime, Criminals and Cellmates*, p. 153; Joan J. Johnson, *Teen Prostitution* (Danbury, Conn.: Franklin Watts, 1992), p. 119.

7. Susan Moran, "New World Havens of Oldest Profession," *Insight on the News* 9 (1993), pp. 12–15.

8. Anastasia Volkonsky, "Legalizing the 'Profession' Would Sanction the Abuse," *Insight on the News* 11 (1995), p. 20.

9. Cited in Johnson, *Teen Prostitution*, p. 97.

10. Cited in Barbara Goldsmith, "Women on the Edge: A Reporter at Large," *New Yorker* 69 (April 26, 1993), p. 65.

11. R. Barri Flowers, *The Adolescent Criminal: An Examination of Today's Juvenile Offender* (Jefferson, N.C.: McFarland, 1990), pp. 59–60; D. Kelly Weisberg, *Children of the Night: A Study of Adolescent Prostitution* (Lexington, Mass.: Lexington Books, 1985), pp. 117–19.

12. Goldstein, *Prostitution and Drugs*, p. 45.

13. *Ibid.*

14. Flowers, *The Adolescent Criminal*, pp. 59–60; Johnson, *Teen Prostitution*, p. 97.

15. Goldstein, *Prostitution and Drugs*, p. 6.

16. *Ibid.*

17. *Ibid.*, pp. 117–18.

18. Weisberg, *Children of the Night*, pp. 117–18.

19. Goldstein, *Prostitution and Drugs*, p, 117. See also Martin A. Plant, "Sex Work, Alcohol, Drugs, and AIDS," in Martin A. Plant, ed., *AIDS, Drugs, and Prostitution* (London: Routledge, 1990), pp. 4–6.

20. Cited in Goldsmith, "Women on the Edge," p. 65.

21. *Ibid.*, p. 74.

22. Volkonsky, "Legalizing the 'Profession' Would Sanction the Abuse," p. 20.

23. Goldsmith, "Women on the Edge," p. 65; Plant, "Sex Work, Alcohol, Drugs, and AIDS," p. 8.

24. W. R. Lange et al., "HIV Infection in Baltimore: Antibody Seroprevalence Rates Amongst Parenteral Drug Abusers and Prostitutes," *Maryland Medical Journal* 36 (1987): 757–61.

25. Cited in A. M. Johnson, "Heterosexual Transmission of Human Immune Deficiency Virus," *British Medical Journal* 296 (1988): 1017–20.

26. J. Van den Hoek et al., "Prevalence and Risk Factors of HIV Infections Among Drug Users and Drug-Using Prostitutes in Amsterdam," *AIDS* 2 (1987): 55–60.

27. Flowers, *Female Crime, Criminals and Cellmates*, pp. 103, 120, 153.

28. Flowers, *The Adolescent Criminal*, pp. 59–60.

29. *Ibid.*, p. 60; Johnson, *Teen Prostitution*, p. 119.

30. Cited in Flowers, *Female Crime, Criminals and Cellmates*, p. 152.

31. Cited in Flowers, *The Adolescent Criminal*, p. 57.

32. Cited in Goldsmith, "Women on the Edge," pp. 65–66.

33. Ronald B. Flowers, *Women and Criminality: The Woman as Victim, Offender, and Practitioner* (Westport, Conn.: Greenwood Press, 1987), p. 128.

34. Volkonsky, "Legalizing the 'Profession' Would Sanction the Abuse," p. 20.

35. Cited in *ibid.*

36. Moran, "New World Havens of Oldest Profession," p. 14.

37. Adrian N. LeBlanc, "I'm a Shadow," *Seventeen* 52 (March 1993), p. 217.

38. *Ibid.*

39. Richard Jerome, "Risky Business: An Honors Student Turns Call Girl —
And Pays with Her Life," *People Weekly* 45, 23 (June 8, 1996): pp. 75–79.

40. "Prostitutes Get Warning About Danger to Lives," *Oregonian* (June 25,
1996), p. B3.

41. Cited in LeBlanc, "I'm a Shadow," p. 217.

42. Cited in Volkonsky, "Legalizing the 'Profession' Would Sanction the Abuse,"
p. 20.

43. Flowers, *Female Crime, Criminals and Cellmates*, p. 156.

44. LeBlanc, "I'm a Shadow," p. 217.

45. See, for example, Paul Recer, "Study: Unfaithful Men Can Spread Cervical Cancer," *Oregonian* (August 7, 1996), p. E6.

46. Johnson, *Teen Prostitution*, pp. 129–30.

47. Goldsmith, "Women on the Edge," p. 66.

48. Flowers, *Women and Criminality*, p. 129.

49. *Ibid.*, p. 130; Jennifer James, "Motivations for Entrance into Prostitution,"
in Laura Crites, ed., *The Female Offender* (Lexington, Mass.: Lexington Books, 1976),
pp. 190–94.

50. Flowers, *Women and Criminality*, p. 130.

51. See, for example, "U.N. Report Finds Increase in Violence Against
Women," *Oregonian* (March 1, 1996), p. A4.

Chapter 10. The Extent of Teenage Prostitution

1. R. Barri Flowers, *The Victimization and Exploitation of Women and Children: A Study of Physical, Mental and Sexual Maltreatment in the United States*
(Jefferson, N.C.: McFarland, 1994), p. 81.

2. Henry Benjamin and R. E. L. Masters, *Prostitution and Morality* (New
York: Julian Press, 1964), p. 161.

3. *Ibid.*, p. 162.

4. Flowers, *The Victimization and Exploitation of Women and Children*, p. 81.

5. *Ibid.*

6. Ronald B. Flowers, *Children and Criminality: The Child as Victim and Perpetrator* (Westport, Conn.: Greenwood Press, 1986), p. 7; Reay Tannahill, *Sex in
History* (New York: Stein and Day, 1980), p. 374.

7. Flowers, *The Victimization and Exploitation of Women and Children*, p. 82.

8. *Ibid.*; Joan J. Johnson, *Teen Prostitution* (Danbury, Conn.: Franklin Watts,
1992), p. 87.

9. Carol Smolenski, "Sex Tourism and the Sexual Exploitation of Children,"
Christian Century 112 (1995): 1079–81.

10. Johnson, *Teen Prostitution*, p. 75; R. Barri Flowers, *Female Crime, Criminals and Cellmates: An Exploration of Female Criminality and Delinquency* (Jefferson,
N.C.: McFarland, 1995), pp. 153–54.

11. Barbara Goldsmith, "Women on the Edge: A Reporter at Large," *New
Yorker* 69 (April 26, 1993), p. 67.

12. Cited in Michael S. Serrill, "Defiling the Children," *Time* 141 (June 21,
1993), p. 52.

13. *Ibid.*

14. Cited in Myrna Kostash, "Surviving the Streets," *Chatelaine* 67 (October 1994), p. 103.

15. Valerie Reitman, "Tokyo's Latest Fad: Teen Prostitution," *Wall Street Journal* (October 2, 1996), p. A8.

16. Serrill, "Defiling the Children," p. 52.

17. Quoted in *ibid.*, pp. 52–53.

18. Cited in Smolenski, "Sex Tourism and the Sexual Exploitation of Children," p. 1079.

19. Flowers, *Female Crime, Criminals and Cellmates*, p. 149; Michael Satchel, "Kids for Sale: A Shocking Report on Child Prostitution Across America," *Parade Magazine* (July 20, 1986), p. 4.

20. R. Barri Flowers, *The Adolescent Criminal: An Examination of Today's Juvenile Offender* (Jefferson, N.C.: McFarland, 1990), pp. 54–55.

21. Sam Meddis, "Teen Prostitution Rising, Study Says," *USA Today* (April 23, 1984), p. 3A.

22. Flowers, *The Adolescent Criminal*, p. 55.

23. *Ibid.*, pp. 49–52, 54–55.

24. U.S. Department of Justice, Federal Bureau of Investigation (FBI), *Crime in the United States: Uniform Crime Reports 1995* (Washington, D.C.: Government Printing Office, 1996), p. 218.

25. *Ibid.*, p. 215.

26. *Ibid.*, pp. 220, 222.

27. *Ibid.*, p. 213.

28. *Ibid.*

29. Flowers, *The Adolescent Criminal*, pp. 62–63.

30. *Ibid.*, pp. 46–47; U.S. Department of Justice, FBI, *Crime in the United States*, p. 213.

31. Jennifer James, *Entrance into Juvenile Prostitution* (Washington, D.C.: National Institute of Mental Health, 1980), p. 17.

32. Flowers, *Female Crime, Criminals and Cellmates*, pp. 150–51.

33. *Ibid.*, p. 105; Mimi H. Silbert, *Sexual Assault of Prostitutes: Phase One* (Washington, D.C.: National Institute of Mental Health, 1980), p. 10.

34. Ronald B. Flowers, *Demographics and Criminality: The Characteristics of Crime in America* (Westport, Conn.: Greenwood Press, 1989), pp. 50–52.

CHAPTER 11. THE CHARACTERISTICS OF GIRL PROSTITUTES

1. Adrian N. LeBlanc, "I'm a Shadow," *Seventeen* 52 (March 1993), p. 216.

2. R. Barri Flowers, *The Adolescent Criminal: An Examination of Today's Juvenile Offender* (Jefferson, N.C.: McFarland, 1990), p. 58; D. Kelly Weisberg, *Children of the Night: A Study of Adolescent Prostitution* (Lexington, Mass.: Lexington Books, 1985), p. 107.

3. Cited in Barbara Goldsmith, "Women on the Edge: A Reporter at Large," *New Yorker* 69 (April 26, 1993), p. 65.

4. LeBlanc, "I'm a Shadow," p. 216.

5. J. Johnson, *Teen Prostitution* (Danbury, Conn.: Franklin Watts, 1992), p. 108.

6. *Ibid.*

7. *Ibid.*, p. 75.

8. Cited in *ibid.*, p. 78.

9. *Ibid.*, p. 87.

10. *Ibid.*

11. *Ibid.*

12. Jennifer James, *Entrance into Juvenile Prostitution* (Washington, D.C.: National Institute of Mental Health, 1980), p. 17.

13. Cited in Anastasia Volkonsky, "Legalizing the 'Profession' Would Sanction the Abuse," *Insight on the News* 11 (1995), p. 21.

14. James, *Entrance into Juvenile Prostitution*, p. 29; Weisberg, *Children of the Night*, p. 94.

15. Sparky Harlan, Luanne L. Rodgers, and Brian Slattery, *Male and Female Adolescent Prostitution: Huckleberry House Sexual Minority Youth Services Project* (Washington, D.C.: U.S. Department of Health and Human Services, 1981), p. 7.

16. "The Enablers," *Juvenile Prostitution in Minnesota: The Report of a Research Project* (St. Paul: The Enablers, 1978), p. 18.

17. James, *Entrance into Juvenile Prostitution*, p. 19.

18. *Ibid.*; "The Enablers," *Juvenile Prostitution in Minnesota*, p. 18; Flowers, *The Adolescent Criminal*, p. 56.

19. James, *Entrance into Juvenile Prostitution*, p. 10; Mimi H. Silbert, *Sexual Assault of Prostitutes: Phase One* (Washington, D.C.: National Institute of Mental Health, 1980), p. 10.

20. Susan Moran, "New World Havens of Oldest Profession," *Insight on the News* 9 (1993): 12–16.

21. Flowers, *The Adolescent Criminal*, p. 56; Dorothy H. Bracey, *"Baby-Pros": Preliminary Profiles of Juvenile Prostitutes* (New York: John Jay Press, 1979), p. 19.

22. Ellen Hale, "Center Studies Causes of Juvenile Prostitution," *Gannet News Service* (May 21, 1981).

23. Silbert, *Sexual Assault of Prostitutes*, p. 15.

24. James, *Entrance into Juvenile Prostitution*, p. 18; Jennifer James, *Entrance into Juvenile Prostitution: Progress Report, June 1978* (Washington, D.C.: National Institute of Mental Health, 1978), p. 53.

25. Maura G. Crowley, "Female Runaway Behavior and Its Relationship to Prostitution," Master's thesis, Sam Houston State University, Institute of Contemporary Corrections and Behavioral Sciences, 1977.

26. Harlan, Rodgers, and Slattery, *Male and Female Adolescent Prostitution*, p. 14.

27. James, *Entrance into Juvenile Prostitution* (1980), p. 88.

28. Harlan, Rodgers, and Slattery, *Male and Female Adolescent Prostitution*, p. 15.

29. Diana Gray, "Turning Out: A Study of Teenage Prostitution," Master's thesis, University of Washington, 1971, p. 25.

30. Crowley, "Female Runaway Behavior," pp. 74–77.

31. See, for example, Katherine MacVicar and Marcia Dillon, "Childhood and Adolescent Development of Ten Female Prostitutes," *Journal of the American*

Academy of Child Psychiatry 19, 1 (1980); Frances Newman and Paula J. Caplan, "Juvenile Female Prostitution as a Gender Consistent Response to Early Deprivation," *International Journal of Women's Studies* 5, 2 (1981), p. 131.

32. R. Barri Flowers, *The Victimization and Exploitation of Women and Children: A Study of Physical, Mental and Sexual Maltreatment in the United States* (Jefferson, N.C.: McFarland, 1994), pp. 81–84.

33. See, for example, *ibid.*; Flowers, *The Adolescent Criminal*, p. 57; Joseph J. Peters, "Children Who Are Victims of Sexual Assault and the Psychology of Offenders," *American Journal of Psychotherapy* 30 (1976): 398–421.

34. Harlan, Rodgers, and Slattery, *Male and Female Adolescent Prostitution*, p. 21.

35. Mimi H. Silbert, "Delancey Street Study: Prostitution and Sexual Assault" (summary of results, Delancey Street Foundation, San Francisco 1982), p. 3.

36. Flowers, *The Adolescent Criminal*, p. 58; R. Barri Flowers, *Children and Criminality: The Child as Victim and Perpetrator* (Westport, Conn.: Greenwood Press, 1986), pp. 82–83.

37. R. Barri Flowers, *Female Crime, Criminals and Cellmates: An Exploration of Female Criminality and Delinquency* (Jefferson, N.C.: McFarland, 1995), p. 152.

38. Crowley, "Female Runaway Behavior," p. 63.

39. Harlan, Rodgers, and Slattery, *Male and Female Adolescent Prostitution*, p. 15.

40. Flowers, *Female Crime, Criminals and Cellmates*, pp. 141–42, 149.

41. Cited in Volkonsky, "Legalizing the 'Profession' Would Sanction the Abuse," p. 21.

42. Flowers, *The Victimization and Exploitation of Women and Children*, pp. 36–44.

43. U.S. Department of Justice, Federal Bureau of Investigation (FBI), *Crime in the United States: Uniform Crime Reports 1995* (Washington, D.C.: Government Printing Office, 1996), pp. 213, 217.

44. *Ibid.*; Flowers, *Female Crime, Criminals and Cellmates*, p. 103.

45. Volkonsky, "Legalizing the 'Profession' Would Sanction the Abuse," p. 21.

46. Myrna Kostash, "Surviving the Streets," *Chatelaine* 67 (October 1994), pp. 103–4.

47. Cited in Johnson, *Teen Prostitution*, p. 97.

48. Flowers, *The Adolescent Criminal*, pp. 59–60; Weisberg, *Children of the Night*, pp. 117–19.

49. Paul W. Haberman and Michael M. Baden, *Alcohol, Other Drugs, and Violent Death* (New York: Oxford University Press, 1978), pp. 18–19.

50. Flowers, *Female Crime, Criminals and Cellmates*, p. 153; Crowley, "Female Runaway Behavior," p. 80.

51. Flowers, *The Adolescent Criminal*, p. 59.

52. Flowers, *Female Crime, Criminals and Cellmates*, p. 153; Weisberg, *Children of the Night*, pp. 117–18.

53. Flowers, *Female Crime, Criminals and Cellmates*, p. 153.

54. Flowers, *Children and Criminality*, p. 97; Judianne Densen-Gerber and S. F. Hutchinson, "Medical-Legal and Societal Problems Involving Children-Child Prostitution, Child Pornography, and Drug-Related Abuse: Recommended Legisla-

tion," in Selwyn M. Smith, ed., *The Maltreatment of Children* (Baltimore: University Park Press, 1978), p. 322.

55. "Crack: A Cheap and Deadly Cocaine Is a Spreading Menace," *Time* 127 (June 2, 1986), p. 18.

56. Flowers, *The Adolescent Criminal*, p. 60.

57. "The Enablers," *Juvenile Prostitution in Minnesota*, p. 75.

58. U.S. Department of Justice, FBI, *Crime in the United States*, pp. 213, 222.

59. "The Enablers," *Juvenile Prostitution in Minnesota*, p. 57.

60. Jennifer James, "Prostitute-Pimp Relationships," *Medical Aspects of Human Sexuality* 7 (1973): 147–63.

61. Bracey, *"Baby-Pros,"* p. 23.

62. *Ibid.*

63. Quoted in Hale, "Center Studies Causes of Juvenile Prostitution."

64. Quoted in Clemens Bartollas, *Juvenile Delinquency* (New York: John Wiley and Sons, 1985), p. 342.

65. James, *Entrance into Juvenile Prostitution: Progress Report.*

66. Flowers, *The Adolescent Criminal*, p. 59; Johnson, *Teen Prostitution*, pp. 105–6.

67. Cited in Johnson, *Teen Prostitution*, p. 131.

68. *Ibid.*

69. Flowers, *The Victimization and Exploitation of Women and Children*, pp. 43–44.

70. Flowers, *Children and Criminality*, pp. 81–83.

71. *Ibid.*

72. James, *Entrance into Juvenile Prostitution* (1980), p. 68.

73. Flowers, *The Adolescent Criminal*, p. 58.

74. Quoted in Patricia Hersch, "Coming of Age on City Streets," *Psychology Today* (January 1988), pp. 32, 35.

Chapter 12. Runaway and Throwaway Girls

1. Ronald B. Flowers, *Children and Criminality: The Child as Victim and Perpetrator* (Westport, Conn.: Greenwood Press, 1986), p. 81; R. Barri Flowers, *The Adolescent Criminal: An Examination of Today's Juvenile Offender* (Jefferson, N.C.: McFarland, 1990), p. 55.

2. Flowers, *The Adolescent Criminal*, p. 49.

3. Flowers, *Children and Criminality*, p. 132.

4. R. Barri Flowers, *Female Crime, Criminals and Cellmates: An Exploration of Female Criminality and Delinquency* (Jefferson, N.C.: McFarland, 1995), p. 141.

5. Cited in Patricia Hersch, "Coming of Age on City Streets," *Psychology Today* (January 1988), pp. 31, 34.

6. Flowers, *Female Crime, Criminals and Cellmates*, pp. 141–56.

7. U.S. Department of Justice, Federal Bureau of Investigation (FBI), *Crime in the United States: Uniform Crime Reports 1995* (Washington, D.C.: Government Printing Office, 1996), p. 374.

8. *Ibid.*, p. 222.

9. *Ibid.*

10. *Ibid.*, pp. 220, 222.

11. *Ibid.*; Flowers, *Female Crime, Criminals and Cellmates*, p. 105; Flowers, *The Adolescent Criminal*, pp. 62–63.

12. Cited in Flowers, *Female Crime, Criminals and Cellmates*, pp. 142–43.

13. *Ibid.*, p. 108; Jennifer James, *Entrance into Juvenile Prostitution* (Washington, D.C.: National Institute of Mental Health, 1980), p. 19.

14. James A. Hildebrand, "Why Runaways Leave Home," *Police Science* 54 (1963): 211–16.

15. Robert Shellow, "Suburban Runaways of the 1960s," *Monographs of the Society for Research in Child Development* 32 (1967): 17.

16. Louise Homer, "Criminality-Based Resource for Runaway Girls," *Social Casework* 10 (1973): 474.

17. Flowers, *Female Crime, Criminals and Cellmates*, p. 144.

18. *Ibid.*, pp. 144, 147.

19. Cited in Hersch, "Coming of Age on City Streets," pp. 31–32.

20. *Ibid.*

21. Flowers, *Children and Criminality*, p. 133.

22. *Ibid.*

23. C. J. English, "Leaving Home: A Typology of Runaways," *Society* 10 (1973): 22–24.

24. Quoted in Stephanie Abarbanel, "Women Who Make a Difference," *Family Circle* 107 (January 11, 1994), p. 11.

25. "'Rat Pack' Youth: Teenage Rebels in Suburbia," *U.S. News & World Report* (March 11, 1995), p. 54.

26. *Ibid.*, p. 51.

27. *Ibid.*, p. 54; Flowers, *The Adolescent Criminal*, p. 51.

28. Cited in Carolyn Males and Julie Raskin, "The Children Nobody Wants," *Reader's Digest* (January 1984), p. 63.

29. Cited in "'Runaways,' 'Throwaways,' 'Bag Kids'— An Army of Drifter Teens," *U.S. News & World Report* (March 11, 1985), p. 53.

30. Males and Raskin, "The Children Nobody Wants," p. 63.

31. Quoted in *ibid.*

32. Cited in Hersch, "Coming of Age on City Streets," p. 31.

33. Abarbanel, "Women Who Make a Difference," p. 11.

34. Quoted in *ibid.*

35. Robin Lloyd, *For Money or Love: Boy Prostitution in America* (New York: Ballantine, 1976), pp. 58–72.

36. "Prostitutes: The New Breed," *Newsweek* (July 12, 1971), p. 78.

37. *Ibid.*

38. Flowers, *Female Crime, Criminals and Cellmates*, p. 146.

39. Hersch, "Coming of Age on City Streets," p. 32.

40. Quoted in Dotson Rader, "I Want to Die So I Won't Hurt No More," *Parade Magazine* (August 18, 1985), p. 4.

41. John Zaccaro, Jr., "Children of the Night," *Woman's Day* (March 29, 1988), p. 137.

42. Hersch, "Coming of Age on City Streets," pp. 32–35.

43. Cited in Zaccaro, "Children of the Night," p. 137.

44. The Runaway and Homeless Youth Act, 42 U.S.C. §§5701–5702 Supp. II (1978); P.L. No. 96–509; 42 U.S.C. §5711 Supp. (1981).

45. R. Barri Flowers, *The Victimization and Exploitation of Women and Children: A Study of Physical, Mental and Sexual Maltreatment in the United States* (Jefferson, N.C.: McFarland, 1994), p. 45.

CHAPTER 13. PIMPS AND GIRL PROSTITUTION

1. Adrian N. LeBlanc, "I'm a Shadow," *Seventeen* 52 (March 1993), p. 216.

2. *Ibid.*; Joan J. Johnson, *Teen Prostitution* (Danbury, Conn.: Franklin Watts, 1992), pp. 108–9.

3. Cited in Johnson, *Teen Prostitution*, p. 75.

4. *Ibid.*, p. 78.

5. *Ibid.*, p. 87.

6. *Ibid.*; R. Barri Flowers, *Female Crime, Criminals and Cellmates: An Exploration of Female Criminality and Delinquency* (Jefferson, N.C.: McFarland, 1995), p. 152.

7. "The Enablers," *Juvenile Prostitution in Minnesota: The Report of a Research Project* (St. Paul: The Enablers, 1978), p. 57.

8. Jennifer James, "Prostitute-Pimp Relationships," *Medical Aspects of Human Sexuality* 7 (1973): 147–63.

9. Dorothy H. Bracey, *"Baby-Pros": Preliminary Profiles of Juvenile Prostitutes* (New York: John Jay Press, 1979), p. 23.

10. Deborah Jones, "Pimped," *Chatelaine* 67 (November 1994), p. 111.

11. Quoted in *ibid.*

12. Johnson, *Teen Prostitution*, p. 79.

13. Susan Moran, "New World Havens of Oldest Profession," *Insight on the News* 9 (1993): 12–16.

14. Johnson, *Teen Prostitution*, pp. 76–77.

15. Cited in *ibid.*, p. 77.

16. *Ibid.*

17. R. Barri Flowers, *The Adolescent Criminal: An Examination of Today's Juvenile Offender* (Jefferson, N.C.: McFarland, 1990), pp. 57–60.

18. Johnson, *Teen Prostitution*, p. 84.

19. Cited in *ibid.*, p. 83.

20. *Ibid.*

21. *Ibid.*

22. *Ibid.*

23. Anastasia Volkonsky, "Legalizing the 'Profession' Would Sanction the Abuse," *Insight on the News* 11 (1995), p. 20.

24. *Ibid.*; Johnson, *Teen Prostitution*, p. 86.

25. Volkonsky, "Legalizing the 'Profession' Would Sanction the Abuse," p. 20.

26. Cited in *ibid.*

27. John G. Hubbell, "Child Prostitution: How It Can Be Stopped," *Reader's Digest* (June 1984): 202, 205.

28. Johnson, *Teen Prostitution*, p. 127.

29. Cited in *ibid.*

30. Flowers, *Female Crime, Criminals and Cellmates*, pp. 113–14, 147, 156; Martin A. Plant, "Sex Work, Alcohol, Drugs, and AIDS," in Martin A. Plant, ed., *AIDS, Drugs, and Prostitution* (London: Routledge, 1990), pp. 1–17.

CHAPTER 14. THE DANGERS OF CHILD SEXUAL ABUSE

1. "Vaccines for the Epidemic of Missing Children," *Psychology Today* 17 (1983), p. 76; R. Barri Flowers, *The Victimization and Exploitation of Women and Children: A Study of Physical, Mental and Sexual Maltreatment in the United States* (Jefferson, N.C.: McFarland, 1994), pp. 46–49.

2. Flowers, *The Victimization and Exploitation of Women and Children*; Kathleen Barry, *Female Sexual Slavery* (Englewood Cliffs, N.J.: Prentice-Hall, 1979); Susan Moran, "New World Havens of Oldest Profession," *Insight on the News* 9 (1993): 12–16.

3. Cited in Ronald B. Flowers, *Children and Criminality: The Child as Victim and Perpetrator* (Westport, Conn.: Greenwood Press, 1986), pp. 86–87.

4. *Ibid.*

5. *Ibid.*, pp. 90–93; Joan J. Johnson, *Teen Prostitution* (Danbury, Conn.: Franklin Watts, 1992), p. 92.

6. 18. U.S.C. §1073 (1980).

7. 128 *Cong. Rec.* 8, 566 (1982).

8. Flowers, *The Victimization and Exploitation of Women and Children*, pp. 53–59.

9. *Ibid.*, pp. 39, 44.

10. P.L. 100–294.

11. *Protecting the Child Victim of Sex Crimes* (Denver: American Humane Association, 1966), p. 2.

12. *Sexual Abuse of Children: Implications for Casework* (Denver: American Humane Association, 1967), p. 10.

13. Karen McCurdy and Deborah Daro, *Current Trends in Child Abuse Reporting Fatalities: The Results of the 1992 Annual Fifty State Survey* (Chicago, Ill.: National Committee for Prevention of Child Abuse, 1993), p. 10.

14. U.S. Department of Health and Human Services, *National Child Abuse and Neglect Data System: Working Paper 2–1991 Summary Data Component* (Washington, D.C.: National Center on Child Abuse and Neglect, 1993), p. 29.

15. Flowers, *The Victimization and Exploitation of Women and Children*, p. 58.

16. Flowers, *Children and Criminality*, pp. 76–83; B. Karpman, *The Sex Offender and His Offenses* (New York: Julian Press, 1962).

17. Cited in Ronald B. Flowers, *Women and Criminality: The Woman as Victim, Offender, and Practitioner* (Westport, Conn.: Greenwood Press, 1987), pp. 61–62.

18. Cited in Anita Manning, "Victims Must Face the Hurt," *USA Today* (January 10, 1994), p. 5D.

19. Cited in Kathy McCoy, "Incest: The Most Painful Family Problem," *Seventeen* 43 (June 1984), p. 18.

20. Flowers, *Women and Criminality*, p. 61.

21. H. Stoenner, *Child Sexual Abuse Seen Growing in the United States* (Denver: American Humane Association, 1972).

22. Flowers, *The Victimization and Exploitation of Women and Children*, p. 63.

23. *Ibid.*, pp. 84–85.

24. *Ibid.*, p. 73.

25. Susan Brownmiller, *Against Our Will: Men, Women, and Rape* (New York: Simon and Schuster, 1975), pp. 278–79.

26. Flowers, *The Victimization and Exploitation of Women and Children*, p. 74.

27. J. M. Reinhardt, *Sex Perversions and Sex Crimes* (Springfield, Ill.: Charles C Thomas, 1957).

28. *Ibid.*

29. Flowers, *The Victimization and Exploitation of Women and Children*, pp. 74–75.

30. *Ibid.*

31. Flowers, *Children and Criminality*, p. 77.

32. Flowers, *The Victimization and Exploitation of Women and Children*, p. 75.

33. *Ibid.*

34. J. L. Mathis, *Clear Thinking About Sexual Deviations* (Chicago: Nelson-Hall, 1972), p. 37.

35. Flowers, *The Victimization and Exploitation of Women and Children*, p. 75; J. C. Coleman, *Abnormal Psychology and Modern Life* (Glenview, Ill.: Scott Foresman and Co., 1972).

36. Flowers, *Children and Criminality*, p. 80.

37. *Ibid.*; Flowers, *The Victimization and Exploitation of Women and Children*, p. 76.

38. Flowers, *The Victimization and Exploitation of Women and Children*, p. 76.

39. Robert H. Morneau and Robert R. Rockwell, *Sex, Motivation and the Criminal Offender* (Springfield, Ill.: Charles C Thomas, 1980), p. 73.

40. Flowers, *The Victimization and Exploitation of Women and Children*, p. 77.

41. P. H. Gebhard, J. H. Gagnon, W. B. Pomeroy, and C. V. Christenson, *Sex Offenders* (New York: Harper and Row, 1965).

42. Flowers, *The Victimization and Exploitation of Women and Children*, p. 77.

43. Richard von Krafft-Ebing, *Psychopathia Sexualis* (New York: Stein and Day, 1965).

44. Flowers, *The Victimization and Exploitation of Women and Children*, p. 77.

45. Morneau and Rockwell, *Sex, Motivation and the Criminal Offender*, pp. 87–89.

46. *Ibid.*

47. Flowers, *The Victimization and Exploitation of Women and Children*, pp. 78–79.

48. Reinhardt, *Sex Perversions and Sex Crimes*; Clifford Allen, *The Sexual Perversions and Abnormalities* (London: Oxford University Press, 1949).

49. Morneau and Rockwell, *Sex, Motivation and the Criminal Offender*, p. 142.

50. Flowers, *The Victimization and Exploitation of Women and Children*, p. 79.

51. Morneau and Rockwell, *Sex, Motivation and the Criminal Offender*, p. 145.

52. Flowers, *The Victimization and Exploitation of Women and Children*, pp. 79–80.

53. David Finkelhor, Linda Williams, Nanci Burns, and Michael Kalinowski, *Sexual Abuse in Day Care: A National Study Executive Summary* (Durham: University of New Hampshire, 1988).

54. National Center on Child Abuse and Neglect, *Research Symposium on Child Sexual Abuse: May 17–19, 1988* (Washington, D.C.: U.S. Department of Health and Human Services, 1988), p. 3.

55. Flowers, *The Victimization and Exploitation of Women and Children*, p. 80.

56. *Ibid.*, p. 59.

57. Flowers, *Children and Criminality*, p. 96.

58. Flowers, *The Victimization and Exploitation of Women and Children*, p. 59.

59. Flowers, *Children and Criminality*, p. 97.

60. Flowers, *The Victimization and Exploitation of Women and Children*, p. 59.

61. *Ibid.*, pp. 84–85; R. Barri Flowers, *The Adolescent Criminal: An Examination of Today's Juvenile Offender* (Jefferson, N.C.: McFarland, 1990), pp. 51, 55.

CHAPTER 15. PORNOGRAPHY AND FEMALE PROSTITUTION

1. R. Barri Flowers, *Female Crime, Criminals and Cellmates: An Exploration of Female Criminality and Delinquency* (Jefferson, N.C.: McFarland, 1995), pp. 148–56; R. Barri Flowers, *The Victimization and Exploitation of Women and Children: A Study of Physical, Mental and Sexual Maltreatment in the United States* (Jefferson, N.C.: McFarland, 1994), pp. 90–93, 179–85.

2. Flowers, *The Victimization and Exploitation of Women and Children*, pp. 91, 184.

3. *Ibid.*, pp. 71–93; R. Barri Flowers, *The Adolescent Criminal: An Examination of Today's Juvenile Offender* (Jefferson, N.C.: McFarland, 1990), pp. 64–65.

4. Ronald B. Flowers, *Women and Criminality: The Woman as Victim, Offender, and Practitioner* (Westport, Conn.: Greenwood Press, 1987), pp. 47–48.

5. Helen E. Longino, "Pornography, Oppression, and Freedom: A Closer Look," in Laura Lederer, ed., *Take Back the Night: Women on Pornography* (New York: William Morrow, 1980), p. 44.

6. Flowers, *The Victimization and Exploitation of Women and Children*, p. 180.

7. Flowers, *Women and Criminality*, p. 48.

8. Cited in Richard Goodall, *The Comfort of Sin: Prostitutes and Prostitution in the 1990s* (Kent, England: Renaissance Books, 1995), p, 186.

9. Frances Patai, "Pornography and Woman Battering: Dynamic Similarities," in Maria Roy, ed., *The Abusive Partner: An Analysis of Domestic Battering* (New York: Van Nostrand Reinhold, 1982), pp. 91–92.

10. *Ibid.*, pp. 93–94.

11. Commission on Obscenity and Pornography, *Technical Report of the Commission on Obscenity and Pornography: Legal Analysis*, Vol. 2 (Washington, D.C.: Government Printing Office, 1971), p. 223.

12. Commission on Obscenity and Pornography, *Report of the Commission on Obscenity and Pornography* (New York: Bantam Books, 1970), pp. 580–81. See also "Keating Indicted in Savings Fraud and Goes to Jail," *New York Times* (September 19, 199), p. 1.

13. U.S. Department of Justice, *Attorney General's Commission on Pornography: Final Report*, Vol. 1 (Washington, D.C.: Government Printing Office, 1986), p. 215.

14. *Ibid.*, p. 216.

15. *Ibid.*, pp. 324–25.

16. *Ibid.*, pp. 465–81, 483–90.

17. Flowers, *Women and Criminality*, p. 53.

18. *Ibid.*, pp. 53–56.

19. Laura Lederer, ed., *Take Back the Night: Women on Pornography* (New York: William Morrow, 1980), pp. 19–20.

20. Kathleen Barry, *Female Sexual Slavery* (Englewood Cliffs, N.J.: Prentice-Hall, 1979), p. 145.

21. Flowers, *Women and Criminality*, p. 128; Flowers, *The Victimization and Exploitation of Women and Children*, pp. 83, 91, 177.

22. Quoted in Hillary Johnson, "Violence Against Women: Is Porn to Blame?" *Vogue* 175 (September 1985), p. 678.

23. Larry Baron and Murray A. Straus, "Sexual Stratification, Pornography, and Rape in the United States," in Neil M. Malamuth and Edward Donnerstein, eds., *Pornography and Sexual Aggression* (Orlando, Fla.: Academic Press, 1984), p. 206.

24. Quoted in Johnson, "Violence Against Women," p. 678.

25. Quoted in William A. Stanmeyer, *The Seduction of Society* (Ann Arbor, Mich.: Servant Books, 1984), pp. 29–30.

26. *Ibid.*, p. 49; Flowers, *Women and Criminality*, p. 54.

27. Stanmeyer, *The Seduction of Society*, p. 49.

28. *Ibid.*, p. 42; Flowers, *Women and Criminality*, p. 54.

29. Flowers, *Female Crime, Criminals and Cellmates*, pp. 108–11; Flowers, *The Adolescent Criminal*, pp. 58–61.

30. Quoted in Alice Leuchtag, "The Culture of Pornography," *The Humanist* 55 (1995), pp. 4–5.

31. *Ibid.*, p. 5.

32. *Ibid.*

33. *Ibid.*, p. 6.

34. *Ibid.*, p. 4.

35. *Ibid.*, p. 6.

36. *Ibid.*

CHAPTER 16. CHILD PROSTITUTION AND CHILD PORNOGRAPHY

1. Rita Rooney, "Children for Sale: Pornography's Dark New World," *Reader's Digest* (July 1983), p. 53.

2. R. Barri Flowers, *The Victimization and Exploitation of Women and Children: A Study of Physical, Mental and Sexual Maltreatment in the United States* (Jefferson, N.C.: McFarland, 1994), pp. 81, 90.

3. Reay Tannahill, *Sex in History* (New York: Stein and Day, 1980), p. 320.

4. *Ibid.*, p. 90

5. *Ibid.*

6. Cited in Michael S. Serrill, "Defiling the Children," *Time* 141 (June 21, 1993), p. 52.

7. Cited in Ronald B. Flowers, *Women and Criminality: The Woman as Victim, Offender, and Practitioner* (Westport, Conn.: Greenwood Press, 1987), p. 48.

8. Cited in Joan J. Johnson, *Teen Prostitution* (Danbury, Conn.: Franklin Watts, 1992), p. 90.

9. Cited in R. Barri Flowers, *The Adolescent Criminal: An Examination of Today's Juvenile Offender* (Jefferson, N.C.: McFarland, 1990), p. 64.

10. Shirley O'Brien, *Child Pornography* (Dubuque, Iowa: Kendall/Hunt, 1983), p. 19; M. Guio, A. Burgess, and R. Kelly, "Child Victimization: Pornography and Prostitution," *Journal of Crime and Justice* 3 (1980): 65–81.

11. Cited in Ronald B. Flowers, *Children and Criminality: The Child as Victim and Perpetrator* (Westport, Conn.: Greenwood Press, 1986), p. 82.

12. Flowers, *The Adolescent Criminal*, p. 64.

13. Flowers, *The Victimization and Exploitation of Women and Children*, p. 91; Johnson, *Teen Prostitution*, p. 90.

14. Flowers, *Children and Criminality*, pp. 82–83.

15. "Child Pornography on the Rise Despite Tougher Laws," *Sacramento Union* (April 7, 1984), p. E6.

16. *Ibid.*

17. *Ibid.*

18. Flowers, *The Adolescent Criminal*, pp. 54–65.

19. Cited in Johnson, *Teen Prostitution*, p. 91.

20. *Ibid.*, pp. 35–36; Carol Smolenski, "Sex Tourism and the Sexual Exploitation of Children," *Christian Century* 112 (1995): 1079–81; Susan Moran, "New World Havens of Oldest Profession," *Insight on the News* 9 (1993): 12–16.

21. Moran, "New World Havens of Oldest Profession."

22. 18 U.S.C. §§2251, 2253–54 (1978).

23. Flowers, *The Victimization and Exploitation of Women and Children*, pp. 92–93.

24. *Ibid.*, p. 93.

25. "Clinton Signs Child Sex Crime Bill," *Facts on File* 55 (1995): 983.

26. The Communications Decency Act was enacted into law on February 8, 1996.

27. Communications Decency Act (1996). See also the following Internet websites: American Civil Liberties Union — http://www.aclu.org/; Electronic Privacy Information Center — http://www.epic.org/.

28. American Civil Liberties Union website.

29. *Ibid.*; Supreme Court ruling, Associated Press, June 26, 1997.

CHAPTER 17. CUSTOMERS OF FEMALE PROSTITUTES

1. R. Barri Flowers, *The Adolescent Criminal: An Examination of Today's Juvenile Offender* (Jefferson, N.C.: McFarland, 1990), pp. 62–63.

2. Susan Bakos, "The Hugh Grant Syndrome: Why Nice Guys Go to Hookers," *McCall's* 123 (November 1995), p. 106.

3. Esther Davidowitz, "Why 'Nice' Men Pay for Sex," *Woman's Day* 56 (August 10, 1993), pp. 101–2.

4. Jennifer James, "The Prostitute as Victim," in Jane R. Chapman and Margaret Gates, eds., *The Victimization of Women* (Beverly Hills: Sage, 1978), p. 176; R. Barri Flowers, *The Victimization and Exploitation of Women and Children: A Study of Physical, Mental and Sexual Maltreatment in the United States* (Jefferson, N.C.: McFarland, 1994), p. 173.

5. Cited in Davidowitz, "Why 'Nice' Men Pay for Sex," p. 100.

6. Bakos, "The Hugh Grant Syndrome," p. 108.

7. *Ibid.*

8. U.S. Department of Justice, Federal Bureau of Investigation (FBI), *Crime in the United States: Uniform Crime Reports 1995* (Washington, D.C.: Government Printing Office, 1996), p. 220.

9. *Ibid.*, p. 373; D. Kelly Weisberg, *Children of the Night: A Study of Adolescent Prostitution* (Lexington, Mass.: Lexington Books, 1985), p. 75.

10. Ronald B. Flowers, *Women and Criminality: The Woman as Victim, Offender, and Practitioner* (Westport, Conn.: Greenwood Press, 1987), p. 129.

11. Laura Trujillo, "Escort Services Thriving Industry in Portland Area," *Oregonian* (June 7, 1996), p. B1.

12. U.S. Department of Justice, FBI, *Crime in the United States*, p. 220.

13. Joan J. Johnson, *Teen Prostitution* (Danbury, Conn.: Franklin Watts, 1992), p. 117.

14. Cited in Bakos, "The Hugh Grant Syndrome," p. 108.

15. Flowers, *The Victimization and Exploitation of Women and Children*, pp. 71–89.

16. Bakos, "The Hugh Grant Syndrome," p. 108.

17. Quoted in *ibid.*

18. Richard Goodall, *The Comfort of Sin: Prostitutes and Prostitution in the 1990s* (Kent, England: Renaissance Books, 1995), pp. 69–79.

19. M. Stein, *Lovers, Friends, Slaves...* (New York: Berkeley, 1974), pp. 317–20.

20. Bakos, "The Hugh Grant Syndrome," p. 108.

21. Davidowitz, "Why 'Nice' Men Pay for Sex," p. 101.

22. *Ibid.*, pp. 101, 106–7; Bakos, "The Hugh Grant Syndrome," p. 108.

23. Stein, *Lovers, Friends, Slaves...*, pp. 1–2.

24. Cited in Johnson, *Teen Prostitution*, p. 131.

25. Cited in Anastasia Volkonsky, "Legalizing the 'Profession' Would Sanction the Abuse," *Insight on the News* 11 (1995), p. 20.

26. Flowers, *The Adolescent Criminal*, p. 60; R. Barri Flowers, *Children and*

Criminality: The Child as Victim and Perpetrator (Westport, Conn.: Greenwood Press, 1986), pp. 81–82.

27. "The Enablers," *Juvenile Prostitution in Minnesota: The Report of a Research Project* (St. Paul: The Enablers, 1978), p. 75.

28. Johnson, *Teen Prostitution*, p. 119; R. Barri Flowers, *Female Crime, Criminals and Cellmates: An Exploration of Female Criminality and Delinquency* (Jefferson, N.C.: McFarland, 1995), p. 153.

29. Quoted in Davidowitz, "Why 'Nice' Men Pay for Sex," p. 100.

30. Cited in Linda Lee, "The World (and Underworld) of the Professional Call Girl," *New Woman* (January 1988), p. 62.

31. Cited in Barbara Goldsmith, "Women on the Edge: A Reporter at Large," *New Yorker* 69 (April 26, 1993), p. 65.

32. *Ibid.*

33. Martin A. Plant, "Sex Work, Alcohol, Drugs, and AIDS," in Martin A. Plant, ed., *AIDS, Drugs, and Prostitution* (London: Routledge, 1990), pp. 1–17.

34. Flowers, *Female Crime, Criminals and Cellmates*, pp. 153, 156.

35. Flowers, *The Adolescent Criminal*, pp. 63–64.

36. Cited in Paul Recer, "Study: Unfaithful Men Can Spread Cervical Cancer," *Oregonian* (August 7, 1996), p. E6.

37. Quoted in *ibid.*

38. Volkonsky, "Legalizing the 'Profession' Would Sanction the Abuse," p. 22; "In Oregon, Portland Enacted an Ordinance in December," *Oregonian* (March 5, 1996), p. A5.

39. Volkonsky, "Legalizing the 'Profession' Would Sanction the Abuse," p. 22.

40. "In Oregon, Portland Enacted an Ordinance in December," p. A5.

41. Volkonsky, "Legalizing the 'Profession' Would Sanction the Abuse," p. 22.

42. "In Oregon, Portland Enacted an Ordinance in December," p. A5.

43. *Ibid.*

44. *Ibid.*; "Prostitution Stings Catch 20 People and 16 Vehicles," *Oregonian* (March 21, 1996), p. D6.

45. Alice Leuchtag, "Merchants of Flesh: International Prostitution and the War on Women's Rights," *The Humanist* 55, 2 (1995), p. 14.

46. Carol Smolenski, "Sex Tourism and the Sexual Exploitation of Children," *Christian Century* 112 (1995), p. 1080.

47. Leuchtag, "Merchants of Flesh," p. 12.

48. *Ibid.*, p. 15.

49. Margot Hornblower, "The Skin Trade," *Time* 141 (June 21, 1993), p. 44.

50. *Ibid.*

51. Smolenski, "Sex Tourism and the Sexual Exploitation of Children," p. 1080.

52. Leuchtag, "Merchants of Flesh," p. 14.

53. *Ibid.*

54. *Ibid.*, p. 15.

55. Smolenski, "Sex Tourism and the Sexual Exploitation of Children," p. 1079.

CHAPTER 18. MALE PROSTITUTION

1. R. Barri Flowers, *The Victimization and Exploitation of Women and Children: A Study of Physical, Mental and Sexual Maltreatment in the United States* (Jefferson, N.C.: McFarland, 1994), p. 82.

2. Robin Lloyd, *For Money or Love: Boy Prostitution in America* (New York: Ballantine, 1976), p. 211.

3. U.S. Department of Justice, Federal Bureau of Investigation (FBI), *Crime in the United States: Uniform Crime Reports 1995* (Washington, D.C.: Government Printing Office, 1996), pp. 213, 220.

4. *Ibid.*, pp. 220, 222.

5. *Ibid.*, p. 220.

6. *Ibid.*, p. 226.

7. *Ibid.*, pp. 233, 242, 251, 260.

8. S. Caukins and N. Coombs, "The Psychodynamics of Male Prostitution," *American Journal of Psychotherapy* 30 (1976): 441–51.

9. *Ibid.*, p. 441

10. Donald M. Allen, "Young Male Prostitutes: A Psychosocial Study," *Archives of Sexual Behavior* 9 (1980): 399–426.

11. Dan Waldorf and Sheigla Murphy, "Intravenous Drug Use and Syringe-Sharing Practices of Call Men and Hustlers," in Martin A. Plant, ed., *AIDS, Drugs, and Prostitution* (London: Routledge, 1990), pp. 109–31.

12. *Ibid.*

13. Allen, "Young Male Prostitutes," p. 418.

14. *Ibid.*, pp. 419–20.

15. *Ibid.*

16. *Ibid.*, pp. 409–18.

17. N. Coombs, "Male Prostitution: A Psychosocial View of Behavior," *American Journal of Orthopsychiatry* 44 (1974): 782–89.

18. Richard Green, *Sexual Science and the Law* (Cambridge, Mass.: Harvard University Press, 1992), p. 194.

19. C. Earls and H. David, "A Psychosocial Study of Male Prostitution," *Archives of Sexual Behavior* 18 (1989): 401–19.

20. Caukins and Coombs, "The Psychodynamics of Male Prostitution," p. 446; Green, *Sexual Science and the Law*, p. 194.

21. Coombs, "Male Prostitution," pp. 782–89.

22. Earls and David, "A Psychosocial Study of Male Prostitution," pp. 401–19.

23. See, for example, Caukins and Coombs, "The Psychodynamics of Male Prostitution," p. 450; D. MacNamara, "Male Prostitution in American Cities: A Socioeconomic or Pathological Phenomenon?" *American Journal of Orthopsychiatry* 35 (1965): 204.

24. Caukins and Coombs, "The Psychodynamics of Male Prostitution," p. 450.

25. *Ibid.*, pp. 446, 450; Green, *Sexual Science and the Law*, p. 194.

26. Caukins and Coombs, "The Psychodynamics of Male Prostitution," p. 446.

27. Joan J. Johnson, *Teen Prostitution* (Danbury, Conn.: Franklin Watts, 1992), p. 118.

28. Green, *Sexual Science and the Law*, pp. 193–96; Allen, "Young Male Prostitutes," p. 422; R. Barri Flowers, *The Adolescent Criminal: An Examination of Today's Juvenile Offender* (Jefferson, N.C.: McFarland, 1990), pp. 61–62.

29. Lloyd, *For Money or Love*, p. 211.

30. U.S. Department of Justice, FBI, *Crime in the United States*, p. 220.

31. *Ibid.*

32. *Ibid.*; Flowers, *The Adolescent Criminal*, pp. 62–63.

33. Flowers, *The Adolescent Criminal*, p. 61; U.S. Department of Justice, FBI, *Crime in the United States*, p. 220.

34. Quoted in Alfred Danna, "Juvenile Male Prostitution: How Can We Reduce the Problem?" *USA Today* 113 (May 1988), p. 87.

35. *Ibid.*, p. 88.

36. Flowers, *The Victimization and Exploitation of Women and Children*, p. 87.

37. Cited in Hilary Abramson, "Sociologists Try to Reach Young Hustlers," *Sacramento Bee* (September 3, 1984), p. A8.

38. Tamar Stieber, "The Boys Who Sell Sex to Men in San Francisco," *Sacramento Bee* (March 4, 1984), p. A22.

39. D. Kelly Weisberg, *Children of the Night: A Study of Adolescent Prostitution* (Lexington, Mass.: Lexington Books, 1985), p. 61.

40. Johnson, *Teen Prostitution*, p. 110.

41. Weisberg, *Children of the Night*, p. 19.

42. *Ibid.*, p. 40.

43. Johnson, *Teen Prostitution*, p. 110.

44. *Ibid.*, pp. 111–12.

45. Sparky Harlan, Luanne L. Rodgers, and Brian Slattery, *Male and Female Adolescent Prostitution: Huckleberry House Sexual Minority Youth Services Project* (Washington, D.C.: U.S. Department of Health and Human Services, 1981), p. 22.

46. Allen, "Young Male Prostitutes," pp. 399–426.

47. Weisberg, *Children of the Night*, p. 58.

48. U.S. Department of Justice, FBI, *Crime in the United States*, pp. 220, 222.

49. *Ibid.*

50. Cited in Stieber, "The Boys Who Sell Sex to Men," p. A22.

51. Weisberg, *Children of the Night*, pp. 124–28.

52. Flowers, *The Adolescent Criminal*, pp. 62–63; R. Barri Flowers, *Female Crime, Criminals, and Cellmates: An Exploration of Female Criminality and Delinquency* (Jefferson, N.C.: McFarland, 1995), pp. 105–8.

53. Weisberg, *Children of the Night*, p. 75.

54. Flowers, *The Adolescent Criminal*, pp. 60–63; Johnson, *Teen Prostitution*, pp. 110–13, 124–28.

55. Flowers, *The Victimization and Exploitation of Women and Children*, pp. 88–89; Waldorf and Murphy, "Intravenous Drug Use and Syringe-Sharing Practices of Call Men and Hustlers," pp. 109–27.

56. M. A. Chiasson, A. R. Lifson, R. L. Stoneburner, W. Ewing, D. Hilderbrandt, and H. W. Jaffe, "HIV–1 Seroprevalence in Male and Female Prostitutes in New York City," *Abstracts from the Sixth International Conference on AIDS* (Stockholm, Sweden, June 1988).

57. U. Tirelli, E. Vaccher, S. Diodatao, R. Biosio, P. De Paoli, and D. Crotti, "HIV Infection Among Female and Male Prostitutes," *Abstracts from the Third International Conference on AIDS* (Washington, D.C.: U.S. Department of Health and Human Services and the World Health Organization, 1987); U. Tirelli, D. Erranto, and D. Serraino, "HIV–1 Seroprevalence in Male Prostitutes in Northeastern Italy," *Journal of Acquired Immune Deficiency Syndromes* 1 (1988): 414–15.

58. Martin A. Plant, "Sex Work, Alcohol, Drugs, and AIDS," in Martin A. Plant, ed., *AIDS, Drugs, and Prostitution* (London: Routledge, 1990), pp. 7–8.

59. Waldorf and Murphy, "Intravenous Drug Use and Syringe-Sharing Practices of Call Men and Hustlers," pp. 109–10.

CHAPTER 19. LAWS AND PROSTITUTION

1. R. Barri Flowers, *Female Crime, Criminals and Cellmates: An Exploration of Female Criminality and Delinquency* (Jefferson, N.C.: McFarland, 1995), p. 103.

2. *Ibid.*; Anastasia Volkonsky, "Legalizing the 'Profession' Would Sanction the Abuse," *Insight on the News* 11 (1995), p. 21.

3. Flowers, *Female Crime, Criminals and Cellmates*, p. 105; R. Barri Flowers, *The Adolescent Criminal: An Examination of Today's Juvenile Offender* (Jefferson, N.C.: McFarland, 1990), pp. 60, 62.

4. Flowers, *Female Crime, Criminals and Cellmates*, p. 105.

5. *Ibid.*, p. 103.

6. *Ibid.*

7. *Ibid.*

8. *Ibid.*

9. *Ibid.*, p. 101; Susan Joffe, "I Was a Heidi Fleiss Call Girl," *Cosmopolitan* 217 (December 1994): 198–201.

10. "Prostitution Stings Catch 20 People and 16 Vehicles," *Oregonian* (March 21, 1996), p. D6.

11. Esther Davidowitz, "Why 'Nice Men' Pay for Sex," *Woman's Day* 56 (August 10, 1993), pp. 100–101.

12. *Caesar's Health Club v. St. Louis County*, 565 S.W. 2d 783 (1978), *cert. denied* 439 U.S. 955 (1978); Richard Green, *Sexual Science and the Law* (Cambridge, Mass.: Harvard University Press, 1992), p. 197.

13. *Morgan v. City of Detroit*, 389 F. Supp. 922 (E.D. Mich. 1975).

14. *IDK, Inc. v. Clark County*, 836 F. 2d 1185 (9th Cir. 1988).

15. *Ibid.*, p. 1195.

16. *Coyote v. Roberts*, 502 F. Supp. 1342 (R.I. 1980), 523 F. Supp. 352 (R.I. 1981).

17. "In Oregon, Portland Enacted an Ordinance in December," *Oregonian* (March 5, 1996), p. A5.

18. "Nasty Attack of Seizure," *Time* 147 (March 18, 1996), p. 80.

19. Richard Goodall, *The Comfort of Sin: Prostitutes and Prostitution in the 1990s* (Kent, England: Renaissance Books, 1995), p. 200.

20. Cited in James Bovard, "Safeguard Public Health: Legalize Contractual Sex," *Insight on the News* 11 (1995), p. 20.

21. Laura Miller, "Prostitution," *Harper's Bazaar* 3400 (March 1995), p. 210.

22. 42 U.S.C. §§5101–5106 (1974), as amended by the Child Abuse Prevention

and Treatment and Adoption Reform Act of 1978, P.L. No. 95–266, 92 Stat. 205 (1978).

23. 42 U.S.C. §§5101–5106 (1974).

24. Ronald B. Flowers, *Children and Criminality: The Child as Victim and Perpetrator* (Westport, Conn.: Greenwood Press, 1986), p. 189.

25. P.L. 93–247 (1974); P.L. 100–295 (1992); R. Barri Flowers, *The Victimization and Exploitation of Women and Children: A Study of Physical, Mental and Sexual Maltreatment in the United States* (Jefferson, N.C.: McFarland, 1994), pp. 196–97.

26. Child Abuse, Domestic Violence, Adoption and Family Services Act of 1992, P.L. 100–295 (1992).

27. Flowers, *The Victimization and Exploitation of Women and Children*, pp. 196–97.

28. *Ibid.*, p. 197.

29. U.S. Department of Health and Human Services, *National Child Abuse and Neglect Data System: Working Paper 2 1991 Summary Data Component* (Washington, D.C.: National Center on Child Abuse and Neglect, 1993), pp. 1, 6.

30. Flowers, *The Victimization and Exploitation of Women and Children*, p. 197.

31. Juvenile Justice and Delinquency Prevention Act of 1974, P.L. 93–415 (1974).

32. *Ibid.*, Title II, Part B., Sec. 223 (a) (12) (1974).

33. Runaway and Homeless Youth Act, 42 U.S.C. §§5701–5702 (Supp. II, 1978).

34. Flowers, *Children and Criminality*, p. 190; D. Kelly Weisberg, *Children of the Night: A Study of Adolescent Prostitution* (Lexington, Mass.: Lexington Books, 1985), pp. 196–97.

35. Flowers, *Children and Criminality*, pp. 191–92; 128 *Cong. Rec.* 8, 566 (1982).

36. 18 U.S.C. §1073 (1980).

37. "Funding for Missing Children Center Wins OK," *Sacramento Bee* (June 5, 1984), p. A4.

38. Flowers, *Children and Criminality*, p. 192.

39. 18 U.S.C. §§2251, 2253–54 (1978).

40. *Ibid.*; Flowers, *The Victimization and Exploitation of Women and Children*, pp. 198–99.

41. "Clinton Signs Child Sex Crime Bill," *Facts on File* 55 (1995): 983.

42. Cited in Carol Smolenski, "Sex Tourism and the Sexual Exploitation of Children," *Christian Century* 112 (1995), p. 1079.

43. See the following Internet websites: American Civil Liberties Union — http://www.aclu.org/; Electronic Privacy Information Center — http://www.epic.org/; Center for Democracy and Technology — http://www.cdt.org/.

44. See the Internet website for the American Civil Liberties Union.

45. *Ibid.*; Supreme Court ruling, Associated Press, June 26, 1997.

46. Flowers, *Children and Criminality*, pp. 192–93; Weisberg, *Children of the Night*, p. 202.

47. Flowers, *Children and Criminality*, p. 190–92; Linda Greenwood, "Justices Uphold Law Barring Child Pornography," *New York Times* (July 3, 1982), p. 1.

48. Flowers, *Children and Criminality*, p. 191.

49. *Ibid.*; Weisberg, *Children of the Night*, p. 205.

50. Flowers, *Children and Criminality*, pp. 192–93; Weisberg, *Children of the Night*, p. 206.

CHAPTER 20. EXAMINING THE ISSUES OF DECRIMINALIZATION AND LEGALIZATION OF PROSTITUTION

1. Laura Miller, "Prostitution," *Harper's Bazaar* 3400 (March 1995), pp. 208–10.
2. Cited in Anastasia Volkonsky, "Legalizing the 'Profession' Would Sanction the Abuse," *Insight on the News* 11 (1995), p. 20.
3. Cited in Miller, "Prostitution," p. 208.
4. *Ibid.*, p. 210.
5. Quoted in *ibid.*
6. *Ibid.*
7. *Ibid.*
8. *Coyote v. Roberts*, 502 F. Supp. 1342 (R.I. 1980).
9. Quoted in Miller, "Prostitution," p. 210.
10. *Ibid.*
11. Quoted in *ibid.*
12. Cited in Barbara Goldsmith, "Women on the Edge: A Reporter at Large," *New Yorker* 69 (April 26, 1993), p. 77.
13. *Ibid.*
14. *Ibid.*
15. Cited in Richard Goodall, *The Comfort of Sin: Prostitutes and Prostitution in the 1990s* (Kent, England: Renaissance Books, 1995), p. 202.
16. Quoted in James Bovard, "Safeguard Public Health: Legalize Contractual Sex," *Insight on the News* 11 (1995), p. 19.
17. Terry Glover, "The Shame Game: Who Profits from Prostitution," *Playboy* (June 1996), pp. 59–60.
18. Bovard, "Safeguard Public Health," p. 18.
19. Cited in *ibid.*, p. 20.
20. *Ibid.*
21. *Ibid.*
22. *Ibid.*, p. 19.
23. *Ibid.*, pp. 18–20; Goodall, *The Comfort of Sin*, pp. 129–99.
24. Miller, "Prostitution," p. 210.
25. Goodall, *The Comfort of Sin*, p. 103.
26. Alice Leuchtag, "The Culture of Pornography," *The Humanist* 55, 3 (1995): 4–6.
27. Goodall, *The Comfort of Sin*, p. 103.
28. Quoted in Miller, "Prostitution," p. 210.
29. Leuchtag, "The Culture of Pornography," p. 6.
30. Quoted in Miller, "Prostitution," p. 210.
31. Volkonsky, "Legalizing the 'Profession' Would Sanction the Abuse," p. 20.
32. *Ibid.*
33. *Ibid.*; R. Barri Flowers, *The Victimization and Exploitation of Women and Children: A Study of the Physical, Mental and Sexual Maltreatment in the United States* (Jefferson, N.C.: McFarland, 1994), pp. 82–85.

34. Volkonsky, "Legalizing the 'Profession' Would Sanction the Abuse," p. 21.

35. Susan Moran, "New World Havens of Oldest Profession," *Insight on the News* 9 (1993): 12–16.

36. Volkonsky, "Legalizing the 'Profession' Would Sanction the Abuse," p. 21.

37. *Ibid.*

38. Quoted in *ibid.*

39. R. Barri Flowers, *Female Crime, Criminals and Cellmates: An Exploration of Female Criminality and Delinquency* (Jefferson, N.C.: McFarland, 1995), pp. 149–50.

40. *Ibid.*, p. 150.

41. *Ibid.*, pp. 141–56.

42. *Ibid.*, p. 156.

43. Volkonsky, "Legalizing the 'Profession' Would Sanction the Abuse," p. 21.

44. Miller, "Prostitution," p. 210.

45. Volkonsky, "Legalizing the 'Profession' Would Sanction the Abuse," p. 21.

46. *Ibid.*

47. *Ibid.*

48. Flowers, *Female Crime, Criminals, and Cellmates*, pp. 101–14, 148–56.

CHAPTER 21. THE PROSTITUTION OF WOMEN WORLDWIDE

1. Cited in Alice Leuchtag, "Merchants of Flesh: International Prostitution and the War on Women's Rights," *The Humanist* 55, 2 (1995), p. 11.

2. *Ibid.*

3. Susan Ladika, "Booming Slave Trade Lures Europeans," *Oregonian* (June 11, 1996), p. A1.

4. Monika Bauerlein, "The Borderless Bordello," *Utne Reader* 72 (November-December 1995), p. 30.

5. Leuchtag, "Merchants of Flesh," p. 11.

6. Carol Smolenski, "Sex Tourism and the Sexual Exploitation of Children," *Christian Century* 112 (1995), pp. 1079–80.

7. Leuchtag, "Merchants of Flesh," p. 13; Lillian S. Robinson, "Touring Thailand's Sex Industry," *The Nation* 257 (1993): 492–97.

8. Smolenski, "Sex Tourism and the Sexual Exploitation of Children," p. 1080.

9. Leuchtag, "Merchants of Flesh," p. 12.

10. Smolenski, "Sex Tourism and the Sexual Exploitation of Children," p. 1080.

11. Leuchtag, "Merchants of Flesh," p. 12.

12. *Ibid.*

13. *Ibid.*, p. 13.

14. *Ibid.*

15. *Ibid.*

16. Smolenski, "Sex Tourism and the Sexual Exploitation of Children," p. 1080.

17. *Ibid.*

18. Cited in Leuchtag, "Merchants of Flesh," p. 14.

19. Robert I. Friedman, "India's Shame: Sexual Slavery and Political Corruption Are Leading to an AIDS Catastrophe," *The Nation* 262 (1996): 11–20.

20. *Ibid.*, p. 12.

21. *Ibid.*

22. Cited in *ibid.*

23. *Ibid.*

24. *Ibid.*

25. *Ibid.*, p. 14.

26. *Ibid.*

27. *Ibid.*, p. 16.

28. Valerie Reitman, "Tokyo's Latest Fad: Teen Prostitution," *Wall Street Journal* (October 2, 1996), p. A8; Margot Hornblower, "The Skin Trade," *Time* 141 (June 21, 1993), pp. 46–47.

29. Hornblower, "The Skin Trade," pp. 45–47; Ronald B. Flowers, *Minorities and Criminality* (Westport, Conn.: Greenwood Press, 1990), pp. 125–26.

30. Hornblower, "The Skin Trade," p. 47.

31. *Ibid.*

32. *Ibid.*

33. Leuchtag, "Merchants of Flesh," p. 16.

34. *Ibid.*

35. *Ibid.*

36. Hornblower, "The Skin Trade," p. 44.

37. Leuchtag, "Merchants of Flesh," p. 16.

38. *Ibid.*

39. Hornblower, "The Skin Trade," pp. 45–47.

40. Leuchtag, "Merchants of Flesh," p. 15.

41. Quoted in *ibid.*, p. 16.

42. Lynn Darling, "Havana at Midnight," *Esquire* 123 (May 1995), p. 98.

43. *Ibid.*

44. *Ibid.*

45. *Ibid.*, p. 96.

46. *Ibid.*, p. 98.

47. *Ibid.*

48. Cited in Petrien Venema and Jan Visser, "Safer Prostitution: New Approach in Holland," in Martin A. Plant, ed., *AIDS, Drugs, and Prostitution* (London: Routledge, 1990), p. 42.

49. *Ibid.*, p. 41.

50. *Ibid.*, p. 42.

51. Cited in *ibid.*, p. 52.

52. *Ibid.*, p. 49.

53. Dagmar Hedrich, "Prostitution and AIDS Risks Among Female Drug Users in Frankfurt," in Martin A. Plant, ed., *AIDS, Drugs, and Prostitution* (London: Routledge, 1990), p. 163.

54. Cited in Hornblower, "The Skin Trade," p. 45.

55. *Ibid.*, p. 46.

56. Hedrich, "Prostitution and AIDS Risks Among Female Drug Users in Frankfurt," p. 168.

57. Sheron Boyle, *Working Girls and Their Men* (London: Smith Gryphon, 1994), pp. 22, 183–84; Richard Goodall, *The Comfort of Sin: Prostitutes and Prostitution in the 1990s* (Kent, England: Renaissance Books, 1995), pp. 12–13.

58. Goodall, *The Comfort of Sin*, p. 12.

59. Boyle, *Working Girls and Their Men*, pp. 135–36.

60. *Ibid.*, p. 136.

61. *Ibid.*, p. 24.

62. *Ibid.*, p. 5.

63. *Ibid.*, p. 68.

64. *Ibid.*

65. *Ibid.*, pp. 160–62.

66. Cited in *ibid.*, p. 161.

67. Ruth Thomas, "AIDS Risks: Alcohol, Drugs, and the Sex Industry — A Scottish Study," in Martin A. Plant, ed., *AIDS, Drugs, and Prostitution* (London: Routledge, 1990), p. 88.

68. Cited in Goodall, *The Comfort of Sin*, p. 218.

69. *Ibid.*

70. *Ibid.*

71. *Ibid.*

72. *Ibid.*, pp. 209–11; Christine Harcourt and Ross Philpot, "Female Prostitutes, AIDS, Drugs, and Alcohol in New South Wales," in Martin A. Plant, ed., *AIDS, Drugs, and Prostitution* (London: Routledge, 1990), pp. 134–37; Peter May, "Rooting for the Dirty Diggers," *New Statesman & Society* 6 (1993).

73. The 1979 Prostitution Act decriminalizing solicitation was replaced by the 1988 Summary Offenses Act, effectively repealing the decriminalization of prostitution.

74. Goodall, *The Comfort of Sin*, p. 210.

75. *Report of the Select Committee of the Legislative Assembly Upon Prostitution*, Parliament of New South Wales, Australia, 1986.

76. Harcourt and Philpot, "Female Prostitutes, AIDS, Drugs, and Alcohol in New South Wales," pp. 137–38.

77. Cited in *ibid.*, p. 149.

78. *Ibid.*, p. 151.

79. Cited in *ibid.*, p. 145.

80. *Ibid.*, p. 146.

81. Cited in *ibid.*

82. *Ibid.*, p. 139.

83. Cited in Hornblower, "The Skin Trade," p. 48.

84. *Ibid.*, pp. 44, 48.

CHAPTER 22. CHILD PROSTITUTION AND SEXPLOITATION INTERNATIONALLY

1. Margot Hornblower, "The Skin Trade," *Time* 141 (June 21, 1993), p. 44.

2. Cited in "Conference Urges Action Ending Child Sexual Exploitation," *Oregonian* (August 29, 1996), p. A3.

3. See, for example, Carol Smolenski, "Sex Tourism and the Sexual Exploitation of Children," *Christian Century* 112 (1995), p. 1079; Michael S. Serrill, "Defiling the Children," *Time* 141 (June 21, 1993), p. 52.

4. Cited in "Legal and Pervasive Prostitution Draws Young Brazilians," *Oregonian* (June 12, 1996), p. A12.

5. Cited in Myrna Kostash, "Surviving the Streets," *Chatelaine* 67 (October 1994), p. 104.

6. Cited in Serrill, "Defiling the Children," p. 53.

7. *Ibid.*, p. 52.

8. Marlise Simons, "Child Abuse Growing Trend in Sex Market," *Oregonian* (April 30, 1993), p. A4.

9. *Ibid.*

10. Deborah Jones, "Pimped," *Chatelaine* 67 (November 1994), pp. 109–13.

11. *Ibid.*

12. *Ibid.*, p. 110.

13. *Ibid.*

14. *Ibid.*, pp. 109–10.

15. Kostash, "Surviving the Streets," p. 104.

16. Cited in *ibid.*

17. Cited in *ibid.*

18. Jones, "Pimped," p. 109.

19. *Ibid.*

20. Cited in "Legal and Persuasive Prostitution Draws Young Brazilians," p. A12.

21. *Ibid.*

22. Cited in Alice Leuchtag, "Merchants of Flesh: International Prostitution and the War on Women's Rights," *The Humanist* 55, 2 (1995), p. 14.

23. *Ibid.*

24. "Legal and Persuasive Prostitution Draws Young Brazilians," p. A12.

25. Cited in Serrill, "Defiling the Children," p. 52.

26. Robert I. Friedman, "India's Shame: Sexual Slavery and Political Corruption Are Leading to an AIDS Catastrophe," *The Nation* 262 (1996), p. 12.

27. Cited in *ibid.*

28. *Ibid.*

29. *Ibid.*

30. *Ibid.*

31. *Ibid.*, pp. 14–15.

32. Cited in Serrill, "Defiling the Children," p. 52.

33. Lillian S. Robinson, "Touring Thailand's Sex Industry," *The Nation* 257 (1993), p. 494.

34. *Ibid.*, p. 495.

35. *Ibid.*, p. 496

36. *Ibid.*, p. 494.

37. Cited in *ibid.*

38. Serrill, "Defiling the Children," p. 54.

39. Valerie Reitman, "Tokyo's Latest Fad: Teen Prostitution," *Wall Street Journal* (October 2, 1996), p. A8.

40. Cited in *ibid.*

41. Quoted in *ibid.*

42. *Ibid.*

43. *Ibid.*

44. Cited in *ibid.*

45. Sheron Boyle, *Working Girls and Their Men* (London: Smith Gryphon, 1994), pp. 122–27.

46. Hornblower, "The Skin Trade," p. 45.

47. *Ibid.*, p. 46.

48. Cited in Simons, "Child Abuse Growing Trend in Sex Market."

49. Cited in Audrey Magee and Philip Sherwell, "For Girls, Few Choices — All Bad: Seamstress, Servant, or Prostitute?" *World Press Review* 43 (1996): 12.

50. Leuchtag, "Merchants of Flesh," p. 11.

51. Simons, "Child Abuse Growing Trend in Sex Market."

52. *Ibid.*

53. Quoted in Serrill, "Defiling the Children," p. 53.

54. Simon, "Child Abuse Growing Trend in Sex Market."

55. Quoted in *ibid.*

56. Smolenski, "Sex Tourism and the Sexual Exploitation of Children," p. 1080.

57. *Ibid.*

58. Cited in Leuchtag, "Merchants of Flesh," p. 16.

59. *Ibid.*

60. Hornblower, "The Skin Trade," p. 45.

61. Cited in *ibid.*, p. 46.

62. Serrill, "Defiling the Children," p. 53.

63. *Ibid.*; R. Barri Flowers, *Female Crime, Criminals and Cellmates: An Exploration of Female Criminality and Delinquency* (Jefferson, N.C.: McFarland, 1995), pp. 153–57.

CHAPTER 23. AIDS AND FEMALE PROSTITUTION GLOBALLY

1. R. Barri Flowers, *Female Crime, Criminals and Cellmates: An Exploration of Female Criminality and Delinquency* (Jefferson, N.C.: McFarland, 1995), pp. 113–14, 156; Martin A. Plant, ed., *AIDS, Drugs, and Prostitution* (London: Routledge, 1990).

2. Robert I. Friedman, "India's Shame: Sexual Slavery and Political Corruption Are Leading to an AIDS Catastrophe," *The Nation* 262 (1996), p. 12.

3. *Ibid.*

4. *Ibid.*

5. Cited in Alice Leuchtag, "Merchants of Flesh: International Prostitution and the War on Women's Rights," *The Humanist* 55, 2 (1995), p. 12.

6. *Ibid.*; Friedman, "India's Shame," p. 12.

7. Lillian S. Robinson, "Touring Thailand's Sex Industry," *The Nation* 257 (1993): 492–97.

8. Cited in *ibid.*, p. 496.

9. *Ibid.*, p. 497.

10. Leuchtag, "Merchants of Flesh," p. 12.

11. Cited in Robinson, "Touring Thailand's Sex Industry," p. 494.

12. T. Rehle, "Risk Factors of HIV–1 Infection Among Female Prostitutes in Khon Kaen, Northeast Thailand," *JAMA: The Journal of the American Medical Association* 269 (1993): 2825.

13. Cited in Warren Strobel, "Vietnam Joins AIDS Battle, Asia Is Overtaking Africa as the Continent Most Devastated by the Deadly Disease," *Insight on the News* 10 (1994): 26.

14. *Ibid.*

15. *Ibid.*

16. *Ibid.*

17. "HIV Cases in China Nearly Double in Year," *Oregonian* (June 26, 1996), p. A4.

18. *Ibid.*

19. *Ibid.*

20. Robert F. Black, Sara Collins, and Don L. Boroughs, "Shooting Up the Future (Intravenous Drug Use and Subsequent Spread of AIDS in Brazil)," *U.S. News & World Report* 113 (July 27, 1992): 55.

21. *Ibid.*

22. *Ibid.*

23. *Ibid.*

24. Quoted in *ibid.*

25. National Committee on AIDS Control, *AIDS and Prostitution* (Amsterdam: Working Group on AIDS and Prostitution, 1988).

26. Cited in Petrien Venema and Jan Visser, "Safer Prostitution: A New Approach in Holland," in Martin A. Plant, ed., *AIDS, Drugs, and Prostitution* (London: Routledge, 1990), p. 52.

27. J. Van den Hoek et al., "Prevalence and Risk Factors of HIV Infections Among Drug Users and Drug-Using Prostitutes in Amsterdam," *AIDS* 2 (1987): 55–60.

28. See, for example, A. M. Johnson, "Heterosexual Transmission of Human Immune Deficiency Virus," *British Medical Journal* 296 (1988): 1017–20.

29. Cited in Dagmar Hedrich, "Prostitution and AIDS Risks Among Female Drug Users in Frankfurt," in Martin A. Plant, ed., *AIDS, Drugs, and Prostitution* (London: Routledge, 1990), p. 159.

30. *Ibid.*

31. *Ibid.*, pp. 159–74.

32. Cited in Pilar Estebanez, "Prostitution and AIDS in Spain," in Martin A. Plant, ed., *AIDS, Drugs, and Prostitution* (London: Routledge, 1990), pp. 193–94.

33. *Ibid.*, p. 193.

34. Cited in *ibid.*, p. 194.

35. *Ibid.*

36. *Ibid.*, p. 195.

37. Strobel, "Vietnam Joins AIDS Battle"; Alfred Neequaye, "Prostitution in Accra," in Martin A. Plant, ed., *AIDS, Drugs, and Prostitution* (London: Routledge, 1990), pp. 175–85.

38. M. J. Rosenberg and J. M. Weiner, "Prostitutes and AIDS: A Health Department Priority," *American Journal of Public Health* 78 (1988): 418–23.

39. Neequaye, "Prostitution in Accra," p. 175.

40. J. K. Kreiss, D. Koech, F. A. Plummer, K. K. Holmes, M. Lightfoote, P. Piot, A. R. Ronald, J. D. Ndinya-Achola, L. J. D'Costa, P. Roberts, E. N. Ngugi, and T. C. Quinn, "AIDS Virus Infection in Nairobi Prostitutes: Spread of the Epidemic in East Africa," *New England Journal of Medicine* 314 (1986): 414–18.

41. Neequaye, "Prostitution in Accra," pp. 175–81.

42. *Ibid.*, p. 179.

43. *Ibid.*

44. *Ibid.*, p. 183.

45. *Ibid.*, p. 181.

46. *Ibid.*, pp. 181–83.

47. Flowers, *Female Crime, Criminals and Cellmates*, pp. 113–14, 156; R. Barri Flowers, *The Adolescent Criminal: An Examination of Today's Juvenile Offender* (Jefferson, N.C.: McFarland, 1990), pp. 63–64.

48. Cited in Flowers, *Female Crime, Criminals, and Cellmates*, p. 113.

49. *Ibid.*

50. Cited in Patricia Hersch, "Coming of Age on City Streets," *Psychology Today* (January 1988), p. 37.

51. *Ibid.*; Flowers, *Female Crime, Criminals and Cellmates*, p. 156.

CHAPTER 24. RESPONDING TO THE WORLDWIDE TRAGEDY
OF FEMALE PROSTITUTION

1. Cited in Margot Hornblower, "The Skin Trade," *Time* 141 (June 21, 1993), p. 48.

2. *Ibid.*

3. Cited in Michael S. Serrill, "Defiling the Children," *Time* 141 (June 21, 1993), p. 54.

4. Hornblower, "The Skin Trade," p. 48.

5. *Ibid.*

6. *Ibid.*

7. *Ibid.*

8. Quoted in *ibid.*

9. *Ibid.*; Alice Leuchtag, "Merchants of Flesh: International Prostitution and the War on Women's Rights," *The Humanist* 55, 2 (1995), p. 16.

10. Quoted in Hornblower, "The Skin Trade," p. 44.

11. Anastasia Volkonsky, "Legalizing the 'Profession' Would Sanction the Abuse," *Insight on the News* 11 (1995), p. 22.

12. Leuchtag, "Merchants of Flesh," p. 16.

13. Stephanie Abarbanel, "Women Who Make a Difference," *Family Circle* 107 (January 11, 1994): 11–13.

14. Barbara Goldsmith, "Women on the Edge: A Reporter at Large," *New Yorker* 69 (April 26, 1993): 64–67, 74–78.

15. Carol Smolenski, "Sex Tourism and the Sexual Exploitation of Children," *Christian Century* 112 (1995), pp. 1080–81.

16. *Ibid.*, p. 1081.

17. *Ibid.*

18. *Ibid.*

19. *Ibid.*

20. Quoted in *ibid.*

21. Serrill, "Defiling the Children," p. 55.

22. *Ibid.*

23. Cited in *ibid.*

24. Robert I. Friedman, "India's Shame: Sexual Slavery and Political Corruption Are Leading to an AIDS Catastrophe," *The Nation* 262 (1996), p. 20.

25. Cited in *ibid.*

26. *Ibid.*

27. "Conference Urges Action Ending Child Sexual Exploitation," *Oregonian* (August 29, 1996), p. A3.

Bibliography

Abarbanel, Stephanie. "Women Who Make a Difference." *Family Circle* 107 (January 11, 1994): 11–13.

Abramson, Hilary. "Sociologists Try to Reach Young Hustlers." *Sacramento Bee* (September 3, 1984): A8.

Adams, Elizabeth A. "Madam 90210." *Cosmopolitan* 216 (January 1994): 154–57.

Adler, Freda. *Sisters in Crime: The Rise of the New Female Criminal.* New York: McGraw-Hill, 1975.

Allen, Clifford. *The Sexual Perversions and Abnormalities.* London: Oxford University Press, 1949.

Allen, Donald M. "Young Male Prostitutes: A Psychosocial Study." *Archives of Sexual Behavior* 9 (1980): 399–426.

Almodovar, Norma J. *Cop to Call Girl: Why I Left the LAPD to Make an Honest Living as a Beverly Hills Prostitute.* New York: Simon and Schuster, 1993.

Barbera-Hogan, Mary. "Teen Sex for Sale." *Teen* 31 (January 1987): 22.

Baron, Larry, and Murray A. Straus. "Sexual Stratification, Pornography, and Rape in the United States." In Neil M. Malamuth and Edward Donnerstein, eds., *Pornography and Sexual Aggression.* Orlando, Fla.: Academic Press, 1984.

Barrows, Sydney, and William Novak. *Mayflower Madam: The Secret Life of Sydney Biddle Barrows.* New York: Arbor House, 1986.

Barry, Kathleen. *Female Sexual Slavery.* Englewood Cliffs, N.J.: Prentice-Hall, 1979.

Bauerlein, Monika. "The Borderless Bordello." *Utne Reader* 72 (Nov.-Dec. 1995): 30–32.

Benjamin, Henry, and R. E. L. Masters. *Prostitution and Morality.* New York: Julian Press, 1964.

Black, Robert F., Sara Collins, and Don L. Boroughs. "Shooting Up the Future (Intravenous Drug Use and Subsequent Spread of AIDS in Brazil)." *U.S. News & World Report* 113 (July 27, 1992): 55.

Blanchard, Keith. "Young Johns." *Mademoiselle* 100 (May 1994): 130–33.

Bovard, James. "Safeguard Public Health: Legalize Contractual Sex." *Insight on the News* 11 (1995): 18–20.

Boyle, Sheron. *Working Girls and Their Men.* London: Smith Gryphon, 1994.

Bracey, Dorothy H. *"Baby-Pros": Preliminary Profiles of Juvenile Prostitutes.* New York: John Jay Press, 1979.

237

Brownmiller, Susan. *Against Our Will: Men, Women, and Rape*. New York: Simon and Schuster, 1975.

Bryan, James H. "Apprenticeship in Prostitution." *Social Problems* 12 (1965): 287–97.

_____. "Occupational Ideologies and Individual Attitudes of Call Girls." *Social Problems* 13 (1966): 441–50.

Bullough, Vern, and Bonnie Bullough. *Women and Prostitution: A Social History*. Buffalo, N.Y.: Prometheus, 1987.

Burgess, Ann. "The Use of Children in Pornography and Sex Rings." *Legal Response: Child Advocacy and Protection* 2, 4 (1981): 1–10.

Bush, P. J. *Drugs, Alcohol, and Sex*. New York: Marex, 1980.

Campbell, C. A. "Prostitution, AIDS, and Preventive Health Behavior." *Social Science and Medicine* 32 (1991): 1367–78.

Carpenter, Cheryl, Barry Blassner, Bruce D. Johnson, and Julia Loughlin. *Kids, Drugs, and Crime*. Lexington, Mass.: Lexington Books, 1988.

Caukins, S., and N. Coombs. "The Psychodynamics of Male Prostitution." *American Journal of Psychotherapy* 30 (1976): 441–51.

Centers for Disease Control (CDC). "Antibody to Human Immunodeficiency Virus in Female Prostitutes." *Morbidity and Mortality Weekly Report* (1987): 157–61.

Central Statistical Office. *Annual Abstract of Statistics 1995*. London: HMSO, 1995.

Chisholm, Patricia. "Street Warfare: Neighborhoods Try to Control the Hooker Trade." *Maclean's* 108 (July 17, 1995): 35–40.

Choisy, M. *Psychoanalysis of the Prostitute*. New York: Philosophical Library, 1961.

Clinard, Marshall B. *Sociology of Deviant Behavior*. New York: Holt, Rinehart and Winston, 1975.

Cross, Harold. *The Lust Market*. New York: Citadel Press, 1956.

Crowley, Maura G. "Female Runaway Behavior and Its Relationship to Prostitution." Master's thesis, Sam Houston State University, Institute of Contemporary Corrections and Behavioral Sciences, 1977.

Danna, Alfred. "Juvenile Male Prostitution: How Can We Reduce the Problem?" *USA Today* 113 (May 1988): 87–88.

Darling, Lynn. "Havana at Midnight." *Esquire* 123 (May 1995): 96–104.

Darrow, William. "Prostitution, Intravenous Drug Use, and HIV-1 in the United States." In Martin A. Plant, ed., *AIDS, Drugs, and Prostitution*. London: Routledge, 1990.

Davidowitz, Esther. "Why 'Nice' Men Pay for Sex." *Woman's Day* 56 (August 10, 1993): 100–107.

Davis, Kingsley. "The Sociology of Prostitution." *American Sociological Review* 2 (1937): 744–55.

Densen-Gerber, Judianne, and S. F. Hutchinson. "Medical-Legal and Societal Problems Involving Children-Child Prostitution, Child Pornography, and Drug-Related Abuse: Recommended Legislation." In Selwyn M. Smith, ed., *The Maltreatment of Children*. Baltimore: University Park Press, 1978.

Dorfman, L. E., P. A. Derish, and J. B. Cohen. "Hey Girlfriend: An Evaluation of AIDS Prevention Among Women in the Sex Industry." *Health Education Quarterly* 19 (1992): 25–40.

Drummond, Isabel. *The Sex Paradox*. New York: Putnam, 1953.

Ehrlich, Paul. "Asia's Shocking Secret." *Reader's Digest* (October 1993): 69–75.

Enablers, The. *Juvenile Prostitution in Minnesota: The Report of a Research Project*. St. Paul: The Enablers, 1978.

Engel, Margaret. "Many Prostitutes Found to Be AIDS Carriers." *Washington Post* (September 20, 1985): A1.

English, C. J. "Leaving Home: A Typology of Runaways." *Society* 10 (1973): 22–24.

Exner, J., J. Wylie, A. Leura, and T. Parill. "Some Psychological Characteristics of Prostitutes." *Journal of Personality Assessment* 41 (1977): 474–85.

Faris, Robert E. *Social Disorganization.* New York: Ronald Press, 1955.

Fleming, Charles, and Michele Ingrassia. "The Heidi Chronicles." *Newsweek* 122 (August 16, 1993): 50–53.

Fletcher, Connie. "What Cops Know: The Facts About Prostitution." *Cosmopolitan* 212 (January 1992): 170.

Flexner, Abraham. *Prostitution in Europe.* New York: Century, 1914.

Flowers, R. Barri. *The Adolescent Criminal: An Examination of Today's Juvenile Offender.* Jefferson, N.C.: McFarland, 1990.

_____. *Female Crime, Criminals, and Cellmates: An Exploration of Female Criminality and Delinquency.* Jefferson, N.C.: McFarland, 1995.

_____. *The Victimization and Exploitation of Women and Children: A Study of Physical, Mental and Sexual Maltreatment in the United States.* Jefferson, N.C.: McFarland, 1994.

Flowers, Ronald Barri. *Children and Criminality: The Child as Victim and Perpetrator.* Westport, Conn.: Greenwood Press, 1986.

_____. *Demographics and Criminality: The Characteristics of Crime in America.* Westport, Conn.: Greenwood Press, 1989.

_____. *Minorities and Criminality.* Westport, Conn.: Greenwood Press, 1990.

_____. *Women and Criminality: The Woman as Victim, Offender, and Practitioner.* Westport, Conn.: Greenwood Press, 1987.

Freud, Sigmund. *New Introductory Lectures in Psychoanalysis.* New York: W. W. Norton, 1933.

Friedman, Robert I. "India's Shame: Sexual Slavery and Political Corruption Are Leading to an AIDS Catastrophe." *The Nation* 262 (1996): 11–20.

Friedman, Vanessa. "Dialing for Dollars." *Vogue* 185 (September 1995): 416–20.

Gagnon, John H. "Female Child Victims of Sex Offenses." *Social Problems* 13 (1965): 191.

Gebhard, P. H., J. H. Gagnon, W. B. Pomeroy, and C. V. Christenson. *Sex Offenders.* New York: Harper and Row, 1965.

Gibson-Ainyette, I., D. Templer, R. Brown, and L. Veaco. "Adolescent Female Prostitutes." *Archives of Sexual Behavior* 17 (1980): 431–38.

Glover, Edward G. *The Psychopathology of Prostitution.* 2nd ed. London: I.S.T.D., 1957.

Glover, Terry. "The Shame Game: Who Profits from Prostitution." *Playboy* 43 (June 1996): 58–60.

Glueck, Sheldon, and Eleanor Glueck. *Five Hundred Delinquent Women.* New York: Alfred A. Knopf, 1934.

Goldsmith, Barbara. "Women on the Edge: A Reporter at Large." *New Yorker* 69 (April 26, 1993): 64–67, 74–78.

Goldstein, Paul J. *Prostitution and Drugs.* Lexington, Mass.: Lexington Books, 1979.

Goodall, Richard. *The Comfort of Sin: Prostitutes and Prostitution in the 1990s.* Kent, England: Renaissance Books, 1995.

Gray, Diana. "Turning Out: A Study of Teenage Prostitution." Master's thesis, University of Washington, 1971.

Green, Richard. *Sexual Science and the Law.* Cambridge, Mass.: Harvard University Press, 1992.

Greenwald, Harold. *The Elegant Prostitute: A Social and Psychoanalytic Study.* New York: Walker and Co., 1970.

Guio, M., A. Burgess, and R. Kelly. "Child Victimization: Pornography and Prostitution." *Journal of Crime and Justice* 3 (1980): 65–81.

Gup, Ted. "What's New with the World's Oldest Profession." *Cosmopolitan* 219 (October 1995): 236–38.

Haft, Marilyn G. "Hustling for Rights." In Laura Crites, ed., *The Female Offender*. Lexington, Mass.: Lexington Books, 1976.

Hale, Ellen. "Center Studies Causes of Juvenile Prostitution." *Gannett News Service* (May 21, 1981).

Harcourt, Christine, and Ross Philpot. "Female Prostitutes, AIDS, Drugs, and Alcohol in New South Wales." In Martin A. Plant, ed., *AIDS, Drugs, and Prostitution*. London: Routledge, 1990.

Harlan, Sparky, Luanne L. Rodgers, and Brian Slattery. *Male and Female Adolescent Prostitution: Huckleberry House Sexual Minority Youth Services Project*. Washington, D.C.: U.S. Department of Health and Human Services, 1981.

Heard, Nathan C. *Howard Street*. New York: Dial Press, 1970.

Hedrich, Dagmar. "Prostitution and AIDS Risks Among Female Drug Users in Frankfurt." In Martin A. Plant, ed., *AIDS, Drugs, and Prostitution*. London: Routledge, 1990.

Henderson, Andre. "The War Against the Sex Trade." *Governing* 7 (April 1994): 38.

Hersch, Patricia. "Coming of Age on City Streets." *Psychology Today* (January 1988): 28–37.

Hildebrand, James A. "Why Runaways Leave Home." *Police Science* 54 (1963): 211–16.

Hirschberg, Lynn. "Heidi Does Hollywood." *Vanity Fair* 57 (February 1994): 88–92.

Hochstein, Rolaine. "Prostitutes: Happy Hookers or Society's Victims?" *Glamour* 83 (May 1985): 184–91.

Hoigard, Cecilie, and Liv Finstad. *Backstreets*. University Park: Pennsylvania State University Press, 1992.

Hollander, Xavier. *The Happy Hooker*. Detroit, Mich.: Buccaneer Books, 1993.

Holmes, K. K., P. A. Mardh, P. E. Sparling, and P. J. Wiesner, eds. *Sexually Transmitted Diseases*. New York: McGraw-Hill, 1984.

Homer, Louise. "Criminality-Based Resource for Runaway Girls." *Social Casework* 10 (1973): 474.

Hornblower, Margot. "The Skin Trade." *Time* 141 (June 21, 1993): 44–51.

Hubbell, John G. "Child Prostitution: How It Can Be Stopped." *Reader's Digest* (June 1984): 202, 205.

Hutchinson, Jim. "Prostitution's Sickening Trade in Children." *Reader's Digest* (Canadian) (August 1994): 29.

Ignoto, Barbara. *Confessions of a Part-Time Call Girl*. New York: Dell, 1986.

Jackson, Norman, Richard O'Toole, and Gilbert Geis, "The Self-Image of the Prostitute." In John H. Gagnon and William Simon, eds., *Sexual Deviance*. New York: Harper and Row, 1967.

James, J., C. Fosho, and R. W. Wohl. "The Relationship Between Female Criminality and Drug Use." *International Journal of the Addictions* 14 (1979): 115–229.

James, Jennifer. *Entrance into Juvenile Prostitution*. Washington, D.C.: National Institute of Mental Health, 1980.

_____. "Motivations for Entrance into Prostitution." In Laura Crites, ed., *The Female Offender*. Lexington, Mass.: Lexington Books, 1976.

_____. "The Prostitute as Victim." In Jane R. Chapman and Margaret Gates, eds., *The Victimization of Women*. Beverly Hills: Sage, 1978.

_____. "Prostitute-Pimp Relationships." *Medical Aspects of Human Sexuality* 7 (1973): 147–63.

_____. "Prostitutes and Prostitution." In Edward Sagarin and Fred Montanino, eds., *Deviants: Voluntary Actors in a Hostile World*. Morrison, N.J.: General Learning Press, 1977.

_____. "Two Domains of Streetwalker Argot." *Anthropological Linguistics* 14 (1972): 174–75.

James, Jennifer, and J. Meyerding, "Early Sexual Experience and Prostitution." *American Journal of Psychiatry* 134 (1977): 1381–85.

Jerome, Richard. "Risky Business: An Honor's Student Turns Call Girl — And Pays with Her Life." *People Weekly* 45, 23 (June 18, 1996): 75.

Joffe, Susan. "I Was a Heidi Fleiss Girl." *Cosmopolitan* 217 (December 1994): 198–201.

Johnson, A. M. "Heterosexual Transmission of Human Immune Deficiency Virus." *British Medical Journal* 296 (1988): 1017–20.

Johnson, Joan J. *Teen Prostitution*. Danbury, Conn.: Franklin Watts, 1992.

Jones, Deborah. "Pimped." *Chatelaine* 67 (November 1994): 109–15.

Karen, Robert. "The World of the Middle Class Prostitute." *Cosmopolitan* 202 (January 1987): 202–7.

Kostash, Myrna. "Surviving the Streets." *Chatelaine* 67 (October 1994): 103–7.

Ladika, Susan. "Booming Slave Trade Lures Europeans." *Oregonian* (June 11, 1996): A1.

Lange, W. R., F. R. Snyder, D. Lozovsky, V. Kaistha, A. Kaczaniuk, and J. H. Jaffe. "HIV Infection in Baltimore: Antibody Seroprevalence Rates Amongst Parenteral Drug Abusers and Prostitutes." *Maryland Medical Journal* 36 (1987): 757–61.

Lederer, Laura, ed. *Take Back the Night: Women on Pornography*. New York: William Morrow, 1980.

Lee, Linda. "The World (and Underworld) of the Professional Call Girl." *New Woman* (January 1988): 60–63.

Lee, Mark, and Rachel O'Brien. *The Game's Up: Redefining Child Prostitution*. London: Children's Society, 1995.

Lemert, Edwin M. *Social Pathology*. New York: McGraw-Hill, 1951.

Leuchtag, Alice. "The Culture of Pornography." *The Humanist* 55, 3 (1995): 4–6.

_____. "Merchants of Flesh: International Prostitution and the War on Women's Rights." *The Humanist* 55, 2 (1995): 11–16.

Lloyd, Robin. *For Money or Love: Boy Prostitution in America*. New York: Ballantine, 1976.

Lombroso, Cesare, and William Ferrero. *The Female Offender*. New York: Appleton, 1900.

Longino, Helen E. "Pornography, Oppression, and Freedom: A Closer Look." In Laura Lederer, ed., *Take Back the Night: Women on Pornography*. New York: William Morrow, 1980.

McKeganey, Neil, and Marina Barnard. *Sex Work on the Streets: Prostitutes and Their Clients*. Bristol, Penn.: Taylor and Francis, 1996.

McLeod, E. *Women Working: Prostitution Now*. London: Crown Helm, 1982.

MacVicar, Katherine, and Marcia Dillon. "Childhood and Adolescent Development of Ten Female Prostitutes." *Journal of the American Academy of Child Psychiatry* 19, 1 (1980): 148–49.

Magee, Audrey, and Philip Sherwell. "For Girls, Few Choices — All Bad: Seamstress, Servant, or Prostitute?" *World Press Review* 43 (1996): 12.

Males, Carolyn, and Julie Raskin. "The Children Nobody Wants." *Reader's Digest* (January 1984): 63–66.

Mamonova, Tatyana. "USSR: Perestroika, Pornography, and Prostitution." *MS Magazine* 2 (September-October 1991): 12.

May, Peter. "Rooting for the Dirty Diggers." *New Statesman & Society* 6 (1993): 18–23.

Miller, Laura. "Prostitution." *Harper's Bazaar* 3400 (March 1995): 208–12.

Millett, Kate. "Prostitution: A Quartet for Female Voices." In Vivian Gornick and Barbara K. Moran, eds., *Women in a Sexist Society*. New York: New American Library, 1971.

Mohr, Johan W., R. Edward Turner, and M. B. Jerry. *Pedophilia and Exhibitionism.* Toronto: University of Toronto Press, 1964.

Moran, Susan. "New World Havens of Oldest Profession." *Insight on the News* 9 (1993): 12–16.

Morneau, Robert H., and Robert R. Rockwell. *Sex, Motivation, and the Criminal Offender.* Springfield, Ill.: Charles C Thomas, 1980.

Neequaye, Alfred. "Prostitution in Accra." In Martin A. Plant, ed., *AIDS, Drugs, and Prostitution.* London: Routledge, 1990.

Newman, Frances, and Paula J. Caplan. "Juvenile Female Prostitution as a Gender Consistent Response to Early Deprivation." *International Journal of Women's Studies* 5, 2 (1981): 128–37.

O'Brien, Shirley. *Child Pornography.* Dubuque, Iowa: Kendall/Hunt, 1983.

Perkins, Olivia. "I Am a High-Class Call Girl." *Cosmopolitan* 215 (October 1993): 96–100.

Plant, M. L., M. A. Plant, D. F. Peck, and J. Setters. "The Sex Industry, Alcohol, and Illicit Drugs: Implications for the Spread of HIV Infection." *British Journal of Addiction* 84 (1989): 53–59.

Plant, Martin A. *AIDS, Drugs, and Prostitution.* London: Routledge, 1990.

_____. "Sex Work, Alcohol, Drugs, and AIDS." In Martin A. Plant, ed., *AIDS, Drugs, and Prostitution.* London: Routledge, 1990.

_____, and M. L. Plant. *Risk-Takers: Alcohol, Drugs, Sex, and Youth.* London: Routledge, 1992.

Policy Journals. *Crime UK 1988: An Economic, Social, and Policy Audit.* Berks, U.K.: Old Vicarage, 1988.

Pollak, Otto. *The Criminality of Women.* Philadelphia: University of Philadelphia Press, 1950.

Pollock, Joy. "Early Theories of Female Criminality." In Lee H. Bowker, ed., *Women, Crime, and the Criminal Justice System.* Lexington, Mass.: Lexington Books, 1978.

Pomeroy, William B. "Some Aspects of Prostitution." *Journal of Sex Research* 11 (1965): 177–87.

Poudel, Meena. Poverty, "Prostitution, and Women." *World Health* 47 (1994): 10.

Price, Susan. "Why Men Still Stray the Old-Fashioned Way." *Ladies' Home Journal* 110 (November 1993): 174–77.

Reinhardt, J. M. *Sex Perversions and Sex Crimes.* Springfield, Ill.: Charles C Thomas, 1957.

Reinholz, Mary. "An Intimate Look at the Life of a Call Girl." *Cosmopolitan* 217 (August 1994): 110–14.

Reitman, Valerie. "Tokyo's Latest Fad: Teen Prostitution." *Wall Street Journal* (October 2, 1996): A8.

Richardson, John H. "When Glamour Turns Grim: Hollywood's Actress-Hookers." *Cosmopolitan* 213 (September 1992): 252–55.

Roberts, Nickie. *Whores in History.* New York: Harper Collins, 1992.

Robertson, Marjorie. "A Third of Homeless Teenagers Survive by Prostitution." *Society* 28 (1990): 2–4.

Robinson, Lillian S. "Touring Thailand's Sex Industry." *The Nation* 257 (1993): 492–97.

Rooney, Rita. "Children for Sale: Pornography's Dark New World." *Reader's Digest* (July 1983): 52–56.

Rosenberg, M. J., and J. M. Weiner. "Prostitutes and AIDS: A Health Department Priority." *American Journal of Public Health* 78 (1988): 418–23.

Rosenblum, Karen E. "Female Deviance and the Female Sex Role: A Preliminary Investigation." *British Journal of Sociology* 26 (1975): 173–78.

Rosenblum, L., W. Darrow, J. Witte, J. Cohen, J. French, P. S. Gill, J. Potterat, K. Sikes,

R. Reich, and S. Hadler. "Sexual Practices in the Transmission of Hepatitis B Virus and Prevalence of Hepatitis Delta Virus Infection in Female Prostitutes in the United States." *Journal of the American Medical Association* 267 (1992): 2477–81.

Satchel, Michael. "Kids for Sale: A Shocking Report on Child Prostitution Across America." *Parade Magazine* (July 20, 1986): 4–6.

Serrill, Michael S. "Defiling the Children." *Time* 141 (June 21, 1993): 52–56.

Shilts, R. *And the Band Played On.* Harmondsworth, Middlesex: Penguin, 1987.

Silbert, Mimi H. "Delancey Street Study: Prostitution and Sexual Assault." Summary of results, Delancey Street Foundation, San Francisco, 1982.

_____. *Sexual Assault of Prostitutes: Phase One.* Washington, D.C.: National Institute of Mental Health, 1980.

_____, and A. M. Pines. "Occupational Hazards of Street Prostitutes." *Criminal Justice and Behavior* 8 (1981): 395–99.

Simons, Marlise. "Child Abuse Growing Trend in Sex Market." *Oregonian* (April 30, 1993): A4.

_____. "The Littlest Prostitutes." *New York Times Magazine* (January 16, 1994): 30.

Smart, Carol. *Law, Crime, and Sexuality: Essays in Feminism.* London: Sage, 1995.

Smith, G. L., and K. F. Smith. "Lack of HIV Infection and Condom Use in Licensed Prostitutes." *Lancet* 2 (1986): 1392.

Smolenski, Carol. "Sex Tourism and the Sexual Exploitation of Children." *Christian Century* 112 (1995): 1079–81.

Stanmeyer, William A. *The Seduction of Society.* Ann Arbor, Mich.: Servant Books, 1984.

Stein, M. *Lovers, Friends, Slaves....* New York: Berkeley, 1974.

Stieber, Tamar. "The Boys Who Sell Sex to Men in San Francisco." *Sacramento Bee* (March 4, 1984): A22.

Strobel, Warren. "Vietnam Joins AIDS Battle." *Insight on the News* 10 (1994): 26.

Sunlove, Kat. "Putting a Price on Pain." *Harpers* 289 (August 1994): 19–20.

Tannahill, Reay. *Sex in History.* New York: Stein and Day, 1980.

Thomas, Ruth. "AIDS Risks: Alcohol, Drugs, and the Sex Industry — A Scottish Study." In Martin A. Plant, ed., *AIDS, Drugs, and Prostitution.* London: Routledge, 1990.

Thomas, William I. *Sex and Society: Studies in the Social Psychology of Sex.* Boston: Little, Brown, 1907.

_____. *The Unadjusted Girl: With Cases and Standpoint for Behavior Analysis.* New York: Harper and Row, 1923.

Tice, Carole. "Love for Sale." *Utne Reader* 49 (January-February 1992): 37–40.

Trujillo, Laura. "Escort Services Thriving Industry in Portland Area." *Oregonian* (June 7, 1996): B1.

Turner, C. F., H. G. Miller, and L. E. Moses, eds. *AIDS, Sexual Behavior, and Intravenous Drug Use.* Washington, D.C.: National Academy Press, 1989.

Underwood, Nora. "Lust at the End of the Line." *Maclean's* 106 (February 8, 1993): 52–55.

U.S. Department of Justice. *Attorney General's Commission on Pornography: Final Report.* Vol. 1. Washington, D.C.: Government Printing Office, 1986.

_____. Bureau of Justice Statistics. *Sourcebook of Criminal Justice Statistics — 1995.* Washington, D.C.: Government Printing Office, 1996.

_____. Federal Bureau of Investigation (FBI). *Crime in the United States: Uniform Crime Reports 1995.* Washington D.C.: Government Printing Office, 1996.

_____. National Institute of Justice. *Characteristics of Different Types of Drug-Involved Offenders.* Washington, D.C.: Government Printing Office, 1988.

Van den Hoek, J., R. A. Coutinho, H. J. Van Haastrecht, A. W. Van Zadelhoff, and J. Goudsmit. "Prevalence and Risk Factors of HIV Infections Among Drug Users and Drug-Using Prostitutes in Amsterdam." *AIDS* 2 (1987): 55–60.

Venema, Petrien, and Jan Visser. "Safer Prostitution: A New Approach in Holland." In Martin A. Plant, ed., *AIDS, Drugs, and Prostitution*. London: Routledge, 1990.

Volkonsky, Anastasia. "Legalizing the 'Profession' Would Sanction the Abuse." *Insight on the News* 11 (1995): 20–22.

Waldorf, Dan, and Sheigla Murphy. "Intravenous Drug Use and Syringe-Sharing Practices of Call Men and Hustlers." In Martin A. Plant, ed., *AIDS, Drugs, and Prostitution*. London: Routledge, 1990.

Weisberg, D. Kelly. *Children of the Night: A Study of Adolescent Prostitution*. Lexington, Mass.: Lexington Books, 1985.

Winick, Charles, and Paul M. Kinsie. *The Lively Commerce: Prostitution in the United States*. Chicago: Quadrangle Books, 1971.

Wolbert, Ann, ed. *Child Pornography and Sex Rings*. Lexington, Mass.: Lexington Books, 1984.

Woolston, Howard B. *Prostitution in the United States*. New York: Century, 1921.

Index

Acquired Immune Deficiency Syndrome 30
Abuse 121, 151, 160, 192; alcohol 27, 48, 61, 84, 93, 105; child 1, 83, 88, 96, 148–49, 192; child sexual 83, 96, 110–11, 119; drug 14, 19, 27, 33, 40, 44, 47–48, 61, 84, 93, 105, 158, 173, 184; mental 71; physical 27–28, 49, 71, 73, 83, 85, 93, 96; ritualistic sexual 110–11; sexual 1, 27–28, 49, 59, 71, 73, 83, 85, 93, 111, 133, 151; substance 27, 31, 49, 58, 84–85, 97, 98, 104, 111, 118–19, 123, 150, 173; *see also* Crimes; Victimization; Violence
The Admirable Discourses of the Plain Girl 121
Africa 177, 188–89
AIDS ix, x, 1–2, 5, 19–21, 28, 30–36, 40, 55, 60–61, 64, 69, 71, 79, 89, 98, 105, 127, 130–31, 143–44, 147, 154, 166, 171, 175–76, 179, 181–82, 185–90, 191–92, 195; adolescent female prostitutes and 34–35; in Africa 188–89; in Brazil 187; and call girls 60; and child prostitutes 161; in China 187; clients and 130–31; and drug

addicted prostitutes 19–20; and female prostitution 30–36, 89, 104; in Germany 188; and high class call girls 32; in India 179; and IV drug use 30–35, 143; legal prostitution and 21, 147, 157; male prostitutes and 35, 143–44; pimps and 104; prostitution, sexism, and 35; and racial and ethnic minorities 32–33; rate of 31, 33, 36, 185–86; runaway girls and 98; and runaways 34; in Spain 188; and streetwalkers 32, 52–53, 60; and studies on female prostitution 31–32; and teen prostitution 69; in Thailand 180, 186; in the United States 189–90; and unregulated prostitutes 33; in Vietnam 186–87; *see also* Drug use; Drugs; HIV infection
AIDS, Drugs, and Prostitution (Plant) 32
Alcohol abuse 27, 48, 61, 84, 93, 96, 105
Alcohol-related offenses 44
Alcoholism 138; *see also* Abuse, alcohol; Substance abuse

Almodovar, Norma J. 54
Anthony, Jane 159
Antipornography laws 120, 122
Arrests 8, 11–15, 21, 28, 40–45, 55, 72–78, 84, 86, 90–92, 127–28, 131–32, 134–36, 142–43, 145, 148, 155–56, 167; alcohol-related 86, 139; by community size 12–13, 92; by community type 75; comparisons with male arrestees 13; for drug abuse violations 44, 84, 139; by ethnicity 45–46; female 8, 11–15, 40–45; female juveniles 42; by gender 41–42, 73–74, 142; for liquor law offenses 44; for loitering 44, 84, 86, 139; male 8, 42, 127–28, 131–32, 134–36, 139–40, 142–43; male juveniles 42, 139–40, 142–43; of male prostitutes 134–36; in Manila 167; of men 41–42; for other offenses 75–76; for pandering 42; of persons under the age of 18 72–74; for pimping 127; for prostitution and commercialized vice 8, 11–15, 21, 40–45, 72–78, 90, 127, 135–36, 139, 145;

245